ANNE BOLEYN.

VOLUME II.

AMS PRESS

NEW YORK

ANNE BOLEYN

A Chapter of English History

1527—1536.

BY

PAUL FRIEDMANN.

IN TWO VOLUMES.

VOLUME II.

London:

MACMILLAN AND CO.

1884.

Library of Congress Cataloging in Publication Data

Friedmann, Paul.
    Anne Boleyn: a chapter of English history,
1527-1536.

    1. Anne Boleyn, consort of Henry VIII, King of
England, 1507-1536. 2. Great Britain—History—
Henry VIII, 1509-1547.
DA333.B6F8 1973   942.05'2'0924 [B] 76-161795
ISBN 0-404-09050-8

Reprinted from the edition of 1884, London
First AMS edition published in 1973
Manufactured in the United States of America

International Standard Book Number:
Complete Set: 0-404-09050-8
Volume II: 0-404-09052-4

AMS PRESS INC.
NEW YORK, N. Y.

TABLE OF CONTENTS.

CHAPTER IX.

THE NORTHERN CONFEDERACY.

CHAPTER X.

THE CONSPIRACY.

CHAPTER XI.

FISHER AND MORE.

CHAPTER XII.

THE COLLAPSE OF THE NORTHERN ALLIANCE.

CHAPTER XIII.

THE RESULT OF HENRY'S POLICY.

CHAPTER XIV.

THE DEATH OF CATHERINE.

CHAPTER XV.

JANE SEYMOUR.

CHAPTER XVI.

CHARLES V. AND ANNE.

CHAPTER XVII.

THE ARREST.

CHAPTER XVIII.

ANNE'S LAST DAYS.

CHAPTER XIX.

CONCLUSION.

APPENDIX.

NOTE A.

NOTE B.

NOTE C.

NOTE D.

NOTE E.

NOTE F.

NOTE G.

ANNE BOLEYN.

CHAPTER IX.

THE NORTHERN CONFEDERACY.

ON the 31st of March, in deference to the wish of du Bellay, a consistory was held, and the cardinals were asked, with a copy of Castillon's letter of the 6th before them, to reconsider their verdict, and in any case to postpone the publication of the sentence. To the first of these requests the cardinals answered that the letter was so vague, and Henry was so untrustworthy, that there was no reason why the sentence should be recalled.[1] As to the second request, neither the pope nor the cardinals were very eager that the sentence should be immediately published; they wished to know first whether Charles V. would give effect to it, and what Francis meant ultimately to do in the matter. The cardinals would not, however, bind themselves by any formal promise.

Du Bellay, finding that all his efforts were in vain, took his leave and set out for France. Happening to

[1] Cardinal of Jaen to Covos, March 30, 1534, *loc. cit.*

B

meet Carne and Revett at Bologna, he told them of the sentence and of what the cardinals had said, and held out hopes that even yet the sentence might be revoked ; but the English agents were not very sanguine that his anticipations would be realised.[1] They stopped where they were, and shortly afterwards started for England. Du Bellay himself travelled rather quickly, and in the middle of April he was back at the French court.

The courier whom du Bellay had despatched with tidings of the sentence had travelled with extraordinary speed, and had arrived at the French court on the
1st, or on the morning of the 2nd of April. Francis, fearing that Henry would proceed to dangerous measures if the unwelcome intelligence were not communicated to him in as gentle a way as possible, sent de la Pommeraye post haste to the English court, which he was able to reach on the 4th of April.[2]

Henry received the news exactly as Francis had foreseen ; but he did not allow himself to be carried away by his rage. For the more he heard of the
consistory of the 23rd of March the more he perceived the need of caution. The fact that all the French cardinals had stayed away, and that all the Italians of the French faction had voted against him, suggested to him the same doubts as those which du

---

[1] Carne and Revett to Henry VIII., April 7, 1534, *State Papers*, vol. vii. p. 552 ; and Cyfuentes to Charles V., April 26, 1534, British Museum, Add. MSS. vol. 28,586, fol. 238.

[2] E. Chapuis to Charles V., April 5, 1534, Vienna Archives, P.C. 229, i. fol. 74 ; and Francis I. to Henry VIII., British Museum, Cotton MSS. Cal. E. i. fol. 35.

Bellay had for a moment entertained. He suspected CHAP. IX. that Francis, while giving him fair words, had for some reason secretly betrayed him. That cardinals could vote according to their conscience seemed incredible to Henry.

In this state of perplexity Henry was afraid to commit himself further. The league with Luebeck had not been concluded, the German Protestant princes stood aloof, Scotland was hostile and Ireland in open rebellion, while in England itself discontent had by no means been allayed by Cromwell's energetic measures. The loss of the protection of Francis in these circumstances might mean total ruin : it was a danger even Henry did not underrate. So he resolved, first of all, to make sure of the French alliance.

A few days after de la Pommeraye's arrival, Lord *English embassy* Rochford and Sir William Fitzwilliam were sent on *to France.* a special embassy to France. They met the French *April 21,* king at Coussy on the 21st of April, and were *1534.* splendidly entertained by him and by his sister the Queen of Navarre.[1] In the intervals between the feasts and the ceremonies they delivered their message. Henry requested, first, that Francis should abandon his alliance with the pope ; next, that he should invade Milan, but without taking subsidies from Clement ; third, that he should adopt in France measures similar to the new English laws (which the ambassadors explained) ; fourth, that a meeting of the two kings should be arranged ; fifth, that Francis should refuse to give the hand of his daughter

[1] Martin Valles to F. de los Covos, April, 1534, British Museum, Add. MSS. 28,586, fol. 244.

CHAP. IX.   Madeleine to James V. of Scotland. While making
these requests, Henry offered to contribute further
towards the subsidies paid to the German princes.[1]

*Answer to
Henry's
demands.*
April 24,
1534.

On the 24th the ambassadors received a detailed
answer to their offers and demands. To the first
point Francis replied that he had no alliance with
the pope. On Henry's account he had steadily refused at Marseilles to conclude any such alliance;
and had the King of England been less obstinate,
and sent a proxy, all would have gone in his favour.[2]
As to the invasion of Milan, this was not a propitious
time, but if ever Francis attempted to conquer Milan
he would not, for the sake of trifling subsidies, put
himself under obligations to Clement.[3] With regard

[1] Reply given by Francis I. to Rochford and Fitzwilliam,
Paris, Bibl. Nat. MSS. Français, vol. 3,005, fol. 129. The instructions said by Mr. Gairdner, *Letters and Papers*, vol. vii. p.
195, to have been addressed to Rochford and Fitzwilliam, do
not agree very well with this answer. I am inclined to think,
therefore, that they are not those which were really given to
the two ambassadors.

[2] Reply to Rochford and Fitzwilliam, *loc. cit.*: "Et premierement quant au propoz quilz luy ont tenu de vouloir habandonne
le pape. Le dict Seigneur a respondu quil na nulle alliance avec
luy. Par quoy nestant en nulle sorte son allie il ne peult et ne
scauroit riens rompre en cest endroict. Et la cause qui la garde
de sallier avec le dict pape a ete la faulte du pouvoir que navoient
point les ambassadeurs de son dict bon frere luy estant a
Marseille. Au moyen de quoy il ne voulut rien traicter tout
seul."

[3] *Ibid.*: "Quant a lemprinse de Milan dont iceulx ambassadeurs luy ont aussi parle. Le dict Seigneur a tres bien entendu
tout ce quilz luy ont dit de la part de son dict bon frere touchant
la dicte emprinse, mais quil ne se voulsist point ayder en nulle
sorte dudict pape . . . Cognoissant tres bien le dict Seigneur
quant a ce poinct la petite ayde quil pourroit avoir dudict pape

to the new statutes made in England, Francis did not blame Henry for them, but he saw no reason why he should follow a similar course.[1] To the proposed meeting he had no objection; and the marriage of the princess Madeleine he was ready to forego. The contribution towards the subsidies in Germany would be gladly accepted.

But Francis in his turn put a question. Charles V., having urged the pope to give sentence against Henry, could not honourably stand still now that his advice had been taken; he would be obliged to execute the papal mandate. Censures would be issued at Rome against the King of England and against his aiders and abettors; and Francis, if he continued to support Henry, would also be excommunicated, and would be attacked by those who were to carry out the sentence. His territory was much more exposed than England, and the war would begin on his frontiers. If he were assailed, what would his good brother of England do for

qui ne scauroit estre que de cent·ou deux cents mil escus, parquoy il sest tres bien garde de se vouloir obliger envers luy pour si peu de chose que cela. Mais de faire la guerre a ceste heure le dict Seigneur ny veoit pas grand propoz."

[1] Reply to Rochford and Fitzwilliam. *loc. cit.* : "Touchant les nouvelles ordonnances faictes par le dict Seigneur Roy dangleterre en son royaume. Le dict Seigneur Roy son bon frere a tres bien entendu tout, ce que les dicts ambassadeurs luy en ont dict. Et veu quil ny a rien contre le droict divin et loultrage quon a faict a icelluy son bon frere, il ne les scauroit trouver maulvaises et luy semble bien quil neust sceu faire de moins. Mais quant a luy de faire le semblable veu quil na pareille occasion et que ce seroit se perturber et travailler actendu quil est en repoz il luy semble ne le devoir faire."

him ? On how large a sum of money might Francis reckon ?[1]

Two days after having received this reply, the English ambassadors left Coussy to return to England. Henry was in no way offended by the venality of the French king. On the contrary, he regained the confidence he had nearly lost, and instructed Sir John Wallop, his resident ambassador in France, to thank Francis for his good-will, and to exhort the friends of the English alliance to persevere in their efforts to establish it.[2] A few days later a second despatch was addressed to Wallop, the draft of which was largely corrected by the king himself. It treats of the proposed interview, and shows what undue importance Henry attached to this display of friendship. It also affords fresh proof of his insincerity. All his corrections are couched in ambiguous terms, and neither in the reply to Roch-

---

[1] Reply to Rochford and Fitzwilliam, *loc. cit.* : " Plus a prie le dict Seigneur Roy iceulx ambassadeurs de remonstrer de sa part a son dict bon frere comme estans de presens le pape et lempereur desesperez il fault que icelluy empereur face de deux choses lune ; ou quil vienne a lexecution de la sentence ou que a sa tresgrande honte, apres lavoir faict donner il laisse les choses comme elles sont ; ce que le dict Seigneur Roy ne peult croyre quil face, puys que il en est si avant. Parquoy venant a lexecution sera force de user de fulminations et mectre en proye non seulement le royaume de son dict bon frere, mais pareillement touts ceulx qui luy ayderont. De quoy ne voulant le dict Seigneur sexcuser de faire laide et diffension a son dict bon frere tel quil doibt . . . indubitablement luy sera le premier assailly, parquoy . . desire il bien scavoir le cas advenant quel ayde es secours il auroit de luy."

[2] Henry VIII. to Sir John Wallop, R.O. Box I, and Gairdner, *Letters and Papers*, vol. vii. p. 252.

ford and Fitzwilliam, nor in the other papers referring to the negotiation, is there any trace whatever of promises which he repeatedly speaks of as having been made by Francis. Henry would only undertake "not vehemently to press" the French king immediately to make laws like those which had just been passed in England against the authority of the pope. He asserted, however, that Francis had pledged himself, "if the bishop of Rome gave him some reasonable occasion," to "do as much or more" than Henry had done.[1] Francis now sent de la Guiche to the English court, and to him Henry expressed a wish that the meeting should take place in August. At the same time he asked that a French fleet should be equipped to watch over his safety while he was crossing the Channel, and to protect the English coasts while he was away ; and that a strong French force should be assembled at Ardres, lest Charles V.—of whom he was mortally afraid— should make a bold dash at the walls of Calais and capture him in his strongest fortress.[2] In the beginning of June, de la Guiche returned with this message to Francis.

May, 1534.

June 7, 1534.

In the meantime the government were taking strong measures against all those who seemed inclined to side with the pope. In the statute settling the succession to the crown on the children of Anne, there was a clause by which it was enacted that all adult subjects should be sworn to observe the Act. Immediately after the close of the session the oath

Arrest of More and Fisher.

[1] Henry VIII. to Sir John Wallop, R.O. Box R, 10c.
[2] Answer to de la Guiche, *State Papers*, vol. vii. p. 559.

was tendered to those whose sentiments it seemed desirable to test, and nearly every one outwardly submitted. But two men of equal fame and eminence, Sir Thomas More and Fisher, Bishop of Rochester, refused. More expressed his willingness to recognise the order of succession established by parliament; but he declined to accept the whole contents of the statute—in other words, to acknowledge the legality of the divorce and of Henry's marriage with Anne. Persisting in his refusal, he was committed for a short time to the custody of the abbot of West-
April 16, 1534. minster, and on the 16th of April was sent to the Tower.[1] To the same place, for the same offence, Fisher was also sent, having previously been attainted and imprisoned on a charge of misprision of treason in connection with the pretensions of Elizabeth Barton, the nun of Kent. In order to intimidate those who might be tempted to follow the example of Fisher
April 20, 1534. and More, Elizabeth Barton and her associates were executed on the 20th.[2]

The oath tendered to Catherine.
May, 1534.
A few days later a royal commission waited on Catherine, and required her to take the oath. This was a gratuitous piece of insolence, for nobody could expect Catherine to comply; but it was made an excuse for depriving her of all those servants who would not swear to the statute. When Catherine refused, she was threatened with death and shut up in her chamber, and her Spanish servants were

[1] E. Chapuis to Charles V., April 16, 1534, Vienna Archives, P.C. 229, i. fol. 83.

[2] J. Husee to Lord Lisle, April 20, 1534, Gairdner, *Letters and Papers,* vol. vii. p. 208.

placed under arrest.[1] Chapuis strongly remonstrated,
and the king, feeling that he had gone too far, gave
way. Catherine was again allowed the use of her
rooms, and her Spanish servants were set free.[2]

The government had now done all it could, and
still but little had been achieved. Neither Catherine
nor Mary had yielded, and although most of Henry's
subjects had taken the oath it was pretty certain that
they would willingly break it if they found an opportunity. Anne, who hated Catherine and her daughter,
was enraged by what she considered a feeble and
vacillating policy. She cordially despised Henry's
weakness, as she called it; she wanted him to carry
out his threats, and to rid her of her rival.

There was a chance that Anne herself might be
able to do that from which Henry shrank; for she
hoped that if he went to France she would be
entrusted with the direction of the government during
his absence. She had been overheard to say to her

[1] E. Chapuis to Charles V., May 29, 1534, Vienna Archives,
P.C. 229, i. No. 37 : "Il envoya bientôt apres devers la Royne
larchevesque de Yorch, les evesques de Duren et de Chestry
et aultres personnes, que oultres plusieurs estranges propos luy
dirent quelle regardast a ce quelle feroit, car si elle refusoit de
jurer et obeyr elle encourroit peyne de la vie, et comme elle ma
envoye dire luy parlairent dun gibet; quoy ouyant la dicte
Royne, elle leur demanda lequel deulx devait estre le bourreaulx
et que sil estoit question la faire morir que ce fust en public non
point en secret. En la fin refusant de jurer ils la confinarent en
ung quartier de son logis, les demoiselles furent serrees en une
chambre, ses confesseur, medecin et apothiquaires deffendus de
parler a elle et de non sortir du logis, de quoy adverty . . . ."

[2] E. Chapuis to Charles V., June 7, 1534, Vienna Archives,
P.C. 229, i. fol. 109.

CHAP. IX.

brother that, when the king was away and she was regent, she would have Mary executed for her disobedience. Rochford warned her of the king's anger if she took so bold a step without his command, but Anne vehemently answered that she did not care and that she would do it even if she was burned or skinned alive for it.[1] Chapuis, who tells the story, may have exaggerated a little, but there can be no doubt that his account is substantially true.

Anne's plans thwarted.

In April Anne had told Henry that she was once more with child.[2] Perhaps she herself believed what she so greatly wished; perhaps the announcement was only a feint to revive her waning influence, or to provide her with an excuse for remaining at home. In any case it had a very different result from that which she expected.

The violence of Anne's temper had begun to alarm Henry, and as the time for the interview approached he became very unwilling to allow her to act as regent. Rather than this, he was ready to give up the meeting he so eagerly coveted. Her supposed pregnancy was a sufficient pretext for breaking off the engagement; and in the beginning of July he sent Lord Rochford to France to obtain, through the influence of Marguerite of Navarre, the postponement of the visit till April, 1535. Rochford was to say that Anne in her present state would be loath to see her husband leave her. Besides, she wished very much to meet the Queen of Navarre, and as she could not travel at this

July 9, 1534.

---

[1] E. Chapuis to Charles V., June 23, 1534, Vienna Archives, P.C. 229, i. fol. 44.

[2] *State Papers*, vii. p. 565.

time she would be exceedingly disappointed if the interview were not put off. This reason Francis gladly accepted, for he was no longer desirous of conferring with Henry, whose proceedings annoyed him more and more. So the question of the meeting was allowed to drop, and Anne's hopes of a regency were nipped in the bud.

In the course of this summer Henry and Anne *Indepen-* were mortified by an incident which attracted general *dence of* *the Lords.* attention. Lord Dacres of Greystock, warden of the western marches towards Scotland, had been one of the foremost opponents of the divorce. He had had frequent quarrels with Anne's friend, the Earl of Northumberland, who was warden of the eastern and middle marches ; and he may have had some hand in the trick which the Countess of Northumberland, his sister-in-law, had tried to play in 1532. Northumberland had brought a long list of complaints against Dacres, and had at last been allowed to accuse him of treason. Early in May, Dacres and his cousin Sir *May,* Christopher were arrested, and the former was brought *1534.* to London to be tried by his peers, while the goods of both were seized for the king's use.[1]

An acquittal in cases in which the crown prosecuted for high treason was a thing scarcely heard of in the annals of Tudor justice. Almost everybody, therefore, expected a conviction ; and the northern gentlemen and the courtiers disputed about the lands of the men about to be attainted.[2] The wife and the

---

[1] Inventories of May 9 and 14, 1534, R.O. Henry VIII., Box Q.
[2] E. Aglionby to Cromwell, June 28, 1534, R.O. Henry VIII., Box Q.

father-in-law of Dacres were forbidden to make suit for his life.[1] The Duke of Norfolk summoned twenty-one peers who were believed to be strong adherents of the court, and on the 9th of July they sat. The depositions and indictments having been read, the king's attorney asked for judgment of high treason. Dacres pleaded not guilty, offered a brief defence, and left himself in the hands of his peers. The lords then retired, and when after a short consultation they returned, Norfolk as high steward put to them the usual question. Lord Mordaunt, being lowest in rank, was asked first, and to the astonishment of the court he replied, " Not guilty." Peer after peer following his example, the prisoner was acquitted.[2]

July 9,
1534.

Henry keenly felt this blow at his absolute authority. That the lords should dare to acquit a man whom he accused of high treason was a dangerous precedent ; and in ordinary circumstances he would have turned angrily against the woman for whose sake he had aroused their opposition. Happily for Anne, he still believed her to be with child, and the hope of being father to a Prince of Wales overcame every other feeling in Henry's breast.

Henry
and Anne
in the
midland
counties.

The rest of the summer Henry and Anne employed in a progress through the midland counties ; and both did their utmost to win the hearts of those whom they met. In some instances they may have succeeded, but in general, under the surface, there remained the same discontent as before. Anne was

[1] Earl of Shrewsbury to Cromwell, June 29, 1534, R.O. Henry VIII., Box Q.

[2] R.O. Baga de Segretis, Bundle VI.

no longer equal to the exertion of keeping her temper
in difficult circumstances; and by a single moment
of insolence she sometimes undid what she seemed to
have accomplished by days of condescension and
flattery. She began to feel tired and disheartened.

As time went on she became aware that she had *Widow*
been mistaken about her condition; and, as if to add *Carey.*
to her annoyance, her sister, who had now been a
widow for seven years, could not hide that she had
those hopes which Anne lacked. Fair widow Carey
had fallen in love with William Stafford, a soldier of
the retinue of Calais, and it was afterwards pretended
that she had married him. However this may have
been, she was now about to bear him a son. The
affair being rather scandalous, poor Mary was sent
from court, and had to ask Cromwell to obtain at
least a small pittance for herself and her new lord.[1]

At last Anne was obliged to tell Henry that she *Henry's*
was not pregnant. It was no agreeable duty, for *disap-*
she felt sure that he would resent the failure of his *pointment.*
hopes. And she was right. He immediately ceased
to show her the attention and courtesy he had paid
her during the last few months; and the court soon
understood that her influence had declined.[2]

While Anne was thus beset with difficulties, she *Aliena-*
was losing the assistance of her best and most powerful *tion of*
Francis I.

[1] E. Chapuis to Charles V., December 19, 1534, Vienna
Archives, P.C. 229, i. No. 70; and Mary Stafford to Cromwell,
Gairdner, *Letters and Papers*, vol. vii. p. 612.

[2] E. Chapuis to Charles V., September 24, 1534, Vienna
Archives, P.C. 229, i. No. 57; and Cyfuentes to Charles V.,
September 20, 1534, British Museum, Add. MSS. vol. 28,587,
fol. 31.

CHAP. IX.
—

ally, Francis I. The reasons for his change of policy were of a mixed kind. Personally, Francis was pretty indifferent to religion and to the papacy; but the great majority of his people still adhered to the old forms. The imprisonment of two men so far-famed as Fisher and More had excited strong indignation, and the execution of the observant friars had been resented by their whole order. The members of this order were among the principal preachers in France, and they made the French pulpits ring with denunciations of Henry's cruelty. If Francis continued to show favour to the King of England, and especially to the faction now in power, he was in danger of losing the support of his own subjects.

But this was not all. The policy of Henry might not only cost Francis the goodwill of his subjects and the friendship of the pope, it might deprive him of the position he had gained in Germany.

Francis and political parties in Germany.

At the time of Luther's revolt there was a twofold agitation in the German lands, the one for religious reform, the other for political change in a democratic sense. Luther put himself at the head of the former movement; the latter he decidedly opposed. Most of the princes, nobles, and patricians of the towns in central Germany associated themselves with him; and when the peasants rose under Muenzer to overthrow the aristocratic government, they were defeated with the help of Luther's most enthusiastic friends.

In Switzerland the reformation initiated by Zwingli was less conservative in politics. Still, it kept within bounds; it was politically respectable. Zwinglians and Lutherans had lately grown to be on friendly terms, the small differences of dogma having been nearly explained away, so that Francis was able to favour the one without offending the other.

Northern Germany was in a very different position. In that part of the country there had been no democratic rising, but the democratic idea steadily gained ground. In the towns the old oligarchies, one after another, were displaced, and a more popular form of government was introduced. The cities so constituted were generally on bad terms with the neighbouring princes and nobles, although there was no open war of any importance until 1533. Nominally, most of the northern towns had adopted Lutheranism, but their Lutheranism was not always orthodox ; their divines did not absolutely submit to Wittenberg.

Francis had formed an alliance with the Zwinglians, who furnished him with strong contingents of Swiss troops, and with the Lutherans, who opposed his enemy, Charles V. With the ever-shifting factions of the northern towns he had nothing to do. He would not trust such fickle communities ; nor did he believe that Charles would ever find in them real enemies. Far from Austria, the northern towns had little to fear from the emperor ; and they hailed with pleasure those measures by which he diminished the power of their neighbours the princes. Their pleasure was in no way diminished by the fact that many of the princes agreed with them about religion.

It was of course the French king's chief wish to widen the breach between the Protestant princes and Charles ; and a good opportunity seemed to offer itself when, on the 5th of January, 1531, Charles's brother Ferdinand was somewhat irregularly elected King of the Romans. Duke John, elector of Saxony, who had not been properly summoned, protested against the election, and all the Lutheran princes refused to recognise Ferdinand as their superior. They were joined by Duke William of Bavaria, who had formerly been a vigorous opponent of the Lutherans. Although, next to the electors, he was the most eminent Catholic prince, he had long been jealous of the grow-

ing power of Austria; and, at the diet of Augsburg in 1530, he had been exasperated by the action of Charles in granting to Ferdinand the vacant dukedom of Wuertemberg. By this arrangement Bavaria had been nearly enclosed by Austrian territory, and had been cut off from her allies. Political reasons thus drove the Catholic duke to seek the alliance of the Protestants.

Francis had been closely watching these events; his agents, Guillaume du Bellay of Langey, Gervase Wein and others, keeping him well informed of all

that went on. In May, 1532, he promised to pay 100,000 crowns to the discontented princes if they would resist by force Ferdinand's claims to royal power;[1] and when the offer was accepted, he deposited the sum at Ingolstadt in Bavaria. The war, however, was postponed on account of a new inroad of the

Turks. All Germany united to repel the common foe, who, baffled at Guenz by the stout defence of Jurischitz, and opposed by an excellent army under Charles V. himself, had to retreat with heavy loss. The danger from the Turks having come to an end,

[1] Receipt of Dukes William and Lewis of Bavaria, Paris, Bibl. Nat. MSS. Fr. vol. 3,016, fol. 76.

and the emperor having gone to Italy, the moment *CHAP. IX.*
for beginning the war seemed to have arrived; but
the confederates hung back, and perhaps no battle
would have been fought but for an event which
disturbed all Ferdinand's calculations.

Christopher, the son of the banished Düke Ulrich *Wuertem-*
of Wuertemberg, was kept in a kind of confinement *berg*
restored to
at the imperial court. In the winter of 1532 he *its native*
duke.
managed to escape, reached Bavaria, and threw
himself on the duke's protection. He was well
received, and his cause was taken up by the duke
as well as by the Schmalkaldic and other princes.
Francis I. was friendly to him, and Guillaume du
Bellay delivered a long and pathetic speech in his
favour. Ferdinand, alarmed by the popularity of the
young duke, offered him compensation; but Christopher insisted that Wuertemberg must be given up.
Negotiations were now begun between Francis and
Philip, Landgrave of Hesse, who, as an old friend
of Christopher's father, was most eager to serve him.
After the conference at Marseilles the French king
proceeded to Lorraine, where, in January 1534, he *January*
met the Landgrave at Bar le Duc, and arrived at an *28, 1534.*
understanding with him. Francis deposited an addi-
tional sum of 200,000 crowns with the duke of Bavaria,
and bought from Ulrich the county of Moempelgard,
with its dependencies in the free county of Burgundy,
for 184,000 ducats. With this money the Landgrave
raised an army, and advanced rapidly by an unexpected
route towards Wuertemberg. Ferdinand was abandoned by all his friends. His own troops tried to
make a stand, but on the 13th of May, at Laufen, they *May 13,*
1534.

CHAP. IX. were utterly routed ; and about the end of the month
Wuertemberg was in the hands of its native duke, and
Philip of Hesse was fast advancing towards Bohemia.
In this emergency, without consulting the emperor,
who might have been less compliant, Ferdinand accepted a treaty of peace, which was signed a few
June, days later at Cadan in Bohemia. Ulrich retained
1534. Wuertemberg, the Protestant princes and towns were
not to be molested, and in return Ferdinand was
acknowledged as King of the Romans.

Francis, who did not at all wish for so speedy
a settlement, protested against what he considered a
breach of faith on the part of the Protestants. They
answered with recriminations, asserting that the
behaviour of the friends of Francis had forced them
to act as they had done. And there was a good deal
of truth in what they said. Philip of Hesse had
concluded the treaty of Cadan, in order to be free to
withstand a grave danger with which he and all
German princes were threatened from the north.

February Early in the spring of 1534 the Anabaptists had
27, 1534. obtained possession of the town of Muenster in
Westphalia ; and as Muenster was but fifty miles
from the dominions of Philip, he and his people were
exposed to no small peril. The surrounding lords
and princes had raised some troops, and were trying
to shut the Anabaptists up in the town they held ;
but in these endeavours they were hampered by the
action of Luebeck and its allies.

Stephen The mission of Stephen Vaughan to Germany had
Vaughan's failed. Ignorant alike of the German language, of
mission. German customs, and of German policy, he had acted

in the most clumsy way, addressing himself, of all CHAP. IX.
men, to the one who was most sure to reject Henry's
advances. John Frederic, elector of Saxony, to
whom Henry's political methods were repugnant, was
little disposed to enter into a league with him, and
declined to run any risk on his behalf. Vaughan, *September 5, 1533.*
being dismissed from the Saxon court with a very
decided refusal, lost heart, and did not proceed to
Cassel, where the Landgrave might have given him
a better reception. He returned to Flanders without
having succeeded in any of his objects.[1]

But if the German princes, the friends of Francis I., *Henry and Luebeck.*
disliked Henry's proposals, the German burghers were
not of the same mind. The negotiations between
Luebeck and Henry had been going on without inter-
ruption. The messengers from Luebeck, who at the
end of October had arrived in England to ask for the *October, 1533.*
release of Marcus Meyer, had in general confirmed
the account he had given of the state of affairs in
North Germany and Denmark.[2] They had even
added further information. Frederic I. of Denmark
having died on the 10th of April, 1533, at Gottorp, *April 10, 1533.*
his eldest son Christian was the principal candidate
for the Danish throne; but Christian had refused
either to form an alliance with Wullenwever and the
town, or to bind himself faithfully to respect their
privileges. The Luebeckers, therefore, opposed his
election, while the nobles and prelates supported him,

---

[1] Stephen Vaughan to Henry VIII., September 6, 1533, *State Papers*, vol. vii. p. 501; and S. Vaughan to Cromwell, September 25 and October 21, 1533, *State Papers*, vol. vii. pp. 509 and 516.

[2] Senate of Luebeck to Henry VIII., October 1, 1533, R.O. Henry VIII. Box I.

CHAP. IX.   and the Danish estates were as hostile to the pretensions of Luebeck as the young duke himself.[1]

December,   In the beginning of December the English secretary
1533.   who had been sent to Luebeck returned. It was
remarked that after his arrival the king was in good
humour, and was particularly careful to treat Marcus
Meyer with distinction.[2] The secretary had found
Wullenwever quite ready for the alliance Meyer had
proposed, and the city had appeared not only eager to
assert its privileges, but well able with its confederates
to execute its designs.

The   The proposed alliance seemed likely to be attended
proposed
northern   by very great advantages. If Denmark were gained,
con-
federacy.   landsknechts and horsemen might be collected there
and maintained at a small cost ; and from Jutland
a force might easily be brought over to Hull or
Newcastle, especially if Hanseatic hulks assisted in
transporting them. Norway and Skonen might be
taken soon after Denmark, and then a great northern
Protestant democratic league might be formed under
the presidency of Henry. The king could not withstand the fascination of so vast a scheme. He did
not, indeed, immediately grant all the demands of the
Luebeckers, but he agreed to send an ambassador to
the town, and asked that in return Luebeck plenipo-
tentiaries should come to England.[3] About the same

[1] G. Waitz, *Luebeck unter J. Wullenwever ;* Paludan Mueller,
Grevenfeide, etc.

[2] E. Chapuis to Charles V., December 9, 1533, Vienna
Archives, P.C. 228, i. fol. 141 ; and E. Chapuis to Charles V.,
December 16, 1533, Vienna Archives, P.C. 228, i. fol. 148.

[3] E. Chapuis to Charles V., December 23, 1533, Vienna
Archives, P.C. 228, i. fol. 153.

time it was decided to send agents to the other *CHAP. IX.*
maritime towns, to the King of Poland, to the
Woywode, and to the German princes, to win their
favour for the league.[1] As to Marcus Meyer himself,
on Sunday, the 7th of December, he was made a *December*
Knight of the Rose, and received a chain worth a *7, 1533.*
hundred pounds, with the promise of a yearly pension
of two hundred and fifty crowns. After this he left
for Luebeck to work in Henry's interest.[2]

On the 15th of January, 1534, Meyer arrived at *January*
Luebeck.[3] He communicated to Wullenwever Henry's *15, 1534.*
message, and induced the burgomaster to send a
secretary to England to make a formal request for
help in the projected war against Denmark. The *Wullen-*
secretary reached London in February, and promised *wever's*
offers.
that if Henry granted the Luebeckers money for the *February*
undertaking, they would not only repay the sum, but *19, 1534.*
pay him twice as much from the revenues of Denmark.
If he did not choose to appear as one of Duke Christian's enemies, a German prince (Count Christopher of
Oldenburg was meant) would carry on the war ; and
this prince would become tributary to England for
any amount he might receive. To these proposals
they wished to have a speedy reply.[4]

Henry gave the secretary a very cautious answer. *Henry's*
He encouraged Wullenwever to persevere in his bold *reply.*

[1] *State Papers*, vol. i. pp. 413, 414.

[2] E. Chapuis to Charles V., December 9, 1533, Vienna
Archives, P.C. 228, i. fol. 140 ; and Gairdner, *Letters and Papers*
vol. vii. p. 110.

[3] Bartholdt, *Juergen Wullenwever von Luebeck.*

[4] British Museum, Cotton MSS. Nero, B. iii. fol. 105, and
Wurm, p. 17.

CHAP. IX. and warlike policy, and to refuse to negotiate with the
Dutch.   He said he could not lightly embark on so
weighty an enterprise ; but he wished an embassy to
be sent to him, that he might treat with duly
accredited ministers; and he ended by offering
Wullenwever a pension.[1]   Early in March the
secretary left with this reply.[2]

January,
1534.

He had been preceded by Dr. Thomas Lee, or
Leigh, whom Henry had sent in January to negotiate
on the spot an alliance with the Hanseatic towns.[3]   At
Luebeck, Lee seems to have done his best to persuade
the town to adopt an active policy ; and he was so far
successful that the authorities made serious preparations for an attack upon Duke Christian.   Wullenwever
had long been in negotiation with Count Christopher
of Oldenburg, formerly a clergyman and canon of the
chapter of Cologne, but now a soldier of some repute.
Count Christopher had levied about 3,000 landsknechts,

May 12,
1534.

with whom, on the 12th of May, he appeared before
Luebeck.   He sent a message to the town asking for
ships to carry his troops to Denmark, where he
intended to restore King Christian II. ; and on the
following day he went himself to confer with the
town council, which decided by a majority, in consequence of fiery speeches of Wullenwever and his
adherents, to help the count in his undertaking.

[1] Henry VIII. to Wullenwever, British Museum, Cotton MSS.
Nero, B. iii. fol. 106.

[2] E. Chapuis to Charles V., March 7, 1534, Vienna Archives,
P.C. 229, i. fol. 54.

[3] Warrant to Cromwell, January 31, 1534, R.O. Henry VIII.
Box Q.

Marcus Meyer, afraid perhaps that the council might draw back, resolved to adopt a course by which it would be absolutely committed. At the head of a small band of chosen followers he secretly left the town, and on the 14th surprised the castle of Trittau, *May 14, 1534.* a stronghold of the Duke of Holstein, which was of great importance to the Luebeckers. Being thus *Luebeck declares war against Duke Christian* compromised, they had no alternative but to declare war against the duke ; and Count Christopher's troops, together with a few Luebeckers, invaded the duchy.[1]

The war having once began, it was much easier to *An embassy sent by Luebeck and Hamburg to England.* induce the town council to send an embassy to England to negotiate an alliance with the king. On the 30th of May the ambassadors left, and were joined on their way by others from Hamburg, which *May 30, 1534.* had also listened to the eloquence of Paget and Lee. Shortly afterwards, on the 16th of June, two ships *June 16, 1534.* flying the colours of Luebeck and of Hamburg sailed up the Thames ; and when they had anchored, the ambassadors from the two towns were landed by the barges and taken in great state to their lodgings. The servants of the Luebeckers were all dressed in red, and, as if to characterise the spirit of their town, wore as motto, *Si deus pro nobis, quis contra nos?* Those of Hamburg, clad in plain black, had a more sedate inscription : *Da pacem, Domine, in diebus nostris.*[2]

On the 24th the Hanseatic ambassadors were

---

[1] Waitz, *Luebeck unter Juergen Wullenwever ;* Paludan Mueller, *Grevenfeide,* etc.

[2] E. Chapuis to Charles V., June 23, 1534, Vienna Archives, P.C. 229, i. fol. 115.

CHAP. IX. received in state at Hampton Court. The chief of
June 24, the Luebeckers, Dr. Otto Adam von Pack—a man
1534. famous for his intrigues in central Germany—
addressed a long laudatory speech to the king, who
gave a gracious reply, and referred the ambassadors
for further negotiations to his ministers.[1] Soon afterwards, at several meetings, the conditions of the
proposed league were discussed.[2]

The war in Denmark. While negotiations were proceeding at the English
court, the war was being carried on in the north. Duke
Christian had soon collected a force sufficient to repel
the invaders, and on the mainland the Luebeckers
made no further progress; but Count Christopher
had taken ship at Travemünde with most of his own
June 19, troops. On the 19th of June he set sail, and a few
1534. days later he landed on Seeland. He met with but
July 13, little resistance, the whole country was overrun, and
1534. Copenhagen itself surrendered to the victor.[3]

Negotiations at the English court. So brilliant a beginning seemed likely to facilitate
the conclusion of the Anglo-Luebeck alliance; but
Henry made exorbitant demands without offering any
real assistance in return. The Hamburgers, who had
no pressing need of a close league, soon became very
July, cool. The superintendent of their church, Aëpinus,
1534. had come over to join them, and, after having heard
the case, had declared for the validity of the marriage between Henry and Catherine; so that his

[1] Chapuis to Charles V., July 7, 1534, Vienna Archives, P.C.
229, i. fol. 119.

[2] Chapuis to Charles V., July 16, 1534, Vienna Archives, P.C.
229, i. fol. 123.

[3] G. Waitz, *Luebeck unter Juergen Wullenwever.*

lay colleagues dared not subscribe to the articles
impugning it.[1] Thus Luebeck alone remained to be
treated with, for the Senate of Bremen had refused
to send representatives to join those of the two
towns. Pack went on with the negotiations, but *August 2, 1534.*
could obtain no more than a loan of £3,333 to
the town of Lubeck for the continuance of the war.[2]
His colleagues thereupon returned home, while he
remained for some time longer, plotting and
scheming, and ingratiating himself with Henry.[3]

Philip of Hesse was greatly annoyed by the *Irritation of Philip of Hesse.*
proceedings of the Luebeckers. The capture of
Trittau, without any previous declaration of war, was
contrary to his ideas of right and honour; and he was
made uneasy by the state of ferment into which most
of the north German towns had been thrown. He
was also alarmed by the threatening movements of
the free peasants of Ditmarschen, who seemed disposed
to begin a new peasants' war. If Duke Christian were
left to fight his way alone, the princes of northern
Germany might have to face a huge and threatening
democratic confederacy.

The negotiations of Henry with Luebeck were well
known, and it was equally notorious that he had
shown special favour to Marcus Meyer, the first
aggressor in this war. Moreover, it was suspected

---

[1] E. Chapuis to Charles V., July 27, 1534, Vienna Archives,
P.C. 229, i. fol. 124; and E. Chapuis to Charles V., January 28,
1535, Vienna Archives, P.C. 229½, i. fol. 9.

[2] Paludan Mueller, *Aktstykers til de Nordens historie,* i. p. 265,
etc.

[3] E. Chapuis to Charles V., September 10, 1534, Vienna
Archives, P.C. 229, i. fol. 137.

CHAP. IX. that he secretly encouraged the Anabaptists. The
German princes, therefore, were very wroth against
him, and their anger was in some measure extended
to Francis, his ally and friend. Thus Philip of Hesse
considered himself fully justified in signing the treaty
of Cadan, against which Francis protested. When
the treaty had been signed, some of Philip's troops
were sent to Muenster, while others went to reinforce
the Duke of Holstein. Ferdinand was no longer the
chief enemy; the men who had to be fought were
John of Leyden and Juergen Wullenwever, who
was backed by King Henry of England.

Francis expresses disapproval of Henry's policy. Francis, dreading the loss of all his influence in
Germany, and wishing to retain the friendship of the
pope and the loyal attachment of his people, had made
no secret of his disapproval of Henry's policy. He and
his ministers had spoken in very strong terms about
Anne, and had more than once hinted that they were
quite ready to abandon the English alliance. These
utterances had been carefully reported to the emperor;
and Clement VII., shortly before his death, had again
tried to negotiate an alliance between Charles and
Francis.

Charles V. wishes to conciliate Francis. Charles had good reasons for wishing to be on
friendly terms with Francis. The Turks had again
assembled in some force on the frontier, and had made
frequent inroads on Austrian territory; and the
famous Admiral Khairredin Barbarossa had left
Constantinople and seized Tunis, where he had secured
an excellent harbour at the Goletta from which
he threatened the shores of Italy and Spain. As
Barbarossa and Soliman were in constant communica-

tion with Francis, Charles apprehended an alliance CHAP. IX.
between the French and the Turks. This he wished
to prevent by conciliating the French king, hoping
meanwhile to strike a crushing blow at Khairredin.
Henry, Count of Nassau, was sent from Palencia to *August*
the French court to negotiate an alliance with *12, 1534.*
Francis.

By paragraphs 24—30 of his instructions Nassau *Proposed*
was directed to speak privately about a marriage *marriage*
between
between the Duke of Angoulême, the youngest son of *the Duke*
Francis, and the Princess Mary of England. He was *of An-*
goulême
to point out that in all probability Angoulême would *and Mary*
thereby succeed to the crown of England, so that a *of*
England.
better match could not be found for him.[1] In making
this proposal Charles wished not only to benefit Mary,
but to bribe Francis to forsake the alliance of Henry.
For if the French king accepted his offer, the match
could be concluded only by joint pressure on the
King of England; and if such pressure were exer-
cised, the alliance between Francis and Henry would,
of course, be dissolved, and there would be less danger
of a great coalition against the emperor.

Some time after the arrival of Henry of Nassau at
the French court, finding Francis rather stubborn
about Italian affairs, he suggested the idea of Mary's
marriage. The French ministers eagerly listened to *The*
the proposal; but they were not ready to accept it. *proposal*
rejected.
Francis said he was bound by ties of honour to Henry,
and added the more sensible remark that Charles V.
was offering what he had not got. Mary was still in
the power of her father, who, on hearing of the proposed

---

[1] *Papiers d'Etat de Granvelle*, vol ii. p. 146.

CHAP. IX.

October 20, 1534.

marriage, might do away with her ; and then the only result for Francis would be the lasting enmity of Henry and Anne. In a letter of the 20th October from Blois, Charles was apprised of the objections of Francis and of the failure of Nassau's negotiation.[1]

[1] *Papiers d'Etat de Granvelle,* vol. ii. p. 221.

CHAPTER X.

THE CONSPIRACY.

IN 1533, after the coronation of Anne, the discontented elements of the nation had been scattered and unorganised; and before they had had time to coalesce, Cromwell's quick hand had carried the principal measures of the government. But at the trial of Lord Dacres the peers had become aware of their own strength; they had learned that they were nearly all secretly disaffected, and that the crown would not easily obtain from them a verdict against any member of their order. Knowing this, they grew bolder; they opened their minds to one another, and looked about for remedies for the maladies of the time. *Reviving confidence of Catherine's friends. July, 1534.*

The lords having numerous adherents among the gentry, they very easily formed a strong party of resistance. As early as the 17th of September, 1534, Eustache Chapuis received a message from two rich and influential gentlemen, who, afraid of exciting suspicion, would not come to his house, but asked him to meet them as if by chance at an appointed place in the fields. The ambassador went, and they openly told him that they wanted the emperor's help *Secret interviews with Chapuis. September 17, 1534.*

CHAP. X. against the tyranny of the king.[1] Several ladies, thinking that their movements were less watched, dared to go to the ambassador's house, and brought Chapuis the same request in their own and in their husbands' names. So strong were the feelings of these fair plotters that one of them, a lady of high rank, forgot all prudence. She threw herself on her knees before Chapuis, and implored him to obtain the emperor's aid. Happily for her, her gentlewomen and the servants of Chapuis stood far off, and although they saw her kneel they could not hear what she said.[2]

Lord Hussey. A week later a person of very considerable importance appeared on the scene, and communicated

---

[1] E. Chapuis to N. de Granvelle, September 23, 1534, Vienna Archives, P.C. 229, ii. fol. 79 : " Mgr je ne vous scaurais escripre davantaige de nouvelles de par de ca de ce que verrez aux lettres a sa Ma^te saulf que ce peuple ne me laysse vivre a force dimportunite pour me faire escripre et solliciter a sa dicte Majeste de pourveoir au remede dyci avant que les choses se gastent plus et soy offrant lopportunite des affaires dirlande. Et ny a point six jours que deux seigneurs de sorte et estat non me ousant venir trouver en la maison me requererirent saillir aux champs pour deviser avec moy que ne fut que pour me parler de ce que dessus et masseurer que a la moindre motion de Sa Majeste presque tout le royaulme se declareroit."

[2] *Ibid.* : " Plusieurs dames de la part de leur mari et daultres men sont venus parler et me feist lune ces jours presque grant honte car en presence de ses demoiselles et serviteurs questoient beaulcop assistans aussi les miens elle se gecte devant moy a deux genoux pour moy recommander la dicte affaire dont deppendoit non seullement le salut de la Royne et princesse mais aussi de tant de povres ames. Ceulx questoient en la compaignie veirent les larmes et facon de faire mais ilz ne sceurent de quoy se traictoit."

with Chapuis. This was Lord Hussey, who until CHAP. X.
1533 had been lord chamberlain to the Princess
Mary. He owned very large estates in the midland
counties, and had considerable influence at court. He
now sent word that before leaving town he wished
privately to speak with the ambassador. To prevent
suspicion they had only a short conference, Hussey *September*
briefly stating that most of the nobility were ex- *29, 1534.*
tremely dissatisfied with the government, that they
had consulted together, and that they wished to be
assisted by imperial troops in forcing Henry to
dismiss Anne, and to give up the course he was
pursuing. For further particulars he referred Chapuis
to Lord Darcy, another member of the conspiracy.

The ambassador, eager to know the whole business, *Lord*
sent on the following day a confidential agent to *Darcy.*
Darcy, who immediately disclosed their designs at
greater length. In the northern counties alone, he
said, there were already sixteen earls and barons, who
in this matter were all of the same opinion.[1] If the
emperor sent men of war and a few troops to the *Scheme of*
mouth of the Thames, and if a band of good hack- *the con-*
butters, some experienced officers and a supply of *spirators.*
arms and ammunition were landed in the north, the
lords would rise against the king. They would unfurl
the imperial standard, adding a crucifix to it.[2] Their

---

[1] E. Chapuis to Charles V., September 30, 1534, Vienna
Archives, P.C. 229, i. fol. 139 : " Et que au quartier du nort dont
il estoit il scavoit bien quil y avoit seze contes et autres groz . . .
que sont de son oppinion." The abstract of this letter, printed
in Mr. Gairdner's Calendar, is not quite correct.

[2] *Ibid.* : " Et plus moyennant lassistence de Vostre Majeste

forces were already considerable—Darcy himself
undertook to raise eight thousand men—and many
others would certainly join them.   Of his associates
Darcy named but two, the Earl of Derby and Lord
Dacres of Greystock, the peer who had just been
acquitted of a charge of high treason.   Of possible
opponents in the north, Darcy knew of none except
the Earl of Northumberland ; and he might be easily
arrested, as he had no following, and his own servants
would not support him.   Charles was advised to
befriend James V. of Scotland, who secretly aspired
to the hand of his cousin, Princess Mary ; and the
intention of the conspirators seems to have been to
proclaim James and Mary under the auspices of the
emperor as feudal overlord.   According to Darcy,
they had no doubt of success.

September
30, 1534.   The communication was so important, the details
given by Darcy seemed so likely to be accurate, that
Chapuis wrote at once to the emperor to ask for
instructions.   He did not venture to offer an opinion
directly, but he clearly showed that he thought the
plan feasible ; and he was persuaded that if it could
be carried out it would be of the greatest advantage.[1]

Charles V.
and the
con-
spiracy.   Charles received the ambassador's letter just after
the Count of Nassau had been despatched to the French
court.   From a simply political point of view, the
offer was tempting enough, since it might enable
the emperor to obtain a firm footing in England, and
secure for him a strong alliance against France.   It

vouldroit faire dresser la banniere du crucifix ensemble celle de
Vostre Majeste."
   [1] E. Chapuis to Charles V., September 30, 1534, *loc. cit.*

had also a most seductive aspect for Charles's fancy. He was the last emperor who seriously thought of regaining the power that had been wielded by Charles the Great. He dreamt of being recognised as the supreme lord of the western world, of establishing that monarchy which Dante had praised, which was to heal all wounds and strife, and to extend the rule of Christendom over the whole earth. Two kingdoms had been foremost among those which had refused to submit to the authority of the Kaiser—France and England. Long ago an English king had been obliged to take an oath of fealty to the emperor, but Richard I. had forgotten his promises as soon as he had recovered his liberty, and they had been wholly disregarded by his successors. For more than three centuries no emperor had pretended to exercise power in England, and only a few forms remained to remind the curious and the learned of the ancient tie.

But now the English nobles, writhing under the tyranny of Henry, appealed to the emperor. Admitting their dependence upon him, they wished to legalise their rising by fealty to the higher lord, and offered to unfurl his standard. The English leopards were to be superseded by the Roman eagle, the imperial power in England was to become a reality. It was a splendid prospect, and the resolution to turn from it must have cost Charles V. a bitter pang. But dreamer as the emperor was, he was also a keen and farsighted politician. For the present, with Soliman, Barbarossa, and Francis I. threatening him, he could not wish for a rising which

CHAP. X. might prove the signal for general war. He wanted
to fight Barbarossa separately, and for that purpose
it was necessary to have peace with France, which
rebellion in England would render impossible. So
the English were to wait until Tunis was taken.

Chapuis was ordered to give general assurances of
good will, and to remain in communication with
Hussey, Darcy, and their confederates, but not to go
any further. He was directed, too, to obtain
Reginald information about Reginald Pole, regarding whom
Pole. the emperor had lately received a report from Venice,
describing him as a person of some importance.[1]
With this part of his instructions Chapuis easily
complied. Reginald was closely related to Lord
Abergavenny, the ambassador's old friend, to the
Earl of Westmoreland, and to Lord Latimer; and his
mother, Countess of Salisbury in her own right, had
been the governess of the princess and was
universally respected and admired. Lord Montague,
the elder brother of Reginald, and Sir Geoffrey Pole,
his younger brother, had already communicated with
Chapuis, and were ready to fight for Mary; and
Chapuis thought that if a rising took place, and if
imperial troops were sent to support it, his presence
would add considerably to the popularity of the
insurrection.[2]

Chapuis received his instructions at a moment

[1] Mr. Hardy's *Report upon Venetian Archives*, p. 69; and
Chapuis to Charles V., November 3, 1534, Vienna Archives,
P.C. 229, i. fol. 151.

[2] Chapuis to Charles V., November 3, 1534, Vienna Archives,
P.C. 229, i. fol. 151.

when it seemed as if no rising would be necessary CHAP. X.
to drive Anne from power; for during the few weeks
which had elapsed between the despatch of his letter
and the arrival of Charles's reply, the conservative
party had gained an important ally. In the spring
of 1534 Henry had already shown signs of being
weary of the woman he now called his wife.
Eighteen months of possession were a long time *Henry's*
for so fickle a lover, and he had begun to pay *new*
marked attention to a young and very handsome *favourite.*
lady at court. Who she was I have not been able
to discover; neither Chapuis nor the French ambassador mention her name in the despatches
which have been preserved. The only thing certain
is, that she was not Anne's later rival, Jane
Seymour.

Henry's affection for Anne had seemed to revive
when she had led him to believe that there was again
a chance of his having a male heir; but when she
was obliged to confess that she had been mistaken
he returned to the young lady, and paid court to her
in a more public manner than ever. Anne became *September*
very angry, and in her bold and overbearing way *1534.*
tried to send her rival away from court. But she
presumed too much on Henry's weakness, overlooking
the fact that she had no authority except what she
derived from the influence she exerted over him. As
soon as he heard of her attempt to interfere with his
amours, he sent her a most insulting message, informing her that she had good reason to be content with
what he had done for her, because if it were still to
be done he would not do it. Let her, he said,

CHAP. X. remember where she had come from, and not be
overbearing.[1]

The new favourite proved to be a strong adherent
of Catherine;[2] and she went so far as to send a
message to Mary to be of good cheer, for things
might change very soon. Whenever she could,
she would do her best to serve the princess.[3]

*Declining
influence
of Anne.*

In proportion as the power of the lady increased,
that of Anne decreased; and the courtiers, ever
ready to abandon a falling favourite, were eager to
desert Anne, whom most of them hated. They soon
had an opportunity of showing how little they really
cared for her. In October Mary and little Elizabeth
were taken to Richmond from the More, where they
had been spending the autumn, and where Mary had
been visited by the gentry of the neighbourhood.
When they were at Richmond, Anne, attended by

*October
22, 1534.*

many ladies and gentlemen, went to see her daughter.
No sooner had she gone in to Elizabeth than the
whole throng of courtiers, the Dukes of Norfolk and
Suffolk at their head, went to pay their respects to
Mary. It was impossible for Anne to console herself

---

[1] E. Chapuis to Charles V., September 24 1534, Vienna
Archives, P.C. 229, i. fol. 139.

[2] E. Chapuis to J. Hanart, October 13, 1534, Vienna Archives,
P.C. 229, ii. No. 60: "Monsr lambassadeur . . . le Roy depuis
quelques jours a commence destre amoureux dune tres belle et
tres adroicte demoiselle et va journellement croissant lamour et
le credit et la bravete de la concubine decroissant; et y a quelque
bon espoir que continuant la dicte amour les affaires de la Royne
et princesse aux quelles la dicte damoyselle est tres affectionee
se porteront bien."

[3] E. Chapuis to Charles V., October 13, 1534, Vienna Archives,
P.C. 229, i. fol. 142.

even by an outburst of anger at the honour shown to her enemy; she had meekly to submit to what she could not but consider a deliberate affront.[1]

Of course the Boleyn faction tried every means to avert the dangers by which they were confronted. Lady Rochford, Anne's sister-in-law, began to intrigue against the favourite, hoping indirectly to shake her credit and to oblige her to leave court. But the plot was detected, and the king in his rage inflicted on her the fate she had tried to prepare for Anne's rival; so that Anne was now deprived of the company both of her sister and of her sister-in-law.[2] Occasionally she attempted to hold her ground, and once she complained of the insolence with which the favourite treated her, but Henry turned his back on her and went away. Her family shared her disgrace. Sir Francis Brian having brought an action against

[1] E. Chapuis to Charles V., October 24, 1534, Vienna Archives, P.C. 229, i. fol. 147: "Mercredi avant que de partir de Mur elle fust visitee de presque tous les gentilshommes et gentilzfemmes de la court, quelque fascherie quen eust la dame. Avant hier jeudi estant a Richemont avec la petite garse, la vint la dame pour veoir sa fille accompagnee des deux ducs de Norphocq et Suffocq et daultres que trestous la vindrent visiter et saluer et une partie des dames que fust chose nouvelle, et ne voulut sortir de sa chambre jusques la dame fust partie pour non la veoir." Mr. Gairdner's abstract of this letter is not quite correct.

[2] E. Chapuis to J. Hanart, October 13, 1534, Vienna Archives, P.C. 229, ii. fol. 85: "Ung homme de la dicte princesse me vient de dire que le dict Roy avoit faict vuider de la court la femme du Seigneur de Rocheffort, pource quelle avoit conspire avec la dicte concubine de procurer et tenir main de par ung moyen ou aultre faire vuider de la court la dicte damoiselle;" and E. Chapuis to Charles V., October 13, 1534, loc. cit.

Lord Rochford, the influence of Henry was exerted in favour of Brian.[1]

The moment seemed favourable for an attempt to re-establish good relations between Henry and the Holy See. In September Clement VII. had fallen dangerously ill, and the king had ordered Gregorio da Casale to repair at once to Rome to watch events, and, if possible, to induce the pope on his death-bed to recall his sentence.[2] The French ambassador, who had been asked to use his influence for the same purpose, had hesitated to do so, but Casale had nevertheless remained at Rome working for his patron. Shortly afterwards Clement died, and Cardinal Farnese, formerly accounted a staunch friend of King Henry, was chosen in his place. Paul III.—so the new pope decided to call himself—adopted a moderate tone, and showed himself anxious for a reconciliation. He spoke with the Cardinal of Lorraine, the most important of the French members of the sacred college, and the cardinal promised to go himself to England to bring the king back to his allegiance to Rome.[3] Casale wrote in a very hopeful manner, and the conservative party in England strained every nerve to profit by the opportunity.

[1] E. Chapuis to Charles V., December 19, 1534, Vienna Archives, P.C. 229, i. fol. 164.

[2] G. da Casale to J. du Bellay, September 22, 1534, Paris, Bibl. Nat. MSS. Français, vol. 19,751, fol. 113; and G. da Casale to Cromwell, September 24, 1534, *State Papers*, vol. vii. p. 570.

[3] G. da Casale to Norfolk, October 15, 1534, *State Papers*, vol. vii. p. 574; and G. da Casale to Rochford, October 15, 1534, *State Papers*, vol. vii. p. 575.

All this was well known at the French court, and Francis and his ministers resolved to take advantage of it. Although they had refused the overtures made by Charles V. for a marriage between Mary and the Duke of Angoulême, they had not broken off the negotiation. What they really desired was a marriage between Mary and the dauphin. If this could be brought about, Anne would be easily disposed of, for Henry would either fall with her, or he would have to give her up. In the latter case he would have to take back Catherine, from whom no further issue was to be expected. England would then, after the death of Francis, be united to France; and the new kingdom, commanding both sides of the Channel, would be the foremost power in Europe. Such were the hopes entertained by the French government; but it was not to be supposed that Charles would readily assent to a scheme that might be so perilous for the empire. The French saw that only by clever intrigue could they hope to persuade him to sanction the substitution of the dauphin for Angoulême.

CHAP. X.
The dauphin and the Princess Mary.

The first thing they had to do was to keep up the distrust between Henry and Charles, and to obtain as much as possible from Henry's fears. About the end of October Philippe de Chabot, admiral of France, was sent on a special mission to England, and although his instructions do not seem to have survived, sufficient evidence remains as to his charge. He was to tell Henry that Charles had proposed through the Count of Nassau two marriages, one between his son Philip and the youngest daughter of

October 20, 1534.

Chabot's mission to England.

Francis—which was true—the other between the dauphin and Mary—which was not true. Moreover, he was to say that Charles had offered Francis the duchy of Milan after the death of the reigning duke, and in the meantime a pension of 100,000 crowns. This also was untrue, for the offer was to hold good only if the duke should die childless, and the sum was much smaller. After this Chabot was to assure Henry that Francis intended to remain faithful to him, and to reject Charles's proposals. But Henry was to be asked to forego the title of King of France, and to accept in exchange a very chimerical title to certain estates in the Low Countries which were to be taken by Henry himself from Charles. Francis desired to be relieved of the obligation to pay the pensions due on account of the treaty of Amiens, and Chabot was to beg Henry to reconsider his policy towards Rome, and either to submit to the pope at once or to reopen the negotiations so suddenly broken off in the spring.[1]

These instructions were very cleverly drawn, for, by a treaty signed in 1518, Mary and the dauphin had actually been betrothed, and Chabot was to base his negotiations on this treaty. If Henry repudiated it, he would set the dauphin free to marry the Infanta Doña Juana, a match which of course would strengthen the Spanish influence in France and draw

---

[1] Reply to Chabot de Brion's proposals, *State Papers*, vol. vii. p. 584; E. Chapuis to Charles V., November 28 and December 19, 1534, Vienna Archives, P.C. 229, i. fol. 157 and 164; and Palamede Gontier to Chabot, February 5, 1535, Lelaboureur, *Memoires de Mr. de Castelnau*, vol. i. p. 405.

Francis away from England. If, on the contrary, to CHAP. X.
prevent the match with the infanta, Henry admitted
that the betrothal was still valid, the game of
Francis would be half won. It was a disagreeable
dilemma for the King of England, and still more
disagreeable for the Boleyns.

Chabot left the French court on the 20th of *October 20, 1534.*
October,[1] and having a very numerous train, he
travelled slowly. On the 8th of November he
arrived at Calais, and on the 11th he crossed to
Dover.[2] Here he waited for his servants and horses,
so that his entry into London was delayed until the
20th.[3] The admiral found a state of things very *November 20, 1534.*
different from that which he had expected. The
conservative party seemed to have no influence whatever; and the English government, instead of showing
any desire for a reconciliation with Rome, was quietly
pursuing the opposite course.

Henry and his advisers were certainly not ignorant *The English govern-ment and the con-spirators.*
of the state of public feeling and of the conspiracy
which was being formed, for Cromwell's spies must
have warned him of what was going on. But the
government was not in a position to take proceedings against the conspirators. It might have secured
from a packed jury the conviction of some of the
lesser malcontents; but it could not venture to

[1] Girolamo Penizon to Cromwell, October 22, 1534, R.O.
Henry VIII. Box Q, fol. 81.
[2] *Chronicle of Calais*, p. 45; and Lord Rochford to Norfolk,
November 11, 1534, Gairdner, *Letters and Papers*, vol. vii. p. 535.
[3] E. Chapuis to Charles V., November 18, 1534, Vienna
Archives, P.C. 229, i. fol. 153; and J. du Mouchiau to Lady Lisle,
November 23, 1534, Gairdner, *Letters and Papers*, vol. vii. p. 548.

CHAP. X. attack the leaders of the movement. An attempt to bring any of the lords to trial would almost certainly have failed, and failure in a matter of so much importance would have seriously damaged the authority of the crown. Fortunately for ministers, they knew that the conspirators now hoped to gain their object by some less dangerous method than open rebellion. Moreover, the winter was setting in, a most unpropitious time for an insurrection. English peasants could not lie out in cold and damp, and if a force were raised against Henry, however powerful it might seem to be, it would dwindle away before the inclemency of the season.

Henry compelled to develop his policy. The government made use of the respite to strengthen itself for the coming struggle. Henry had, indeed, no choice but to go forward with the task he had begun. If he retreated now, he would encourage the opposition, and lose, perhaps, not only all that accession to the prerogative which he had gained during the last few years, but a great part of the authority which had long been obnoxious to peers and commoners alike. He would have to sacrifice his trustiest and ablest ministers, and to substitute for them at the council board the very men who resisted his pretensions. He would become so weak a king, while the peers would become so elated and so popular, that the olden times of York and Lancaster might be revived, and in the midst of the turmoil the Tudor king might disappear. It was, therefore, absolutely necessary to complete the measures which had been taken for the assertion of the royal supremacy.

Parliament met on the 4th of November, and CHAP. X. ministers introduced a number of bills which clearly showed that neither the growing dislike of Henry for Anne, nor his fancy for her rival, had altered his policy. First of all came the famous Act of Supremacy, by which the king was to be declared the only supreme head on earth of the Church of England. This bill was easily carried : a fort- night after the opening of the session, two days before Chabot arrived in London, it had already passed.[1]

The Act of Supre- macy. November 4, 1534.

November 18, 1534.

The admiral, being convinced that the Act of Supremacy was due to Anne's influence, took pains to indicate that the feelings of his master towards her had greatly changed. For two days after he had been received by Henry he did not even mention her name, so that at last the king asked whether he would not go and see the queen. "As it pleases your highness," was the cold answer. He had no message for her ; and he showed that he would wait upon her only out of courtesy to the king.[2] While Chabot strongly marked his indifference to Anne, he begged for permission to see the Princess Mary. His ap- plication was refused, but he found means to let it be generally known that the request had been made. And when his gentlemen and servants were asked whether a marriage had been arranged between the dauphin and the infanta, they asserted that no such

Chabot at the English court.

November 22, 1534.

---

[1] Chapuis to Charles V., November 18, 1534, Vienna Archives, P.C. 229, i. fol. 153.

[2] Chapuis to Charles V., November 28, 1534, Vienna Archives, P.C. 229, i. fol. 157.

CHAP. X.   plan was thought of.   How could it be?   Was not
           the dauphin betrothed to the princess?[1]

At the same time both Chabot and the resident
French ambassador, Morette, were ostentatiously polite
to Chapuis; and in the same spirit Chapuis responded
to their advances.   There was a show of cordiality
between the two embassies which boded no good to
Henry and Anne.

On hearing from Chabot what his instructions
were, Henry tried a counter move.   He could not
see why the dauphin should marry Mary, who was
illegitimate; but might not Angoulême marry
Elizabeth?   Chabot did not absolutely reject the
proposal, as it would not necessarily prevent the
other match, and Henry might be persuaded to give
a considerable dowry.   But the French representative
was careful to leave the impression that he was not
satisfied.[2]

*December
1, 1534.*
An incident which occurred on the evening before
Chabot's departure from England well depicts Anne's
position.   On the 1st of December there was a ball
at court, and the admiral sat with Henry and Anne
on a raised platform looking at the dances.   Palamede
Gontier, treasurer of Brittany and chief secretary to
the embassy, being in the hall, Henry wished to
present him to Anne, and went to fetch him.   Anne
kept her eyes on the king as he made his way through

[1] Chapuis to Charles V., December 5, 1534, Vienna Archives,
P.C. 229, i. No. 68.

[2] Reply to Chabot de Brion, *State Papers*, vol. vii. p. 584;
and E. Chapuis to Charles V., December 5, 1534, Vienna Archives,
P.C. 229, i. fol. 160.

the crowd, and saw that he stopped before reaching
Gontier, and forgot everything in the conversation of
a young lady—her rival. By constant tension of
mind, Anne's health had been very much impaired ;
and she burst into a fit of hysterical laughter which
lasted for several minutes. The admiral, indignant
at her behaviour, angrily asked whether she laughed
at him ; and although Anne, on regaining her composure, tried to explain, she could not allay his
resentment. Chabot reported the incident with
remarks by no means flattering to Anne.

Next day, while Chabot was standing in the hall of
his house, Sir William Fitzwilliam, Sir Nicholas Carew,
Cromwell and other ministers of Henry came to pay
their respects to him. He received them with marked
coldness, but when Chapuis was announced Chabot
went to meet him, greeted him most amiably, and,
leaving the Englishmen to themselves, drew the
imperial ambassador aside to assure him of his good-
will and to complain of Henry. These demonstrations
were intended as much for the English as for Chapuis,
the admiral wishing it to be clearly understood that

---

[1] E. Chapuis to Charles V., January 14, 1535, Vienna Archives,
P.C. 229½, i. fol. 1 : "Le soir du festin que le Roy luy feist que
feut la veillie de son partement estant assiz aupres de la dame
pendant que lon dansoit, sans occasion ne propoz se meit a rire
le plus desmesurement du monde de quoy le dit admiral monstra
estre bien marry et fronsant le nez luy dict : comment madame
vous mocquez Vous de moy ou quoy ? Dont apres avoir saouler
son ris sexcusa vers luy disant quelle se ryoit a cause que ce
Roy luy avoit dit quil alloit demander le secretaire dudict admiral
pour lenvenir vers elle pour luy faire feste et que le dict Roy
avoit rencontre en chemin une dame que luy avoit fait oblye le
surplus. . . ."

CHAP. X. he was decidedly displeased with the king and with
Anne.[1]

*Bill for
enforcing
obedience
to Act of
Supre-
macy.* Chabot had really some reason to complain of
Henry's behaviour. Even while he was in England
a bill was brought in by the government to enforce obedience to the Act of Supremacy. By this
bill it was to be made high treason to deny to the
king and queen or their heirs the dignity, style and
name of their royal estate, or to call them heretic,
schismatic, or infidel.[2] The measure met with considerable opposition; and after long and animated
debates in both houses it was passed only when the
government accepted two amendments intended to
mitigate its severity. The first of these was that the
Act should not take effect until the first of February
following, when it would be generally known, and
nobody would be likely to incur its penalties unawares.
The second amendment seemed even more important,
for it decreed that only malicious denial of the king's
title should be considered high treason. This clause
was introduced for the purpose of shielding persons
who, like Fisher and More, would offer no opinion on
the question.

*Fisher
and More.* Fisher and More had now been prisoners for many
months. The severity with which they had at first
been treated had soon been relaxed; they had been
allowed to obtain books and writing materials, to see
their friends, and to enjoy the liberties of the Tower—
that is, to take a walk either in the inner garden or

---

[1] E. Chapuis to Charles V., December 5, 1534, Vienna Archives,
P.C. 229, i. fol. 160.

[2] Statutes of the Realm, 26 Henry VIII., cap. xiii.

on the leads behind the battlements. But after the
passing of the Act of Supremacy they were asked
by the council, which went to the Tower for the
purpose, to accept the new law. Both desired to be
excused ; whereupon, to punish them for their obstinacy, the privileges they had enjoyed were withdrawn. Their books and writing materials were
taken from them, and they could correspond only by
stealth.[1]

Had the bill creating new kinds of treason passed
in its original form, the two prisoners might have
suffered immediately. As it was, the rigour of their
confinement was not to last very long, and for a
moment they were to have a chance of regaining
their freedom. The last month of 1534 was particularly disagreeable to Henry. Chabot, as already
said, had plainly shown that he was no longer the
friend he had been ; and, as he had hitherto been
very favourable to Henry and Anne, this was an
ominous sign. Nor was it much more encouraging
that although couriers came from France none of them
brought an answer to the proposals made to the French
admiral. Chabot had, indeed, travelled home rather
slowly, but even this could not account for the delay.
Henry was also troubled by tidings which reached
him from Spain. A considerable body of troops was
being raised in that country, ships were being got
ready, and an important expedition was clearly
about to be undertaken. As the King of England
was not aware of the real object of these preparations,

---

[1] *More's Works*, p. 1446 ; and Interrogatory of J. Fisher, § 5,
printed by J. Lewis, in *Life of J. Fisher*, vol. ii. p. 410.

CHAP. X. he became somewhat suspicious. There were ships enough in the Biscayan harbour to bring over the whole force to the English shores, and he had no fleet to intercept them, nor an army to withstand the troops if they landed.[1]

In these circumstances Henry thought it expedient to conciliate his enemies both abroad and at home. Although most rigorous measures had been passed, the government began to act warily, and the first to feel the good effect of the change were the prisoners in the Tower. Their confinement was once more made less strict; they were allowed to write and receive *February,* letters, and to see their friends.[2] Nay, if a letter of
1535. Palamede Gontier, printed by Lelaboureur, may be considered good evidence, Fisher was even permitted to leave the Tower on bail, and to repair to the court at Westminster.[3] In any case, from the end of December to the middle of February, they were treated with comparative favour. And so were Catherine and Mary, who during this period were not molested by messages from the council.

Henry At the same time it was thought that some arrange-
and ment might be come to with Charles V.; and in Paris,
Charles V. towards the end of December, Sir John Wallop tried to open negotiations with Viscount Hanart, the imperial ambassador at the French court. Hanart did

---

[1] Hanart to Granvelle, January 14, 1535, British Museum, Add. MSS. 28,587, fol. 207.

[2] *More's Works*, p. 1450.

[3] Palamede Gontier to P. Chabot de Brion, February 5, 1535, Lelaboureur, *Memoires de Mr. de Castelnau*, vol. i. p. 405, *et seq.* See Appendix, Note E.

not pay much attention to these overtures, but CHAP. X. neither did he refuse to listen to them. A few weeks later, on the 20th of January, Wallop returned to *January 20, 1535.* the subject. He called on Hanart, and stated that he had consulted some of his friends in England, and that in their opinion a compromise might be arrived at on the following basis. Let the emperor promise not to proceed in the matter of the divorce by violence as long as Henry lived ; and in the mean-time the queen would be treated well, and otherwise matters would remain in suspense. Hanart was very reserved, but he wrote an account of the conversation to Granvelle and asked for instructions.[1]

The time seemed in every way propitious for a reconciliation. The credit of the Boleyns was daily decreasing, their enemies were becoming more aggressive, and persons belonging to the class who like to be on the winning side were forsaking Anne and her relatives. She knew this, and was in great anguish of mind. She could not conceal from herself that the ally on whom she had most firmly reckoned, Francis I., was disposed to desert her cause ; and she clearly understood that without his help the emperor could not be resisted. If Francis formed an alliance *Francis and Charles V.* with Charles against England, Henry might save himself by speedy submission, but Anne would have to be sacrificed.

Happily for her, the antagonism between Charles and Francis was so deep-rooted that a real alliance was impossible. After Chabot's return Francis had hesi-

[1] Hanart to Granvelle, January 31, 1535, British Museum, Add. MSS. 28,588, fol. 70.

CHAP. X.   tated, for the offers made by the emperor seemed very
tempting.   But the French king was well aware that
the expedition which was to be undertaken against
Khairredin was meant to deprive him of an ally;
and he suspected that Charles's proposals were intended to amuse him and to keep him quiet while
Tunis was being conquered.   While he was balancing
between two courses open to him, he received news
which filled him with indignation against the emperor.
A rumour had gone abroad in Germany that Francis
had agreed to abandon the German Lutheran princes;
and the French, rightly or wrongly, traced the report
to an imperial source.   If it were not contradicted
he would lose the friendship of his German allies, and
would not be able, as heretofore, to levy landsknechts

January 18, 1535.   to fight his battles.   On the 18th of January Francis
saw Viscount Hanart, to whom he violently com-
plained of what he had heard.   The viscount tried
in vain to explain the thing away: he could not
appease the king's anger or lull his suspicions.[1]
Incensed against the emperor, Francis bethought

January 21, 1535.   himself once more of the English alliance.   An
answer to Henry's proposals was made out, and three
days after Hanart's audience Palamede Gontier
took it to the English court.

But even now the long expected message was by
no means what Anne would have liked.   The con-

Anne's despondency. February 2, 1535.   ditions of Francis were rather hard.   No wonder,
then, that she looked haggard and worn, and that
when, two days after his arrival, Gontier saw her at a

[1] J. Hanart to Charles V., January 31, 1535, British Museum,
Add. MSS. 28,587, fol. 207.

ball at court and gave her a letter from Chabot, she
betrayed her anxiety. She complained that by coming
so late he had made the king very suspicious. It
was necessary, she said, that Chabot should put
matters right, for she found herself in even greater
difficulties than before her marriage. She entreated
Gontier to pray the admiral in her name to look after
her affairs, of which she could not, unhappily, inform
him at such length as she wished, because of the
prying eyes of the king and the courtiers. She added
that she would not be able to write, nor would she
have an opportunity of seeing him again, and even
now she dared not remain with him any longer.
And so she left him, and the treasurer followed Henry
into the ball-room wondering what all this meant.
"I assure you, my lord," he wrote to Chabot, "by
what I can make out she is not at her ease." [1]

Immediately after his arrival, Gontier had been
called to court, and had had a long audience of
the king. First of all the marriage of Elizabeth
with the Duke of Angoulême, which Henry had
proposed, was spoken of. It would be necessary,
Palamede Gontier said, that Elizabeth should be made
perfectly sure of her rank, as the Duke of Angoulême
could not marry a woman whose social and political
status was a matter of doubt. Henry angrily protested that Elizabeth was the undoubted heir to the
crown, and generally recognised as such; but if any
doubt remained in the mind of Francis, he might
easily set it at rest by obliging the pope to recall
the sentence given by Clement, and to declare the

Negotia-
tions
between
England
and
France.
January
31, 1535.

[1] P. Gontier to Chabot de Brion, February 5, 1535, *loc. cit.*

marriage with Catherine to have been null and void from the beginning. Henry was most anxious that this should be done, for reasons which Gontier perhaps guessed, and which ought to have made the French reluctant to commit themselves any further in the matter.

Gontier went on to state what portion Francis would expect the little girl to bring to him and to his son. It was nothing less than the renunciation by Henry of the title of King of France, and the extinction of all pensions, arrears, or payments which the French were by treaties bound to make to him—a sum of about 120,000 crowns a year. At this exorbitant claim Henry's anger broke forth, and he could not for some time regain his equanimity. In the end he said that 50,000 crowns of perpetual pension he was ready to give up, but the sixty thousand which were to be paid to him personally during life he would not relinquish. No decision was arrived at, and as it had grown late the conference was postponed to the following day.

February 1, 1535. Early next morning Palamede Gontier went to Cromwell's house at Austinfriars. The French had hitherto shown little attention to the secretary, having failed to realise the full extent of his power. They now tried to make up for past neglect. Gontier brought complimentary messages from the king and from the admiral, and threw out broad hints that Cromwell would profit by supporting the demands of France. The secretary listened politely, and professed goodwill towards Francis; but he made no positive promise or answer. Although Gontier flattered himself

that he had made some impression on him, Cromwell
remained at heart as anti-French as he had ever been.

From Austinfriars the treasurer took his way to
Westminster, where he met the Dukes of Norfolk and
Suffolk, both of whom showed themselves most
friendly. Gontier remained at court until after dinner,
when he was called into the royal presence. Henry
was still angry at the extravagant claims of Francis,
and complained of the negotiations which had been
kept up with the emperor. The following day was
Candlemas, and Gontier went to the royal chapel.
After the service Henry invited him into his closet,
and in a more pacified tone began to talk about the
proposed meeting between himself and the French
king. He was much gratified to hear that the Queen
of Navarre and the daughters of Francis were to come
to the interview. This flattered his vanity, and put
him in better humour. The audience ended with a
significant request from the French king. Lord
Rochford and Sir Nicholas Carew were rival candidates for the next vacant garter, and Francis asked
that it might be bestowed on Carew. Henry promised
to remember his good brother's wishes.[1]

February 2, 1535.

That same evening—the evening of the ball at
which Gontier met poor Anne—the royal council drew
up the official answer to the French proposals. It
was even less favourable than the reply given by
the king. The perpetual pension he had declared
himself willing to resign, the council would not part
with. As to the marriage, they proposed that commissioners should be sent at Whitsuntide to Calais,

[1] P. Gontier to Chabot de Brion, February 5, 1535, *loc. cit.*

CHAP. X.   there to debate the conditions. Should the admiral
be one of them, the Duke of Norfolk, Sir William
Fitzwilliam, and Cromwell would go to meet him.
Neither the father nor the brother of Anne were to
take part in the negotiations which would settle the
future fate of her daughter—another certain sign of
their disgrace.   The time of the conference was
intentionally fixed at a distant date, that Francis
might try to obtain from Paul III. a reversal of the
sentence given by Pope Clement.[1]

Morette's
dinner
party.
February
3, 1535.

The English opponents of Henry's policy were
now in high spirits. On the day after the ball at
court, Morette gave a great dinner party, at which
the Dukes of Norfolk and Suffolk, Sir William
Weston, prior of St. John, Lord Abergavenny, and
other influential adherents of the papacy were present.
Palamede Gontier told them of the *auto da fé* at
Paris lately, when Francis himself with his sons had
marched in the procession and had watched the torturing and burning of a good number of Protestants.
The English lords were delighted to hear of this,
and praised Francis for what he had done.   There
could be no doubt, Gontier wrote to Chabot, as to
what they themselves would like to do in England.[2]

Henry
forced to
choose
between
Catherine
and Anne.

Henry was at this time in a state of great perplexity. Annoyed by Anne's jealousy, and angry
with her for not having borne him the son and heir

[1] Henry VIII. to Chabot de Brion, *State Papers*, vol. vii.
p. 596; Chabot de Brion to Henry VIII., April 17, 1535, *State*
Papers, vol. vii. p. 592; and P. Gontier to Chabot de Brion,
February 5, 1535, *loc. cit.*

[2] Gontier to Chabot de Brion, February 5, 1535, *loc. cit.*

he had expected, he was anxious to be rid of her;
and the most natural way of accomplishing his purpose seemed to be a second divorce. Cranmer, he
felt sure, would make no difficulties, but would declare
the second marriage, like the first, to be null and void.
Having thought the matter over, he opened his mind
to some of his most trusted counsellors. Who they
were does not appear; but their answer averted the
blow which he thought of striking at Anne. If the
king, they replied, wished to repudiate Anne, he must
restore the rights of Catherine, and acknowledge
Mary as his heir and successor.[1] Henry had hoped
that the marriage with Catherine might still be
dissolved by the pope, and that he would then be
delivered from all difficulty. He had overlooked the
fact that even if Paul III. revoked his predecessor's
sentence it would be extremely dangerous to discard
Anne after all that had been done in her favour. The
Catholics would be as hostile as before, and he would
excite the enmity of the Protestants, who would
decline to believe in new scruples of conscience. As
his advisers urged, therefore, it was necessary for
him to make up his mind whether he would have
Catherine or Anne for wife; the choice lay with him,
but was limited to these two. This was at last made
apparent to Henry, and on his decision the fate of
Anne depended.

[1] E. Chapuis to Charles V., May 2, 1536, Vienna Archives,
P.C. 230, i. fol. 80: "Et plustost se fust declaire ce dict Roy
neust est que quelcung de son conseil luy donnoyt entendre que
ne sauroyt separer de la dicte concubyne sans tacitement con-
firmer non seullement le premier mariaige mais aussy que plus il
crainct lautorite du pape."

CHAPTER XI.

FISHER AND MORE.

Cromwell decides to support Anne.

ANNE and her friends were in serious peril, and she might have succumbed at once had she not regained the help of Cromwell. The secretary had not been much impressed by Gontier's fair words; he was still hostile to France, and saw with apprehension the growing power of the aristocratic party and of his bitter enemy the Duke of Norfolk. Having identified himself so closely with the measures against the Roman Church, he could not but fear that, if its authority were re-established, he would fare very badly at its hands. In order to prevent the possibility of a reaction, he resolved to support Anne; and perhaps it was he who explained to Henry the danger of a second divorce.

The troubles of the Boleyns had been due in a great measure to the influence of the new favourite, whose reign had now lasted nearly six months—for Henry, rather a long time. It occurred to them that their prospects might be improved if the king were under the dominion of a more friendly beauty; and in the hope that he might be fascinated they brought to

court Anne's pretty cousin, Margaret Shelton, daughter
of the governess of Mary. The scheme may not have
been very dignified, but it was eminently successful.
On the 25th of February, little more than three
weeks after the ball at which Gontier had seen Anne
in despair, Eustache Chapuis wrote: "The lady   *A new*
"who formerly enjoyed the favour of this king does so *favourite.*
February
"no longer; she has been succeeded in her office by a 25, 15. 5.
"first cousin of the concubine, daughter of the new
"governess of the princess."[1]

The defeat of the imperialist favourite led to *The mal-*
renewed agitation among the malcontents, for with the *contents.*
advent of Margaret Shelton disappeared the last hope
that by means of female influence a reversal of policy
might be obtained. Even during the preceding
winter, when it had been found that the fair partisan
of Catherine and Mary was not able to make Henry
altogether obedient to her will, the members of the
opposition had drawn together again, and numerous
recruits had swollen their ranks. In the end of
December, 1534, the only peer north of the Trent *December,*
who had been favourable to Anne, the Earl of North- *1534.*
umberland, professed to be deeply offended by the
insolence of the Boleyns, and to be ready to join the
confederacy against his former love. This was reported
to Chapuis by the earl's physician.[2] The conspirators

[1] E. Chapuis to Charles V., February 25, 1535, Vienna
Archives, P.C. 229½, i. fol. 13: "La damoiselle questoit naguieres
en faveur de ce Roy ne lest plus et a succede en son lieu une
cousine germaine de la concubine quest fille de la moderne
gouvernante de la princesse."

[2] E. Chapuis to Charles V., January 1, 1535, Vienna Archives,
P.C. 229½, i. fol. 34.

CHAP. XI. were rather suspicious of Northumberland, whom they knew to be wayward and fickle, and they warned Chapuis to be very careful in dealing with him;[1] but if Anne's enemies were unable to consider him a trustworthy ally, it was at least certain that she could not regard even him as a faithful friend.

More important men now began to communicate with Chapuis. Lord Sandys, the chamberlain of the household, who had retired from court on the plea of sickness, sent a message to the ambassador by his physician to the effect that it would be easy for Charles V. to conquer England, and that he himself would willingly rise if the emperor would undertake to support an insurrection.[2] A few weeks later, the Marquis of Exeter protested that he was prepared to shed his heart's blood in the cause of Catherine;[3] and Lord Bray, a wealthy peer who was highly *March* 3, esteemed for his learning and energy, applied to 1535. Chapuis for the text of a prophecy that there would be a revolt against the government, and begged for a cipher by means of which some malcontent lords might safely correspond with one another. He also wished to be permitted to speak with Chapuis about these matters. The latter request the ambassador did not think fit to comply with, as it might awaken suspicion, but otherwise he returned a friendly and

[1] E. Chapuis to Charles V., January 28, 1535, Vienna Archives, P.C. 229½, i. fol. 9.

[2] E. Chapuis to Charles V., January 14, 1535, Vienna Archives, P.C. 229½, i. fol. 1.

[3] E. Chapuis to Charles V., February 25, 1535, *loc. cit.*

encouraging answer, asking only that his correspond-
ent would wait for a more convenient season.[1]

In February Mary had fallen seriously ill.[2] After *Mary's*
some time the king allowed the queen's physician to *illness.*
February
attend her, and sent his own physician, Dr. Butts, to *5, 1535.*
consult with him.[3] The two doctors did not limit *Political*
their conversation to medical matters, but very soon *opinions of*
the
began to talk of politics. Dr. Butts made no mystery *doctors.*
of his opinions. He said that the life of the queen *March,*
and the princess might be spared if the king fell *1535.*
ill, since he would then listen to reason and understand his errors, but that otherwise they could be
saved only by the employment of force. It was well
for the king, he added, that the emperor did not know
with how little trouble he might make himself master
of England.[4]

[1] E. Chapuis to Charles V., March 4, 1535, Vienna Archives,
P.C. 229½, i. fol. 42 : "Sire hier vint ung docteur religieux avec
lequel jay de longtemps familiarite qui me vint demander une
pronosticacion que parle de la mutynacion qui doit estre contre
les gouverneurs de ce royaulme de laquelle pronostication chacun
estoit requis de la part de millor Brez, quest ung seigneur scavant
riche et de bon cueur . . . il vouldroit escripre a plusieurs bons
personnages pour selon que pouvoit comprendre dudict religieulx
les inciter contre . . . gouvernemens desperant de la tardance du
remede de Vostre Maieste."

[2] E. Chapuis to Charles V., February 9, 1535, Vienna Archives,
P.C. 229½, i. fol. 22.

[3] E. Chapuis to Charles V., February 25, 1535, *loc. cit.*

[4] E. Chapuis to Charles V., April 25, 1535, Vienna Archives,
P.C. 229½, i. fol. 74 : "Il a dit au dict de la Royne quil ny avoit
que deux moyens pour remedier aux affaires des Royne et princesse, et a ceulx de tout le royaulme. Le premier estoit si dieu
vouloit visiter ce roy de quelque petite maladie, lors oultre que
de luy mesmes se recougnoistroit, il prendroit aussy en pacience

The aim of the conspirators being to proclaim Mary, Chapuis feared that if the signal for revolt were given she would be put to death; and he had sounded her whether she would be ready to save herself by flight. Finding that she was willing to do whatever might seem to him to be expedient, he decided that if he received the emperor's permission, and if Mary remained at Greenwich, she should be carried off and put on board a light rowing vessel which would carry her to Flanders; but in consequence of her illness this plan had to be abandoned.[1] It happened about this time that several of Anne's adversaries (among them her uncle, Sir Edward Boleyn) were dining with Chapuis; and with them he made an appointment to go on the Saturday following to Lord Darcy, with whom he was anxious to confer about measures for the princess's safety. Much to the disappointment of Chapuis, this engagement could not be fulfilled; and, knowing the watchfulness of Cromwell's spies, he did not venture

March 6, 1535.

to go alone. He despatched a confidential agent, however, and to this messenger Darcy said that if civil war were proclaimed he believed Henry would send Catherine and Mary to the Tower, and keep them

---

et de bonne part les remonstrances que luy en seroynt faictes; lautre moyen seroit dattempter la force . . . et que tardant lung ou laultre remede elles estoient en dangier de leur vie, et que bien en prenoit au dict Roy son maistre que V. Mte nestoit bien informee de la facilite quil y auroit de venir a chief de lemprinse dont seroit maintenant la propre saison."

[1] E. Chapuis to Charles V., February 9 and 25, and March 4, 1535, *loc. cit.*

there as hostages for his own security.[1] Now, Sir
William Kingston, captain of the king's guard and
constable of the Tower, had entered into correspondence
with the conspirators, and had declared himself a
devoted adherent of the two ladies. If they were
entrusted to him, they would be in no danger whatever.[2] This intelligence, which was confirmed from
other quarters, somewhat reassured the ambassador;
but as a thoroughgoing adherent of the king might
be put in Sir William Kingston's place, Chapuis was
still of opinion that Mary ought to be removed from
England. In April she was taken to Eltham, and he
hoped that it might be possible to have her conveyed
from that place to the river below Gravesend. If
men were sent in pursuit, they would probably wish
her good speed and take care not to overtake her.[3]

---

[1] E. Chapuis to Charles V., March 7, 1535, Vienna Archives,
P.C. 229½, i. fol. 46.

[2] E. Chapuis to Charles V., March 4, 1535, Vienna Archives,
P.C. 229½, i. fol. 42: "Que me faict croire que survenant la
dicte evocacion ce roy ne se hasteroit de faire oultraige ausdites
dames actendant lissue des affaires. Il est a penser quil sen
saisiroit et les feroit mectre en la tour et croys que en tel cas les
dictes royne et princesse ne seroint tant a son commandement
quil penseroit bien, pour estre le cappitaine a ce que il monstre
serviteur de vostre maieste et des dictes dames et homme de bien
ayant communique avec aucuns des susmencionez;" and E.
Chapuis to Charles V., March 7, 1535, *loc. cit.*: "Je suis seur
que tumbant elles en main et garde de celluy dont rescripvis
dernierement quelles seroyent hors de dangier et ne desire moings
le bien que les autres comme ay sceu encoires aujourdhuy de bien
bonne part et ne desire que locasion de pouvoir monstrer sa
bonne volente."

[3] E. Chapuis to Charles V., April 5, 1535, Vienna Archives,
P.C. 229½, i. fol. 64: "la maison ou elle gist est a douze mille de

CHAP. XI. The chief difficulty would be to get her out of the
house, which was strongly guarded by a body of
royal servants under the command of Sir John
Shelton.[1]

The government, knowing much of what was going
on, caused the chief conspirators to be closely
watched, and when some of them applied for permission to leave the court it was not granted. Cromwell
wished to keep them near, so that they might always
be surrounded by spies.[2]

Illness of
Cromwell.
March 3,
1535.
While Anne and her party—thanks to Margaret
Shelton—seemed to be recovering their power, they
were threatened by a new danger. Early in March,
Cromwell caught a severe cold, and was obliged to keep
his room for a few days.[3] Impatient at the confine-

March 6,
1535.
ment and wishing to speak with Chapuis, he went out
too soon,[4] had a relapse to which he did not pay

ceste riviere et quant pourroit une fois tenir la dicte princesse a
cheval il seroit plus aise de la saulver quil nestoit a grinuic, car
lon lembarqueroit plus avant que gravesen de la ou est tout le
dangier de ceste riviere;" and E. Chapuis to N. de Granvelle,
April 5, 1535, Vienna Archives, P.C. 229½, iii. fol. 4: "et
serreroient les yeulx donnant une benediction a ceulx qui la
saulveroient."

¹ E. Chapuis to Charles V., April 5, 1535, *loc. cit.*: "et que
la ou elle estoit maintenant yl ny avoit ordre de soy saulver de
nuyt."

² E. Chapuis to Charles V., January 1, February 25, and
March 23, 1535, *loc. cit.*

³ E. Chapuis to Charles V., March 4, 1535, Vienna Archives,
P.C. 229½, i. fol. 42: "Quil sestoyt hier trouve malade dune
reume que luy avoit faict enfler ung yeul et la joue."

⁴ E. Chapuis to Charles V., March 7, 1535, *loc. cit.*: "Le
VIᵐᵉ Cremuel me vint trouver ne layant pu faire premier a cause
de son indisposicion."

sufficient attention, and on Monday, the 22nd, broke CHAP. XI.
down altogether. He seems to have suffered from *March* 22,
inflammation of the lungs. For a fortnight his life 1535.
was in danger, and for nearly three weeks he could
not transact any business.[1] During this time his
enemies, the friends of Catherine and Mary, tried
to exercise some influence on Henry, and he seemed
not unwilling to hear them ; but Cromwell recovered,
and at once destroyed their hopes. Whoever had
dared to speak in favour of the queen and the princess
was soundly rated and threatened by the secretary.[2]

Before Cromwell's illness, it had been determined
that the form of oath which had been prepared
towards the close of the session, and to which the
clergy attending convocation had been compelled to
subscribe, should be imposed upon all who were
suspected of hostility to the new measures.[3] Now
another step in the same direction was taken ; a
proclamation was issued against those who still adhered to the pope, or who used his name or style
in the service of the Church.[4] Strict inquiry was to

[1] Diarium Petri Suavenii, edited by C. F. Wegener, *Aars-beretninger*, vol. iii. pp. 234 to 236: "Sabato (March 6) re-nunctiatum, non dari otium ad me audiendum propter raucedinem et nescio quam valetudinem malam." . . . "Die lunae post Palmarum (March 22), coepit aegrotare tertiana febri . . . Dominica Quasimodo geniti (April 4) accessi ad aedeis Crumwelli propterea quod dicebatur nonnihil convaluisse. Nemo invenie-batur, qui me adesse vellet significare . . . Die Jovis (April 7) . . . jam nonnihil convaluisset et homines ad se admitteret."

[2] E. Chapuis to Charles V., April 17, 1535, Vienna Archives, P.C 229½, i. fol. 68.

[3] Palame Gontier to Chabot de Brion, February 5, 1535, *loc. cit.*

[4] Henry VIII. to the Earl of Sussex, April 17, (1535), Strype,

CHAP. XI.   be made, and offenders were to be severely punished.
The secular clergy in general offered little opposition,
but there were monks who showed themselves less
yielding.   The priors of the Carthusian monasteries,
men renowned for their ascetic virtue and piety,
assembled at the Charterhouse, near London, and
Priors of   protested against the new edict.   Cromwell summoned
Carthu-   them before him, and as they boldly proclaimed their
sian mon-
asteries.   intention to disobey what they considered an unjust
April 20,   command they were committed to the Tower to await
1535.
judgment.[1]   They were not kept long in suspense.
April 29,   On the 29th of April they were arraigned at the
1535.
Guildhall, found guilty, and condemned to the usual
punishment of traitors.[2]   No mercy was shown to
them; on the 4th of May the three priors and a
May 4,   Brigitin monk from Syon were hanged, cut down alive,
1535.
disembowelled, beheaded and quartered.[3]   The Duke
of Richmond, Henry's bastard son, the Duke of
Norfolk, Wiltshire, Rochford, Norris, and other courtiers went to Tyburn to witness their death.[4]

Memorials, vol. i. part ii. p. 208.   Mr. Gairdner places this letter
in the year 1534, but I think it belongs to 1535, for in the
latter year Tunstall received a similar privy seal: Cuthbert
Tunstall to all men, June 9, 1535, R.O. Henry VIII., anno xxviii.,
bundle ii.

[1] Examination of Carthusian monks, April 20, 1535, R.O.
Henry VIII. Box R, No. 36.

[2] Records of the trial, R.O. Baga de Segretis, Pouch VII. Bundle
I.; and Third Report of the deputy keeper of public records, App.
II. p. 237.

[3] E. Chapuis to N. de Granvelle, May 8, 1535, Vienna
Archives, P.C. 229½, iii. fol. 7.

[4] E. Chapuis to Charles V., May 8, 1535, Vienna Archives,
P.C. 229½, i. fol. 76.

By this time the negotiations about the proposed meeting at Calais had been nearly brought to an end. On the 5th of March, after a stay of five weeks, Gontier had left England to give Francis an account of his mission.[1] On the 25th he came over once more, remaining about a week in England.[2] He took back flattering and promising messages from Henry, to which the admiral of France answered in the same strain. The 23rd of May was fixed as the day on which the commissioners were to assemble, and Henry looked forward with confidence to the result.[3]

Cromwell was less sanguine, for he knew from the beginning what would be the effect of the execution of men so highly respected as the Carthusian monks. The English Observants, Carthusians, and Brigitins were not simply English subjects, they were members of international religious societies which everywhere commanded respect and sympathy. Henry had persecuted those monastic orders which were esteemed by Catholic and Protestant alike, while he favoured the members of confraternities notorious for their sloth, their ignorance, and their immorality. Preachers on the Continent vehemently denounced the cruelty of a king who had caused men like Haughton to be executed, and men like Peyto to be banished. In France the feeling against Henry seems

---

[1] E. Chapuis to Charles V., March 7, 1535, *loc. cit.*

[2] E. Chapuis to Charles V., April 5, 1535, Vienna Archives, P.C. 229½, i. fol. 64.

[3] Henry VIII. to Chabot de Brion, *State Papers*, vol. vii. p. 596 ; and Chabot de Brion to Henry VIII., April 17, 1535, *State Papers*, vol. vii. p. 592.

CHAP. XI to have become intensely bitter, and the English
alliance was most unpopular.[1]

Being certain that in these circumstances the
commissioners at Calais would be unable to agree,
Cromwell resolved to have nothing to do with their
proceedings.   He pretended that he was not yet well
enough to go, and, as the Boleyns had been restored
to favour, Lord Rochford was named in his stead.[2]

May 20,
1535.
May 22,
1535.

On the 19th and 20th of May the English commissioners arrived at Calais, and on the 22nd they
were joined by Chabot, with whom were Genoul-
hiac, master of the horse ; Poyet, president of
the parliament of Paris ; and Bochetel, secretary for
finance.[3]   What Cromwell had foreseen came to pass.

*Demands
of the
French.*

The French would not depart from the conditions
proposed through Palamede Gontier, and they are
said to have added a clause to the effect that if for
any reason, after the conclusion of the treaty, Henry
broke off the match, he would forfeit all pensions and
arrears due to him by the King of France.[4]   On all
the points in dispute the admiral was immovable, so

---

[1] Advertisements from France, October 24 and 25, 1534, R.O.
Henry VIII., Box Q, Nos. 84 and 85 ; and T. Thebalde to Lord
Wiltshire, June 7, 1535, R.O. Henry VIII., Box R, No. 1.

[2] E. Chapuis to Charles V., May 8, 1535, *loc. cit.*

[3] Chronicle of Calais, p. 45 ; and Chabot to Henry VIII.,
April 17, 1535, *loc. cit.*

[4] J. Hanart to Mary of Hungary, June 5, 1535, Brussels,
Archives du Royaume, Negotiations de France, vol. ii. fol. 18 :
"Jentends que sur la matiere de leurs alliance y a de grosses
difficultes sur les demandes que se font pour asseurence du
mariage.   Ceulx de ce couste demandent payne de comise le
tribut et toutes les pensions quil payent chacun an en angleterre
et que la fille soit dois maintenant juree pour princesse."

that after two sittings Norfolk perceived that no
understanding such as Henry desired could be
arrived at.

Lord Rochford crossed to Dover, and galloped straight
to the court to give an account of the French demands.
On his arrival he went at once to his sister, who could   *May* 25,
scarcely bring herself to believe the news he reported.   1535.
On the following days she relieved her feelings by
saying all the ill she could of Francis and of the
French people;[1] and it was observed that whereas
Morette had hitherto been invited to all her parties,
he was henceforth conspicuously absent.[2]

When he had seen the king, Rochford left for
Calais with the same haste with which he had come,
taking with him supplementary instructions to Norfolk.[3] They were to prove fruitless. Francis, in
consenting to treat with Henry regarding the marriage
of Angoulême and Elizabeth, wanted to obtain such

---

[1] E. Chapuis to Charles V., June 5, 1535, Vienna Archives,
P.C. 229½, i. fol. 89 : "Sire apres les deux premieres communi-
cations entre les deputez de ces deux Roys le Sr de Rochefort
partist de Calais et arriva icy le XXV du mois passe et avant
que parler au Roy il sadressa a la dame sa seur et divisa bien
longuement avec elle et ne luy dust rapporter dudict Calais
chose que luy aggreast car et lors et mainteffois depuis ainsy
que ma dict le grant escuyer elle a maulgree et dit mille maulx
et opprobres du Roy de France et generallement de toutte la
nation."

[2] E. Chapuis to Charles V., June 16, 1535, Vienna Archives,
P.C. 229½, i. fol. 97 : "la dame . . . fit plusieurs braves mommeries, elle y appella plusieurs et na ete content lambassadeur
de France dy etre oblye."

[3] Articles and Instructions for Norfolk, *State Papers*, vol. vii.
p. 608.

CHAP. XI. a dowry, in ready money, subsidies, or renunciation
of pensions, as would make it worth his while to
sanction the match without taking into account any
hopes the little girl might have of succeeding to the
English throne. He wished, too, to refrain from
doing anything that would imperil the treaty by
which a marriage between the dauphin and the
Princess Mary had been arranged. And he not only
objected to join Henry in his revolt against the Holy
See, but strongly advised that by some kind of
submission the English schism should be brought to
an end. Henry, on the other hand, desired by the
proposed marriage to make sure of the French alliance,
and he would not accept any conditions which would
render it equally advantageous to Francis to side with
Mary and her adherents. He was not inclined to
give a large dowry, for his vanity revolted against
the idea that his, the great King Henry's, daughter
was not by herself a brilliant match for a younger
son of the French king.[1] He insisted that Angoulême
should be sent over to him, with some idea perhaps
that he would then have a hostage for the good
behaviour of Francis.[2] And he advanced preposterous claims as to the position the young duke was to

[1] Henry VIII. to Chabot de Brion, *State Papers*, vol. vii. p.
596.

[2] Articles and Instructions for Norfolk, *loc. cit.*: "Second-
arylie, touching the traduction hither into this Realme the saide
Duke of Angolesme to be educate and brought up here, the saide
Duke of Norfolk and his colleges shall eftsones in that behalf,
by all meanes they can, presse the saide Admyrall . . . ;" and
Cyfuentes to Charles V., July 16, 1535, British Museum, Add.
MSS. 28,587, fol. 345.

occupy in France, should he by right of his wife CHAP. XI.
succeed to the English crown.[1]

The English commissioners in vain strove to over- *Failure of the negotiations.*
come the resistance of Chabot and his colleagues.
The French no longer stood in urgent need of the
English alliance, since it was open to them, if they
pleased, by accepting the overtures of Nassau, to
come to terms with the emperor. It was Henry who
was now in danger of finding himself confronted by
a hostile coalition ; it was he, the French thought,
who ought to be ready to make sacrifices. But this
he declined to do, and his commissioners succeeded
only in irritating Chabot, who had not forgotten the
abuse showered upon him by Henry and Cromwell
early in the spring, and who had been further angered
by the execution of the Carthusian priors just before
the conference at Calais began.[2] The conference

---

[1] Articles and Instructions, *loc. cit.* : "Thirdely, where as the
kinges Highnes by the said former instructions hathe gyven in
charge to the said Duke of Norfolk and his colleges that amongst
other it be specyallie provyded, in case the saide Duke of
Angolesme shall succede the Kinges Highnes in the emperiall
Crowne of this Realme in the right and title of the saide Lady
Pryncesse, that then his saide dukedom of Angolesme, and all
other his domynyons, landes, and possessions within the realme
of Fraunce, or elles where in any of the Frensh kinges domynyons,
shalbe clerely exonerated and frely discharged, by the consent of
their Parliamentes, from all exactions, servytutes, homages, and
fealties . . . the saide Duke of Norfolk and his colleges shall in
that poynt styke fyrmely to the conducing of the same to
effecte. . . "

[2] Chabot de Brion to Cardinal du Bellay, June 8, 1535, Paris,
Bibl. Nat. MSS. Fr. vol. 19,577 : "Vous entendrez le tout par
ce qui est escript au Roy presentement, Vous asseurant Monsieur que jen voudroys bien estre depesche pour la tricoterie de

CHAP. XI.

having been broken up, Chabot left Calais in a very bad temper on the 14th of June.[1]

The failure of Norfolk and his colleagues had an unhappy effect on the fate of the prisoners in the Tower. After the victory of Anne in February, they had been kept in somewhat closer confinement, but at first they had not been otherwise molested. When Cromwell recovered from his illness, and active measures were taken against the adherents of the pope, they suffered from the change. On the 30th of April, the day after the Charterhouse monks were condemned to die, More was called before some of the royal councillors and warned that if he did not give way he might incur the same penalties as the Carthusians. But his fortitude was not to be shaken ; he refused to yield.[2] On the 4th of May he was again examined, and admonished not to expose himself to the fate of those who had just been led to execution.[3] Subsequently, More, Bishop Fisher, Dr. Abel, the former chaplain of Catherine, and Featherstone, Mary's former schoolmaster, were formally called upon to submit within six weeks ; otherwise, they would be put upon their trial.[4]

They might still have escaped had not the suspicions of the king been aroused by the resolute tone of the French and by the rashness of the pope. The French

mode estrange de marchander quon nous tient qui nest point mon naturel . . ."

[1] Chronicle of Calais, p. 45.

[2] Account of Thomas More, More's Works, ed. 1557, p. 1451.

[3] *Ibid.* p. 1452.

[4] E. Chapuis to Charles V., May 8, 1535, Vienna Archives, P.C. 229½, i. fol. 76.

admiral at Calais had persisted in speaking of CHAP. XI.
Princess Mary; Morette assiduously cultivated the
good will of Chapuis; and Morette's servants talked
very freely about the marriage of Mary and the dauphin.
Henry began to fear that the proposals made by
Count Henry of Nassau, of which Chabot had given
him warning, had been secretly accepted by France,
and that Francis would try to get possession of
Mary in order to make her the dauphin's wife.[1]

The news from Rome was still more disquieting. *Henry*
The papal court had, of course, been informed of the *and the*
disfavour into which Anne had fallen at the end of *Papacy.*
1534, and of the extreme insecurity of her position
during the first two months of 1535.[2] Paul III. then
hoped that Henry, cured of his passion for Anne,
would retrace his steps; and the Cardinal of Lorraine,
the most influential of all the cardinals of the
French faction, promised, as we have seen, to go to
England to bring about a reconciliation.[3] There seemed
to be little doubt that if the cardinal fulfilled his
promise, Henry would submit, as it was inconceivable that he would insult Francis by refusing the
mediation of so great a man. The cardinal, however,
did not go; his place was taken by Chabot; and

[1] E. Chapuis to N. de Granvelle, July 25, 1535, Vienna
Archives, P.C. 229½, iii. fol. 19.
[2] Cyfuentes to Charles V., November 7, 1534, British Museum
Add. MSS. 28,587, fol. 125; and Account from Rome, British
Museum, Add. MSS. 28,586, fol. 9.
[3] G. da Casale to Norfolk, October 15, 1534, *State Papers*,
vol. vii. p. 573: "Lotharingius . . . dicit se velle in Angliam
ad Serenissimum Regem venire;" and G. da Casale to Cromwell,
November 8, 1534, *State Papers*, vol. vii. p. 579.

when the pope complained, it was replied that equally good results might be obtained at the meeting at Calais.[1] Paul III. greatly doubted this, but he did not doubt that the French and Gregorio da Casale were right in the accounts they gave him of a change in Henry's temper and convictions. The pope was not aware that there had been a reaction, that Anne was once more triumphant, and that the favourable opportunity had been lost. Believing that Fisher, who had been so leniently treated at the beginning of the year, continued to enjoy the favour of the king, he allowed himself to be persuaded to make the good bishop a cardinal.[2] This was done on the 21st of May; and Jean du Bellay, Henry's stout friend and advocate, and Girolamo Ghinucci, his former ambassador, were also—at the same consistory —promoted to the dignity of the purple.

Fisher made a cardinal.

May 21, 1535.

As soon as Gregorio da Casale heard of the creation, he strongly protested against it. The pope began to think that he had made a mistake, but as it was now past remedy, he tried to excuse what he had done, saying he had hoped to please rather than to offend the King of England. Casale, fearing that Henry would suspect him of having advised the nomination of Fisher, and that he might lose his pension,[3] asked

[1] Cyfuentes to Charles V., March 3, 1535, British Museum, Add. MSS. 28,587, fol. 243.

[2] G. da Casale to Cardinal du Bellay, May 21 and June 2, 1535, Paris, Bibl. Nat. MSS. Fr. vol. 19,571, fols. 117 and 118.

[3] G. da Casale to Cardinal du Bellay, May 21, 1535, *loc. cit.*: " Hora questa cosa sara giudicata molto male in Inghilterra, maxime da quelli che sa V. S. R^{ma}, dubito che quei tali com

that at least the red hat should not be sent to Fisher; but this request seems to have been disregarded.[1] Shortly afterwards the French ambassador, Charles de Denonville, Bishop of Mâcon, received letters about the execution of the Carthusian monks; and when they were read in consistory, they dispelled any illusion which the pope or the cardinals may still have retained as to Henry's intentions.[2]

Paul III., now seriously alarmed, sent for Denonville, and asked him to beg Francis to intercede for the new cardinal. The ambassador, while promising to write to the king, gave little hope. The imperialists, he said, in order to make Henry suspicious of the good faith of Francis, were pretending that the honour had been granted on the recommendation of the French. If Francis pleaded for Fisher, Henry would probably believe what the imperial agents asserted, and resent his intervention.[3]

Fisher in danger. May 29, 1535.

sospettosi dirano che questo sia stato mio motivo onde nascerebbe la mia ruina totale. . ."

[1] G. da Casale to Cromwell, May 29, 1535, *State Papers*, vol. vii. p. 604 ; and Report of Spy from Boulogne, R.O. Henry VIII., Box R. : "Monseigneur, il passa ung homme mardi la nuyt en engleterre que le pappe envoye au Roy avec ung chappeau rouge pour levesque de Rocestre qui est prisonier en la tour de Londres avec une bulle dexcommunication pour fulminer le Roy sil ne mect le dict evesque dehors et sil luy empesche de prendre le chappeau. Ledict messaigier vint mardi quant Monsgr ladmiral."

[2] G. da Casale to Cromwell, June 1, 1535, *State Papers*, vol. vii. p. 605 ; and the Bishop of Mâcon to Francis I., May 29, 1535, Paris, Bibl. Nat. MSS. Dupuis, vol. 265, fol. 138.

[3] The Bishop of Mâcon to Francis I., May 29, 1535, *loc. cit.*, cipher undeciphered : "Me priant affectueusement Vous vouloir encoires suplier davoir le Cardinal de Rocestre pour recommande

Paul III. was greatly distressed, and once more
protested that he had not intended to displease King
Henry.   He was ready, he declared, to give a
written attestation that he had never been asked
by any prince to 'confer the cardinal's hat on the
Bishop of Rochester.[1]

The Bishop of Mâcon wrote to his master and to
Cardinal du Bellay ; and Nicolas Raince, the French
permanent secretary, also wrote at the urgent request
of the pope.[2]   Moreover, in two letters addressed to
du Bellay, Gregorio da Casale proposed that Fisher
should promise, if his life were spared, to swear to the
statutes in order to be allowed to go to Rome to
receive the red hat.   This would be very advantageous
to Henry, who would be glad to get rid of his

doubtant que sans voustre ayde il nen aura pas moins que les
executez.   Il se dict que les ministres dudict Empereur avoient
escript en flandres de faire publier en angleterre par les marchants
flamens ayant trafficque avecques les angloys que la promotion
dudict Roffence avoit este faicte a voustre poursuite et requeste
affin danimer le dict Roy a lencontre de Vous et seroit bon quil
Vous pleust y faire donner ordre pour y obvier et ouster ce scrupulle
au dict Roy.   Jay adverty noustre dit Sainct Pere de tout cecy
luy remonstrant que au moyen de ce bruit il sera bien difficille
que puissiez persuader ny moyenner affaire du dict Roffence vers
le dict Roy dangleterre."

[1] *Ibid.* : "Il me dict quil feroit telle attestation que Vous
adviseriez que Vous ny autre prince chrestien ne luy feist parler
dudit Roffence, que la verite estoit quil lavoit fait cardinal pour
son scavoir et vertu le cognoissant par ses œuvres estre necessaire
pour le futeur concille, et lavoit plustoust fait cardinal pour en
gratiffier le dit Roy dangleterre que en hayne de luy."

[2] The Bishop of Mâcon to Cardinal du Bellay, June 2, 1535,
Paris, Bibl. Nat. MSS. Fr. vol. 19,577 ; and Nicolas Raince to
Cardinal du Bellay, May 21 (*sic.*), 1535, *ibid.*

opponent.[1] Casale did not say that the scheme had
been approved of by the pope, but he had no doubt
that Paul III. would absolve Fisher from any sin he
might commit in taking the oath.

It is most unlikely that Fisher would ever have con-
descended to save his life by a subterfuge such as
Casale suggested ; he was not the man to forswear
himself, even if he had the secret permission of the
pope to do so. But he does not appear to have been
put to the test. On receiving the letters of Denonville,
Francis asked Henry to spare Fisher's life, and, if
Cardinal du Bellay is to be trusted, Henry answered

---

[1] G. da Casale to Cardinal du Bellay, May 21, 1535, *loc. cit.* :
"Potria anchora S. M^{ta} far intendere al Re dInghilterra che
questa cosa tornera a suo commodo, perche questo vescovo il
quale non ha mai voluto giurare la osservantia de nuovi statuti
fatti in Inghilterra, il che ha dato gran dispiacere al Re, al pre-
sente, si per liberarsi di prigione, si per la gran dignita, forse
fara quel che vuole il Re, perche lo lasci vinire in qua, et cio
seguendo, la M^{ta} Chr^{ma} et quel principe potrano anchora far
capitale di Roffense come dun gran cardinale. Questa cosa
quando fosse con destrezza maneggiata col Re proprio potrebbe
forse riuscire. Ma ci bisogna usare destrezza grande;" and G.
da Casale to Cardinal du Bellay, June 2, 1535, *loc. cit.* : "Sopra
questo affare potria la M^{ta} Chr^{ma} persuadere al Re dInghilterra,
che poi che la cosa e fatta dovrebbe cercare al meno cavarne
qualche utilita. Come saria col liberarlo e lascarlo esser cardinale
farlo assentire et conjurare alla osservatione de statuti, il che
egli non havendo voluto fare infra si trova in prigione. Et forse
glielo fara fare per un tanto premio et honore. Et quando pur
sia per stare nella sua ostinatione si puo mostrare che lascandolo
venire in Francia fara doi effetti, luno che levera questo impedi-
mento dInghilterra laltro che essendo il Chr^{mo} et il Re dInghilterra tanto amici venendo qualche occasione potranno valersi dun
tanto huomo Cardinale."

*Defiant
mood of
Henry.*

that the request should be granted;[1] but, whatever promise the king may have made, he had no mind to fulfil it. He was in an angry and suspicious mood. Not only had the pope dared to confer a high dignity on a rebellious subject of his, but Jean du Bellay, who had seemed to be almost a Protestant, and whom he had always expected to help him in inciting Francis to open rebellion against the papacy, had accepted the red hat. Henry regarded such conduct as little short of treason.[2]

Besides, Gregorio da Casale had written to Cromwell that it was the French who, after the execution of the Carthusians, had spoken most passionately of Henry's cruelty. This confirmed Henry in his belief that he was betrayed by Francis, and that a great league had been formed against him. He felt like an animal at bay, and as he could not touch the pope, or the King of France, or the Bishop of Paris, he resolved to wreak his vengeance on the prisoners in the Tower.

*Henry's
suspicions.*

Henry felt convinced that Fisher had corresponded with the pope, and that his promotion was a part of some vast scheme of the opposition. He considered the bishop his greatest enemy, and believed him to

---

[1] G. da Casale to Cromwell, July 27, 1535, *State Papers*, vol. vii. p. 618.

[2] E. Chapuis to Charles V., June 16, 1535, Vienna Archives, P.C. 229½, i. fol. 97 : "Sire ce Roy a ce que jentends nest seullement picque destre faict ledict evesque Cardinal mais a cause de celluy de Paris auquel en toutes choses avoit grande confidence mesmes pour ce que avant cette creation il se tenoit pour maulvais papiste. Il na aussi gros plaisir de lauditeur de la chambre."

be far more dangerous than in any circumstances he
could have been.[1] When the news of Fisher's
elevation had arrived, Henry had broken out into
violent threats, and had immediately sent a commission
to the Tower to find whether the honour had been
asked for. The cardinal asserted that the pope had
acted of his own free will, but this did not satisfy the
king. Several of the jailers and some friends and
kinsmen of Fisher were arrested on a charge of
having served as his messengers, and were closely
examined. Of course, nothing to their disadvantage
was proved, but still the king was not mollified.[2]

On the 14th a royal commission again examined
Fisher and More, and demanded that they should
accept the Acts of Succession and of Supremacy.[3]
Both refused to make any statement. Thereupon an

[1] E. Chapuis to Charles V., June 30, 1535, Vienna Archives,
P.C. 229½, i. fol. 103 : " Cremuel me dit que le pape estoit cause
de sa mort et que le dict pape avoit faict tres mal et tres follement
de lavoir faict Cardinal actendu que cestoit le pire enemy que le
Roy son maistre eust."

[2] E. Chapuis to Charles V., June 16, 1535, *loc. cit.* : " Sire des
que ce Roy entendict levesque de Rochestre estre cree Cardinal
tres despit et fasche que se trouva il dit et asseura par plusieurs
fois quil dounroit ung autre chappeau audict evesque et quil
envoyeroit apres la teste a Rome pour le chappeaul Cardinal." . . .
" Et cependant pour ce que il ny a legitime occasion de les faire
morir le Roy va serchant sil se trouvera quelque chose contre
eulx, mesme si le dict evesque a fait poursuyte du chappeaul, et
pour ce entendre sont constituez plusieurs prisonniers tant de ses
parents que de ceulx que le gardoient en prison ; " and Examination of J. Fisher, *Archaeologia Britannica*, vol. xxv. p. 99.

[3] Examination of J. Fisher, June 14, 1535, *State Papers*, vol. i.
p. 431 ; and Examination of Sir Thomas More, June 14, 1535,
State Papers, vol. i. pp. 432 to 436.

CHAP. XI. indictment was prepared against the cardinal, and on
June 17, the 17th of June he was brought to trial at West-
1535.   minster.[1] His rights as a peer were disregarded, the
           government holding that by the Act of Attainder
           passed in the autumn of 1534, he had been deprived
Fisher   of his see and of the honour attached to it. A
condemned common jury it was easy to pack and easy to frighten,
and
executed. so a sentence for the crown was obtained, and five
           days later Fisher was led to execution on Tower Hill.[2]
           The extreme penalty of treason had been commuted
           into simple decapitation, and even on the scaffold a
June 22, pardon was offered to him if he would submit.[3] He
1535.   remained firm, spoke a few words to the assembled
           crowd, laid his head on the block, and received the
           stroke of the axe. The king had ordered one of the
           preachers of the modern school to be his confessor,
           and even this man, prejudiced as he must have been
           against Fisher, was loud in praise of his goodness
           and sanctity.[4]

[1] Records of the trial, R.O. Baga de Segretis, Pouch VII.
Bundle II.; and Third Report of the Deputy of Public Records,
App. II. p. 239.

[2] About the date of Fisher's execution there is some uncer-
tainty. It is differently stated as June 21, 22, or even 23.
Lord Herbert says it was June 22, and in this he agrees with the
account given by Chapuis. E. Chapuis to Charles V., June 30,
1535, Vienna Archives, P.C. 229½, i. fol. 103 : "Le xxii yl eust
trenchee la teste au lieu que le duc de boquinguam et nest a
penser le regret et compassion que tout le monde en avoit."

[3] *Ibid.* : "Il fust sollicite a merveilles depuis quil fut sur
lechaffaud de consentir a ce que vouloit le Roy luy offrant sa
grace mais y ny eust ordre et mourust tres vertueusement."

[4] E. Chapuis to Charles V., June 30, 1535, *loc. cit.* : "Il luy
fust donne pour confesseur ung sien grand enemy quest le plus

Meanwhile, Anne did her best to divert Henry's attention from his embarrassments. She organised splendid balls and mummeries, and by cleverly playing, now on his obstinacy, now on his vanity and love of show, she established her old empire over his vacillating mind.[1] It was not, therefore, difficult *Trial and* for the Boleyn party to persuade him that Sir *death of* Thomas More should also be brought to trial. On *More.* the 26th of June a true bill was found against Sir *June 26,* Thomas by the grand jury for Middlesex, and on the *1535.* 1st of July he was led to Westminster Hall to be *July 1,* tried before a special commission.[2] He offered an *1535.* eloquent defence, but it could not have any influence on the jury; he was found guilty, and sentenced to receive the punishment of a traitor. A few days later he was executed, maintaining to the last the quaint humour, the delicate tenderness, the stainless honour, which, with his fine intellectual genius, make him one of the noblest and most attractive figures in English history.

With this last and most illustrious victim Henry's

grand lutherien du monde et faulteur de toutes les diableries que sont yci, si ne cesse il de dire que lon a faict morir lung des meilleurs et plus saincts homme du monde."

[1] E. Chapuis to Charles V., June 16, 1535, *loc. cit.*: " Et pour le desennuyer de ces fascheries la dame luy a ces jours faict ung festin en une sienne maison ou elle fit plusieurs braves mommeries . . . la dicte dame a si bien banquete et momme que a ce que ma aujourdhuy envoye dire la princesse le Roy est plus rasste (*sic.* rassote) delle quil ne fust oncques quest chose qua augmente grandement la craincte de la princesse."

[2] Records of the trial, R.O. Baga de Segretis, Pouch VII. Bundle III.; and Third Report of the Deputy Keeper of Public Records, App. II. p. 240.

CHAP. XI.

*Henry's
cruelty
condemned.*

cruelties, for the moment, came to an end. It soon became apparent that the executions would not have the effect which he had desired and expected. More and Fisher enjoyed so high a fame for piety, virtue, and learning that their death roused a storm of indignation. In England, indeed, most people were afraid to say what they thought, but abroad Henry was loudly and universally condemned. Francis I. spoke very strongly to Sir John Wallop, the English ambassador, and he might have spoken more strongly still had he not known that Wallop was at heart deeply displeased.[1] The French ministers expressed themselves with even greater freedom than their master.[2]

*Measures
proposed
against
Henry at
Rome.
September
1535.*

At Rome the French cardinals no longer opposed the publication of the sentence against Henry. Even Cardinal du Bellay ceased to defend him, and sought only to exonerate Francis from blame for the relations that had hitherto been maintained between France and England.[3] Consistories and congregations met, therefore, to prepare a bull of deprivation and

[1] Cromwell to Sir John Wallop, August 23, 1535, Burnet, *Collectanea,* part iii. book ii. No. xxxv.

[2] A. de Montmorency to Cardinal du Bellay, July 26, 1535, Paris, Bibl. Nat. MSS. Fr. 19,577 : " Apres avoir faict coupper la teste au C^al Rochestot ils ont faict le semblable a Monsieur Morus qui estoient deux tels personnaiges que scavez;" and Gregorio da Casale to —— July 30, 1535, *State Papers,* vol. vii. p. 621, footnote: "Dicunt etiam quod Cardinalis Turnonensis, suis literis Romam missis, hujus hominis mortem descripsit adeo pie, ut ommes commoverit ad lachrymas."

[3] Cardinal du Bellay to Francis I., September 3, 1535, Paris, Bibl. Nat. MSS. Fr. 5499, fol. 206 ; and *Memorial on the English Cause,* ibid. fol. 212.

excommunication; and decisive measures would have
been taken had not the imperial agents at the papal
court suddenly realised that there were formidable
obstacles in the way. They sent a long memoir to
the emperor setting forth their difficulties, and asking
what they were to do.

The pope and the cardinals, they said, shocked by
the execution of the Cardinal of Rochester, wished to
deprive Henry of his throne for the crimes of heresy
and *lesæ majestatis,* England being still reputed at
Rome to be held in fief of the Holy See. But if
this were done, the kingdom would revert to the pope
as feudal overlord, and Princess Mary would lose her
rights. The deprivation might, indeed, be made in
favour of Mary, but such an arrangement could not
be kept secret; the new cardinals would divulge it;
and Henry might treat the princess as he had treated
Cardinal Fisher. Upon the whole, it seemed best that
the pope should deprive Henry without saying in whose
favour he acted; and then the imperial agents might
appear for Catherine and Mary, and claim the vacant
throne for the latter. But as every conceivable plan
would be attended with danger, they did not dare to
come to a final resolution without further instructions.[1]

The result of all this was that the bull of deprivation was not issued. But the indignation against
the King of England remained as strong as ever, and
the only question now was whether the pope was
likely to find a secular prince able and willing to carry
out his sentence.

[1] *Memoir on the English Cause,* British Museum, Add. MSS.
vol. 28,587, fol. 334.

CHAP. XI.

*Henry
and
foreign
Pro-
testants.*

Henry was regarded with hardly less hostility by the majority of foreign Protestants than by Roman Catholics. There had always been a radical distinction between the English and the Continental reformation. The German theologians who broke away from Rome, admitting no authority but that of the Scripture, could not favour a theory of royal supremacy, which if generally acknowledged would have set up, instead of one pope, hundreds of popes.[1] They disliked Henry's proceedings, and feared that he would permanently discredit their cause. For political reasons he had favoured Wullenwever, who was strongly suspected of Protestant heterodoxy; and there is reason to think that he was at least very near entering into negotiations with the Anabaptists at Muenster, who pleased him by giving constant trouble to Mary of Hungary, the regent of the Low Countries.[2] Henry knew how much he was distrusted by moderate Protestants; and, to vindicate his character, he had caused a number of Anabaptists, who had fled from Holland to England, to be arrested in May, and to be brought before a commission. Fourteen of them had refused to retract, and had been burned as heretics.[3] This did not conciliate the German reformers, who continued to suspect Henry of being friendly to John of Leyden.

---

[1] Anton Musa to Stephan Rothe, January 16, 1536, *Corpus Reformatorum*, vol. iii. No. 1389.

[2] Memorandum by Paget, Gairdner, *Letters and Papers*, vol. vii. p. 230.

[3] E. Chapuis to Charles V., June 5, 1535, Vienna Archives, P.C. 229½, i. fol. 89.

The execution of Fisher and More widened the breach between Henry and the Lutherans. Both men had been firm opponents of English Protestantism, but they had also been personal friends of the foremost Humanists ; and they themselves had been among the principal representatives in England of the new learning, on which the German reformation was chiefly based. Like Luther, Fisher maintained the validity of Catherine's marriage, not because he believed in the power of the pope to dispense from a prescription in the Bible, but because he held that there was no prescription of the kind to be found in the Bible ;[1] and in matters about which public opinion was divided this was by no means the only important point on which they agreed. Fisher, therefore, was respected by Luther's followers, while for Sir Thomas More they had the strongest admiration ; and the tidings that two such men had been beheaded filled them with astonishment and horror.[2]

Seeing how violent a commotion he had produced, *Henry* Henry became anxious to justify himself for what he *defended.* had done. Several memorials were drawn up in defence of his conduct, and in one of them, which was evidently intended for the Roman Catholics, especially for the French, the following passage occurs : " First, to assaye the mind of the most christian majesty (oh, subtle craft !) concerning the deliverance of the late bishop of Rochester being in the ende for his

[1] Examination of John Fisher, R.O., Box Q, 155, and B. M. Cotton MSS. Cleopatra, E. fol. 196, etc.

[2] *Glaubwuerdiger Bericht von dem Todt T. Mori*, Strassburg, 1535, and *Beschreibung des Urtheils Herrn T. Morus*, s. l.

CHAP. XI. unfeigned deserving condemned of treason, whom they
after his death (and God's will), to excite the hatred
of all cardinals, name a cardinal, he [the pope] does
say that the labour of the most christian majesty
interposed with his brother the most noble king of
England, was contemned, set at nought, and mocked;
where indeed no such labour was made. And yet
that holy see not content with that lie makes another
open lie and most falsely brings in that the intercession
of the most christian majesty has caused the said
Rochester to die the rather. In this matter I call to
record the conscience of the most christian majesty,
which, forsomuch as he never inter . . . with his
friend in this cause (of whom he knows he may
obtain anything that he desires) not only does see
most manifestly now their lies, but also (such is his
prudence) he has plainly declared that he hates all
treason and inobedience, in so much that he thought
that there should be given no place to . . . neither
prayer in such case for the maintenance of the
commonwealth in his estate."

Especial credit is taken for the manner in which
Fisher was put to death. "He was not killed with
poison, which thing some men do use, he was not
sodden in lead as the solemn use is in certain places,
he was not hanged in a halter, what best agrees for a
traitor, he was not burnt, he was not put to death
with lingering torments, but lost his life with a
sudden stroke of a sworde the which sort of death
in such bitterness is most easy." [1]

[1] Memorial about Fisher's death, R.O. Henry VIII., Box R,
No. 11. I have altered the spelling of the passages above quoted.

This memorial was conceived with much skill, for Francis could not afford to say that he had in vain interfered for Fisher. That would detract from his reputation by showing that he had little influence in England. On the other hand, by remaining silent, he would seem to admit that he had approved of Fisher's execution, since it would be said that if he had not approved of it, he—Henry's greatest friend —would surely have tried to prevent it. The dilemma was a most unpleasant one, and Francis was indignant with Henry for forcing it upon him.

Another memorial, which seems to have been drawn up somewhat later, was intended to allay the indignation of the German Protestants; and in this production (which is in Latin) a virulent attack is made on the character of the dead men. "As you write," *The* the paper begins, "that everywhere in Germany *character of Fisher* the king is believed to have punished More and *and More* Rochester for no other cause than that they sincerely *attacked.* adhered to evangelical doctrine and persistently opposed the king's marriage, we wonder who can be the author of this idle tale."[1] The king's beneficence, equity, piety, and mildness were so well known to the world that his reputation for these qualities could not be easily undermined by calumny.[2]

[1] Latin Memorial about More's and Fisher's death, R.O. Henry VIII., Box S: "Quod scribis passim per Germania idque constantissima fama vulgatum, regem haud aliam ob causam in Moro ac Roffense animadvertisse qua quod Evangelicam doctrinam syncere assererent, et regias item nuptias impugnarent miramur profecto quis ejus fabulæ author esse possit."

[2] *Ibid.*: "Neque enim induci possumus ut credamus erudita Germanorum ingenia tam facile vanissimis vulgo rumoribus posse

CHAP. XI. With what exquisite kindness he had treated King James of Scotland, not holding him responsible for the atrocious misdeeds of his father! What generosity he had shown to Francis I., to whom, out of pure goodness, he had lent 800,000 crowns towards his ransom! The king never prevented the gospel from being preached if it were preached truly and honestly. Why, then, this impudent calumny that More and Rochester were punished because they sincerely adhered to evangelical doctrine and opposed the king's marriage? No one had been more willing than they to swear to the Acts by which the crown was settled on the offspring of Henry and Anne; and More, in his dialogues against Luther, had contended that marriages prohibited in Leviticus are not permitted to Christians. As for what was said about their defence of the gospel, the writer wondered whether any German believed that the gospel had ever had enemies more mischievous than these two.[1] Rochester and More had both written books in which they had bitterly assailed the best leaders of the sect; and in a letter to Erasmus, More had openly stated that he would be a constant enemy of heretics, for so he called those who wanted a purer doctrine. And so he had shown himself.[2] "It makes one

abduci ut quidlibet credant de quolibet et regis benignitatem, equitatem, pietatem, clementiam orbi scimus multo notoria quam ut a quovis calumnie impetu facile subruantur."

[1] Latin Memorial about More's and Fisher's death, R.O. Henry VIII., Box S: "Iam quod de propugnato evangelio fabulantur miramur si quisquam Germanorum sit, qui credat Evangelium nocentiores unquam his duobus hostes habuisse."

[2] Ibid.: "Idem in epistola ad Erasmum (quam Paulo antequam

ashamed," says this virtuous scribe, "to recall what
tortures he invented and inflicted upon those whom
he perceived to be inclined to evangelical truth."
He caused search to be made in all quarters for
heretics, offering great rewards for evidence against
them; and when they were brought before him, he
never committed them to prison "until he had seen
them tortured in a pitiable manner before his eyes."
That More was "of a cruel and fierce temper" might
be judged from this fact, that those whom he caught
"he was in the habit of torturing by a new method
invented by himself." He immediately caused new
shoes to be put upon persons brought before him;
then the victims were tied to stakes, and the
soles of their feet were brought close to a blazing
fire, that, to those who would not confess, the
pain—).[1] Here, unhappily, a sheet of the manuscript has been lost. The document closes with a

---

maiestatis postularetur ediderat) ingenue et palam se perpetuum
hostem hereticis (sic enim purioris doctrine studiosos omnes
appellat) non sine stomacho futurum denunciat. Id quod Archi-
grammateus adhuc regni exactissime haud dubie prestitit."

[1] Latin Memorial about More's and Fisher's death, R.O.
Henry VIII., Box S : "Pudet commemorare quos ille cruciatus ex-
cogitaret exercueratque in eos quos veritati evangelice persenserat
esse addictiores, conquisitos undique et magno interim indicibus
proposito praemio, unquam ante carceribus committere solebat,
quam in oculis suis miserabiliter excruciatos conspixisset. Fuisse
autem Moro atrox et saevum ingenio vel hoc judicat, quod novo
et a se invento questionis genere deprehensos venationis torquere
solitus sit, cruciatus vero erat hujusmodi, Adductos ad se, protinus
novis calceis indui et cippis constringi fecerat. Deinde eorum
plantas igni flagrantissimo admoveri, scilicet ut ne confitentibus
quidem dolor . . ."

prayer that all princes may be able to imitate Henry's
immense goodness of heart.[1]

These accusations against More have been repeated
by some later writers; but there is not a tittle of
evidence that he was guilty of the cruelties imputed
to him.   Such charges conflict with all that we know
of his character and his modes of thought; and to
his contemporaries they were absolutely incredible.
Henry gained nothing by the attempt to tarnish the
fame of one whose virtues were so widely known and
so cordially appreciated.

[1] Latin Memorial about More's and Fisher's death, R.O.
Henry VIII., Box 8: "Quem ut assequi pauci possent, ita ut
omnes principes imitare possent immensam illius misericordiam
precamur, qui gloriosam illam aeternitatis adoptionem, studiosis
misericordie benignissime policitur, fallere non potest."

CHAPTER XII.

THE COLLAPSE OF THE NORTHERN ALLIANCE.

SCARCELY had the blood of More dried on Tower Hill when bad news arrived from every quarter. Besides the ill feeling which the execution of two such men as Fisher and More had produced, political events were everywhere unfavourable to Henry. He was especially disappointed by the course of the war in the north, from which he had expected such great results. Duke Christian, reinforced by troops of the Landgrave, had taken the bold course of attacking Luebeck on its own ground ; and Marcus Meyer had been thoroughly beaten. Cut off from the sea, the town had been forced, on the 18th of November, 1534, to sign a treaty by which the war was to be confined to Denmark. This was of considerable advantage to the duke, who had no longer to fear for his patrimonial estates, and could employ the whole of his forces in reconquering Jutland and in opposing Count Christopher. In his difficulties Wullenwever had written to Cromwell, offering a league on better conditions, and Henry had despatched Christopher Mores to reside as ambassador in Denmark and

The war in Denmark.

October 10, 1534. November 18, 1534.

CHAP. XII.

October
28, 1534.

Allies of
Duke
Christian.

Allies of
Luebeck.

Luebeck.[1] Mores, soon after his arrival at Hamburg, heard of the treaty with Christian, but if he came too late to be of use, his journey did not the less exasperate the German princes.

Two parties were now striving for supremacy in Denmark. Duke Christian was backed by his brothers-in-law, Gustavus Vasa, King of Sweden, and Albert, lately Master, now first Duke of Prussia. The Landgrave, the Duke of Lueneburg, and many other German Protestant princes were favourable to him, and the majority of the Danish nobility and clergy were on his side. Luebeck had as allies Count Christopher of Oldenburg, Count John of Hoya, a brother-in-law of the King of Sweden, whom the latter had deeply offended, Hoya's brother Count Eric, a certain Bernhardt von Melen, who had married a cousin of Gustavus Vasa and had also become a mortal enemy of the king, a Count of Tecklenburg, and a few of the Holstein nobles. The towns of Rostock, Wismar, and Stralsund were as eager in the fray as Luebeck itself. Duke Albert of Mecklenburg, who had married a niece of King Christian II., and the Master of Livonia were decidedly favourable to the town, while the Elector of Saxony maintained a benevolent neutrality. The peasants of Ditmarschen assisted the Luebeckers with money, and took up a threatening position on the frontiers of Holstein. In Denmark itself Luebeck could reckon on the assistance of the democratic elements, not in the towns only, but even among the peasants. In

[1] Wullenwever to Cromwell, October 17, 1534, R.O. Box Q, No. 78 ; and Expenses of Christofer Mores, R.O. Box Q, No. 88.

Jutland the peasantry rose at the call of a partisan of
Christian II., and in a bloody battle at Svendstrup
overthrew the levies of the duke and the nobility.

The two parties would have been pretty equally
matched had it not been for the fact that the adherents of Duke Christian were all of one mind,
desiring simply to place the duke on the Danish
throne, while the adherents of Luebeck were pulling
in different directions.   Count Christopher had
already begun to pursue an independent course,
having obliged the estates of Seeland and Skonen to
take an oath of fealty to him as governor of the
kingdom ; and this had created considerable jealousy.
The intrigues of Wullenwever increased the mutual
distrust.   He was negotiating with three different
pretenders, and the fear of offending any of the three,
and of giving too much power to Count Christopher,
paralysed the action of the town.

While the two parties were confronting each other   *Duke
in this way, Duke Christian obtained a copy of the   *Christian
treaty of alliance which had been proposed between   *sends an
                                                       *ambassa-
Luebeck and the King of England.   To find out   *dor to
                                                       England.
whether the treaty had been actually signed, and, if
possible, to detach Henry from the alliance with
Wullenwever, he sent Peter Schwaben or Suavenius,
one of his most trusty counsellors, as ambassador to
England and Scotland.   The instructions to Schwaben,
written in Latin, and dated from Gottorp, the 20th of   *January
January 1535,[1] contain only a lengthy account of   *20, 1535.*
the facts of Christian's case and a request that Henry
will not favour the Luebeckers.   But it is clear

[1] C. F. Wegener, *Aarsberetninger,* vol. iii. p. 217.

CHAP. XII. from Schwaben's negotiations that he had secret instructions to offer considerable advantages to Henry for the English alliance. He seems to have been authorised to promise nearly as much help as the Luebeckers were to bind themselves by treaty to give.[1] There was this difference between Duke Christian and the Luebeckers, that the former was perfectly able to perform his promise and was a man whose word could be trusted, while the latter found it extremely difficult to levy troops, and each faction in the town was ever ready to repudiate the engagements entered into by its adversaries. Besides, by aiding the duke, Henry would have gained the friendship of his allies, especially of the Hanseatic towns on the German Ocean. Luebeck would have been forsaken by most of its confederates, and would not have been able to do the English king any great harm.

Had Henry been the wise and well-informed king he pretended to be, he would have welcomed Christian's ambassador cordially; for here was an opportunity of forming that great northern Protestant confederacy of which he had so often dreamt. In close alliance with Gustavus Vasa of Sweden and Christian of Sleswick-Holstein, Denmark, Skonen and Norway, enjoying the friendship of the Landgrave, the dukes of Lueneburg, of Pomerania, and of Prussia, he would have been a really powerful king, and might have made himself independent of Francis and well able to hold his own against the emperor. But he

[1] Proposals of P. Schwaben, C. F. Wegener, *Aarsberetninger*, vol. iii. p. 251.

was neither wise nor well informed. He listened
eagerly to the coloured reports and interested advice
of men like Marcus Meyer, Dr. Pack, and Count Eric of
Hoya, who had come over to treat with him.[1] It did not
occur to him that if the Luebeckers were as powerful
as they said they were, they would not for the loan
of 20,000 florins become his dependants. Everything
they told him he believed ; and he promised and
acted accordingly.

When Schwaben arrived at Hampton Court on the *Reception*
28th of February, Cromwell received him civilly, *Schwaben.*
listened to his representations, denied that any treaty *February*
had been actually signed with the Luebeckers, and 28, 1535.
promised a speedy reply.[2] But when on the following
day Schwaben was ushered into Henry's presence, he *February*
was treated less politely. The king would not hear 29, 1535.
him, but began a long discourse, speaking of the
Luebeckers as " our very dear and honoured friends."
He said Christian had no right whatever to rule
Denmark, the throne of which was elective. The
election rested with the people, not with the council ;
and even of the council Christian had but a small part
with him. " Why," asked Henry, " should not I accept
the kingdom of Denmark, which has been offered to
me ?" As to the King of Sweden and Count Christopher,
they would soon rue the day they had taken part
against Luebeck. The people of that town were
very powerful, they had placed Frederic I. on his

[1] E. Chapuis to Charles V., November 3, 1535, Vienna
Archives, P.C. 229, i. No. 62.

[2] Diarium Petri Suavenii, C. F. Wegener, *Aarsberetninger*,
vol. iii. p. 233.

CHAP. XII. throne, and they would be victorious again. "You see," he triumphantly exclaimed, "I too know something of these matters." He continued for some time in this strain, and the ambassador was not even permitted to explain his mission. Schwaben handed in, in writing, the substance of what he had to say; merely informing the king that the Luebeckers had been routed in Skonen and that Marcus Meyer had been killed. Henry laughed at this, and Cromwell also showed himself less friendly than he had been the day before. Schwaben was referred for an answer to the council, and so dismissed.[1]

After this he was kept waiting for many weeks. It seems that Cromwell, who did not quite share his master's confidence in the ultimate success of Luebeck, wished to keep the negotiation open to see what course events would take. But at last Schwaben was sent away with scant courtesy and with an indecisive reply.[2]

April,
1535.

January
13, 1535.

Schwaben had been correctly informed as to the overthrow of the Luebeckers in Skonen; but Marcus

[1] Diarium Petri Suavenii, *loc. cit.* p. 233: "Die lunae sum auditus in horto. De foedere non negavit rex, caussam autem scire voluit, quamobrem sibi oblatum Danicum regnum acceptare non liceret . . . Danicum regnum electivum non haereditarium esse. Lubecenses revera amicos regis . . . electionem non apud consiliarios, sed apud plebem quoque haerere. Paucos ex consiliariis Christiano adhaerere; nihil hoc esse . . . Se quoque aliquid scire . . . Dixi postea de defectione Scanicorum, de caede Lubecensium, de morte Marci Meyers. Eorum nihil creditum est."

[2] Diarum Petri Suavenii, *loc. cit.* p. 240; and E. Chapuis to Charles V., April 18, 1535, Vienna Archives, P.C. 229½, i. fol. 68.

Meyer, who had commanded the troops of the town, had only been made prisoner. He was taken to the strong castle of Warberg on the western coast of Skonen, where he was treated with due honour ; and, as might have been anticipated, he took advantage of the comparative liberty accorded to him to conspire with the town people who were in favour of Luebeck. The result was that on the night of the 11th of March his friends surprised the castle, and made him its commander. But instead of handing it over to the Luebeckers, Meyer behaved at Warberg like an independent prince.[1] A message was sent to Christopher Mores, who was at Copenhagen ; and when Mores went to Warberg on the 26th of May, Meyer asked whether Henry would not help him to hold out and to retrieve all he had lost.[2]

Henry was not at first very much inclined to assist Meyer. He had seen that Peter Schwaben, whom he had received so badly, had, in the main, given him accurate intelligence. Duke Christian had regained the whole of Jutland ; and in the middle of February his captain-general, John von Rantzau, was able to elude the vigilance of the Luebeck fleet, which cruised in the Belt, and to land a strong force in the island of Funen. They seized the coast opposite Jutland, where the Belt is so narrow that the German ships could not prevent communication between the two shores. More troops followed, and shortly afterwards

CHAP. XII.

Meyer in Warberg.

March 11, 1535.

May 26, 1535.

Henry disinclined to help Meyer.

December, 1534.

February 18, 1535.

[1] G. Waitz, *Wullenwever*, vol. ii. pp. 196, 197, and 212.

[2] Accounts of Christofer Mores, R.O. Box Q, No. 88; and E. Chapuis to Charles V., June 30, 1535, Vienna Archives, P.C. 229½, i. fol. 103.

the greater part of the island was in the hands of Rantzau. Nor did matters look more hopeful in Skonen. Marcus Meyer, unable to follow up his success, was soon besieged at Warberg, and the entire kingdom, with the exception of a few fortified towns, was occupied by the joint forces of Duke Christian and the King of Sweden.[1]

Besides, Henry had now recognised that Christian was backed by the great majority of the German Protestants, whose goodwill he was anxious, if possible, to retain. He became, therefore, somewhat cooler in his zeal for Luebeck, Wullenwever, and Meyer, and began to think that he might act as mediator between the contending parties, who were endangering the cause of Protestantism by their political strife. By this means he hoped to earn their gratitude, and to obtain an opportunity of forming a powerful league of which he would be the natural chief. Two embassies were to set out—the one to be composed of Dr. Edward Fox, bishop elect of Hereford, Dr. Nicolas Heath, and Robert Barnes, a personal friend of the Wittenberg divines; the other of Dr. Edward Bonner, Richard Cavendish, and Dr. Adam Pack. The former embassy was to treat with the Elector of Saxony and other German princes;[2] the latter was to go to Luebeck, Denmark, and Holstein to mediate between the belligerents.[3]

---

[1] G. Waitz, *Luebeck unter Juergen Wullenwever,* vol. ii. pp. 186, 187, 220, 221.

[2] *State Papers*, vol. vii. p. 636, foot-note ; *Corpus Reformatorum*, vol. ii. p. 939, foot-note.

[3] G. Waitz, *Luebeck unter Juergen Wullenwever*, vol. iii. p. 469.

But while the ambassadors designate were waiting for their instructions, events on the continent proceeded at a very rapid pace. On the 11th of June, Count John von Hoya marched out at the head of a considerable force to surprise John von Rantzau in his positions near Assens, in the island of Funen. Rantzau, hearing of the movements of Hoya, advanced against him, and gained a great victory at Oxnebjerg; Hoya himself, with Count Tecklenburg and many officers of note, being killed, while most of his troops either shared his fate or were made prisoners.

On the same day on which Hoya was routed there was a naval battle near Bornholm. The Hanseatic fleet had been divided; one part of it, near the island of Funen, hampering the progress of Rantzau, another part, near Bornholm, watching the movements of the Swedish admiral Peter Skram. Skram was in command of a numerous fleet of Swedish and Prussian ships, to which a few Dutch and Danish vessels had been added. He kept his forces well together, and on the 11th of June attacked the Hanseatic squadron off Bornholm. The issue of the battle was doubtful; but the Hanseatic admiral, knowing that Skram would soon be reinforced, retreated towards Copenhagen, where he expected to find the rest of his fleet. Skram, being better informed, did not pursue his adversary, but sailed towards Funen. There, near Svendborg, on the 16th, he attacked the other German squadron, took nine of its best ships, and sunk one vessel. Only a few of the German vessels made their escape.

By these battles, fought within a few days of one

CHAP. XII.

Defeat of Henry's friends.
June 11 1535.

June 11, 1535.

June 16, 1535.

CHAP. XII. another, Luebeck lost its preponderance both on land
and on sea, and the campaign was virtually decided.
July 12 Shortly afterwards Duke Christian crossed the Great
1535. Belt, and landed in Seeland. Copenhagen was too
strong to be stormed, but Duke Albert of Mecklenburg
and Count Christopher were shut up in it, and the
open country remained in Christian's hands.[1]

Henry must have heard at the end of June or in
the beginning of July of the misfortunes of his
friends. Doctor Pack tried to represent matters in as
favourable a light as possible ; and as the king received
messages from Meyer, from Duke Albert, from Count
Christopher, who now offered very favourable conditions, and from Wullenwever, he did not attach
great importance to the lost battles.[2]

Francis, But there was another matter which caused him
Ferdi- much anxiety. Hitherto Francis had rather favoured
nand, and
the the religious dissensions in Germany ; up to the
German summer of 1534 he had certainly not made any serious
Protes-
tants. attempt to heal the schism. The league of Schmalkalden he had encouraged, and he had paid large
subsidies to Philip of Hesse and to the dukes of
Bavaria. He hoped that in return for this aid they
would stand by him in time of need, furnish him
with landsknechts, prevent Ferdinand from giving
help to his brother, the emperor, and threaten the
Low Countries from the south and east. By the
treaty of Cadan, and by the events which followed

---

[1] G. Waitz, *Luebeck unter Juergen Wullenwever.*

[2] Albrecht of Mecklenburg and Christof of Oldenburg to
Henry VIII., May 12 and 15, 1535, *Aktstykker*, vol. ii. pp.
80-82, etc.

it, Francis was taught that he could not rely on his CHAP. XII.
German allies. After the conclusion of that treaty
Ferdinand adopted a friendly tone towards the princes
of the Schmalkaldic league, and showed that he intended to work for Rome in a temperate and conciliatory spirit.[1] The Protestants, being anxious not
to endanger the concessions they had already obtained,
responded with pleasure to his advances. The new
Elector of Saxony proposed to visit Ferdinand at
Vienna, and there was even some talk of a marriage
between the eldest son of the landgrave and a
daughter of the emperor.

To Francis all this was most distasteful; for if
Ferdinand succeeded, he would earn the thanks of
Rome, and make for himself a great reputation; and
even if he failed, he would for a time possess considerable influence at Schmalkalden, at Zuerich, and
at Rome, while Francis would lose his best allies.
There remained but one way out of the difficulty : to
beat Ferdinand on the ground he had chosen, to out-
do him in his efforts to conquer heresy by kindness.
For the first time since the outbreak of Luther's
rebellion Francis really bestirred himself to bring the
schism to an end. In the autumn of 1534 Guillaume
du Bellay and Gervasius Wein were in constant
communication with the Protestant theologians ; and
Philip Melanchthon drew up a list of articles in which *August* 1,
he went so far as to acknowledge the primacy of the 1534.
pope. These articles were declared by the Bishop of
Paris, at whose request they were prepared, to

---

[1] L. von Ranke, *Deutsche Geschichte*, vol. iv. pp. 51-55.

CHAP. XII. be quite acceptable.[1] The pope himself manifested a
desire to meet the German reformers half way, and
at the time of Clement's death there seemed to be a
fair chance of an agreement.[2]

As soon as the new pope was installed, the matter
was taken up again. Paul III. was as anxious to
arrive at an understanding as his predecessor had
been, and in the summer of 1535 the prospect

June 23, appeared so bright that Francis wrote to Melanchthon,
1535. inviting him to visit France to discuss further the
basis for a settlement.[3] Cardinal du Bellay and
his brother strongly urged Melanchthon to accept
the invitation, and the reformer was eager to undertake the journey.[4] The only thing wanted was
the permission of the Elector of Saxony, the prince
whom Melanchthon served ; and Francis wrote to John
Frederic, asking him to give the necessary leave.[5]

[1] Articles by Melanchthon, August 1, 1534, *Corpus Reformatorum*, vol. ii. No. 1205, A : " Concedunt nostri politiam
ecclesiasticam rem licitam esse, quod videlicet sint aliqui episcopi
qui praesint pluribus ecclesiis ; item quod Romanus Pontifex
praesit omnibus episcopis. Hanc canonicam politiam, ut ego
existimo, nemo prudens improbat. . . ; " Melanchthon to Camerarius, September 13, 1534, *Corpus Reformatorum*, vol. ii.
No. 1215 ; and Cardinal du Bellay to Mr. de Saint Caletz
(November, 1534), Paris, Bibl. Nat. MSS. Français, vol. 5499,
fol. 199.

[2] Cardinal du Bellay to Mr. de Saint Caletz, Paris, Bibl. Nat.
MSS. Fr. vol. 5499, fol. 199.

[3] Francis I. to Melanchthon, June 23, 1535, *Corpus Reformatorum*, vol. ii. No. 1279.

[4] Cardinal du Bellay to Melanchthon, June 27, 1535, *Corpus
Reformatorum*, vol. ii. No. 1280 ; and G. du Bellay to Melanchthon,
July 16, 1535, *Corpus Reformatorum*, vol. iv. *Supplementa*, No. 56.

[5] J. Friedrich to Francis I., August 18, 1535, *Corpus Reformatorum*, vol. ii. No. 1303.

Henry became very uneasy when he heard of these negotiations. If the German Protestants were reconciled to the pope, the other northern states would follow their example. England would then remain alone in its schism, and with a disaffected people and hostile neighbours, Henry would be unable to hold out. It was, therefore, of the highest importance to him that both Francis and Ferdinand should fail; only by the maintenance of religious dissension could he hope to find allies against Charles and Paul III.

In the begining of July, Henry decided to send Robert Barnes to Saxony, to counteract the efforts of Francis.[1] Shortly afterwards a letter was received from Sir John Wallop, announcing that Melanchthon was expected at the French court. Thereupon *July 26,* Barnes was ordered to depart with all speed to *1535.* dissuade the great theologian from visiting a country where Protestants had just been cruelly martyred, and to invite him rather to go to England, where he would be sure of a good reception. At the same time Christopher Mundt, a German in the pay of Henry, and Simon Heynes, an English clergyman, were sent *August 1,* to the French court to watch the proceedings of *1535.* Francis, and—in case Melanchthon went to France— to prevent him from effecting a reconciliation with the Holy See.[2]

The French were so provoked by Henry's opposition that he ought to have acted with the greatest caution;

[1] Credentials for R. Barnes, July 8, 1535, *Corpus Reformatorum,* vol. ii. p. 936, foot-note.

[2] Norfolk and Rochford to Cromwell, Burnet's *Collectanea,* part iii. book iii. No. xlii.

but this he was incapable of doing. Christopher Mores had returned from Denmark, and with him had come Gerhard Meyer, the brother of Henry's favourite, Sir Marcus. Gerhard Meyer had asked Henry to assist his brother with men and money, and Mores had reported on what he had seen at Warberg. For the moment the king did not grant Gerhard's request, but while Bonner and Cavendish were waiting for a fair wind to start, Dietrich Hagenow, a captain, arrived with important despatches from Meyer. Meyer offered not only to hand over to officers of King Henry the castle and town of Warberg, but to obtain for him the towns and castles of Malmoe, Landskron, Copenhagen, and Elsinore.[1]

This offer appeared so brilliant that Henry could not resist the temptation to accept it. He thought that with Warberg and the four towns in his possession he might indeed become the absolute umpire in the quarrels between the northern powers, and establish the much-talked-of confederacy. Gerhard Meyer was sent back to his brother with a most favourable message, and shortly afterwards two royal ships were fitted out to sail to Warberg. Between them they were to carry only a hundred English soldiers under Mores and Hagenow, but they were to convey to Meyer a large supply of cannon, powder and shot, hackbuts, pikes, and other munitions of

---

[1] J. Gostwyk to Cromwell, July 31, 1535, R.O. Cromwell letters, xiv. No. 37 ; Bonner and Cavendish to Cromwell, July 24, 1535, British Museum, Cotton MSS. Nero, B. iii. No. 51 ; *Wurm*, p. 27 ; *Waitz*, vol. iii. pp. 179 and 468 ; and *Aktstykker*, vol. i. p. 430.

war. Best of all, a considerable sum of money was to be taken over to Warberg, where Bonner and Cavendish were to go to confer with Meyer.[1]

But before the ships could start, the government received from the captains of some English vessels a message which entirely altered the case. Of the English merchantmen which, in the spring of 1535, had sailed for the Baltic, a few had already, on their outward voyage, been seized by the Duke of Mecklenburg in the Sound and at Copenhagen.[2] Twelve others, which had gone to Dantzig, fell in with a part of Admiral Skram's fleet on their way home. They were stopped and boarded by the Swedes, who treated them as enemies, and took them to Swedish harbours.[3]

The expedition to Warberg now seemed rather hazardous Peter Skram might waylay the royal ships, as he had waylaid the merchantmen in the Baltic, and not only would ships, stores, and money be lost, but clear proof would be obtained of Henry's duplicity. Being thus deprived of an agreeable illusion, Henry violently abused Hagenow, and ordered the soldiers to be dismissed and the ships to be taken back

---

[1] *Waitz*, iii. p. 180; *Aktstykker*, i. p. 459; and Chapuis to Charles V., September 6 and 13, 1535, Vienna Archives, P.C. 229½, i. fols. 123 and 125.

[2] Albrecht of Mecklenburg to Henry VIII., May 12, 1535, *loc. cit.*

[3] Robert Legge, Thomas Gyggs, and William Bolle to ——, September 6, 1535; G. Schanz, *Englische Handelpolitik*, vol. ii p. 487; Christian III. to Henry VIII., November 16, 1535 *ibid.* p. 490; and Report of Dinteville, Paris, Bibl. Nat. MSS. Dupuis, vol. 547, fol. 200.

CHAP. XII. to the Thames.[1]   Poor Marcus Meyer was left vainly
to hope for succour. All he received was a visit from
September, Bonner and Cavendish, who apparently gave him
1535. some money, and exhorted his men to remain true to
him, and to reckon on the help of King Henry.[2]

About the same time that Peter Skram's inconvenient proceedings were reported at the English
court, other intelligence of even worse import came
Fall of from Hamburg. Robert Barnes had arrived there in
Wullen- the beginning of August, and had intended to hold a
wever. disputation with the divines of the place, who, headed
by the famous Aëpinus, condemned the divorce.[3]
While he was preparing to defend his master's cause,
he received new and pressing orders to proceed to
Wittenberg to confer with Melanchthon ; and although he was very unwilling to go—for Wittenberg
was said to be ravaged by the plague [4]—he was, of
course, obliged to obey. Before starting, he heard that
August on the 21st of August a sitting of the council at
21, 1535. Luebeck had led to the total overthrow of the party
of Wullenwever. Wullenwever, indeed, had been allowed to retain the post of first burgomaster of the
town, but his friends had been compelled to leave
the council. Five days later, his position having

[1] E. Chapuis to Charles V., September 25, 1535, Vienna
Archives, P.C. 229½, i. fol. 128.

[2] G. Waitz, *Luebeck unter J. Wullenwever*, vol. iii. pp. 180, 181,
and Regkman's Chronicle.

[3] E. Chapuis to Charles V., January 28, 1535, Vienna, P.C.
229½, i. fol. 9 ; and R. Barnes to Cromwell, August 22, 1535,
British Museum, Cotton MSS. Vitellius, B. xxi. fol. 34.

[4] R. Barnes to Cromwell, August 25, 1535, R.O. *Cromwell
Correspondence*, vol. iii. fol. 78.

become entirely untenable, he resigned his office, and CHAP. XII.
accepted in its stead the administration of a small *August* 26, 1535.
outlying part of Luebeck territory. The mighty
tribune of the north, the great ally of King Henry,
had fallen from his high estate, and had been forced
to make way for his rival and enemy, his predecessor
Broemse.[1]

But even now Henry did not come to the end of
the troubles in which he had involved himself by
association with Meyer and Wullenwever. Wullenwever was too ambitious not to regret the loss of his
power, and the presence of Bonner and Cavendish at *Wullen-wever and the English ambassa-dors.*
Hamburg with a considerable sum of money inspired
him with a hope that he might mend his broken
fortunes. He secretly left his new home, and
presenting himself before the English ambassadors *November* 1535.
suggested the following plan. During the last few
months some four or five thousand landsknechts,
commanded by Uevelacker, formerly a captain under
Count Christopher, had been living idly in the
country between the Weser and the Elbe. Wullenwever proposed to engage these men, and undertook,
after re-establishing his authority in Luebeck, to send
the greater number of them to assist Duke Albert
and to raise the siege of Copenhagen. Bonner and
Cavendish were attracted by the scheme, and promised
Wullenwever ten thousand florins, about sixteen
hundred pounds, of the money they had in their
keeping. They seem even to have advanced a part
of the sum.[2]

[1] G. Waitz, *Luebeck unter Juergen Wullenwever.*
[2] Examination of J. Wullenwever, January 27, 1536, Waitz,

So Juergen Wullenwever, with four of his servants, rode off to meet Uevelacker; and at night he put up at a little inn near Rotenburg. The weather having been raw, he ordered wine, and, continuing to drink, took more than was good either for him or for Henry VIII. He got drunk, and began to brag about his past greatness and his plans for the future. The innkeeper, thinking that all was not right, went out and reported what was going on to Claus Hermelink, a captain of the Archbishop of Bremen. Hermelink was an enemy of Wullenwever, and may have been allured by the money the ex-burgomaster was said to carry; at any rate, he hurried with some of his soldiers to the inn, and seized the drunken man. Next morning Wullenwever found himself a prisoner of Archbishop Christopher of Bremen.[1]

Luebeck unter Juergen Wullenwever, vol. iii. p. 494 : "54, Gefragt, was er leztmals tzu Hamburck mit den Engelischen gehandelt. Daruf bekannt das die Engelischen ime angetzeigt das sie von dem konige in Engeland befelch haben, hertzog Albrechten, wo er ein fues im reich hette, mit einer summa geldes als zehen thausent gulden zu erledigung konig Christierns vorzustreckenn. Doch wollen sie erstlich sich erkundigenn ob die knechte so Ubelacker bei einander hette pfalzgraff Friederichen zustendig, das sein F. G. dieselbigen zu eroberung des reichs Dennemark gebrauchen wolten, als dan wolten sie sich der sachenn mit den knechten nit undernemen. Daruf hat er Wollenweber sich gegen inen erboten, das er selbst zu Ubelacker und den knechten reiten und eigentlich bei innen erkunden wolte, ob sie pfalzgraf Friederich zu gebrauchen in willens. So sei er uf dem wege alhier ins gefencknus gebracht."

[1] Account from Luebeck, November 15, 1535, Waitz, *Luebeck unter Juergen Wullenwever*, vol. iii. p. 469 : "Wollenweber isth hier auszgerithen selb vierde ane wyllen und wyssen des Roths, szo das er isth gekomen zcue Hamborck, von do isth er gerithen

The only piece of good news sent home by the English ambassadors was that Melanchthon was not to go to France. But this was not due to their influence. A letter which Robert Barnes had written to Melanchthon from Hamburg had produced no effect; after receiving it, the German theologian was as eager to go as he had been before.[1] The journey was put off because the elector, John Frederic, refused to sanction it, pretending that he could not spare the services of so great a professor.[2] But it was whispered about that his real reason was that he was afraid of displeasing the emperor and the King of the Romans;[3] and, as this became known in England, the announcement that Melanchthon would not leave home lost a good deal of its value.

On his arrival at Jena on the 18th of September, Barnes found that the elector was just going to start for Vienna on a friendly visit to the King of the Romans.[4] Barnes received no immediate reply to the message he had brought to John Frederic; all that he could obtain was permission to hold a

CHAP. XII.

Henry and the Wittenberg divines.

August 18, 1535.

September 18, 1535.

noch Buchszthehode, von do nam er zwene diener mith, und isth geritthen noch Rodenborch, das hoereth dem bischoffe von Brehmen zcu, do isth er die Nacht ueber geblieben. In summa in der Herberge isth er truncken undt voll worden . . ."

[1] Melanchthon to Camerarius, August 5, 1535, *Corpus Reformatorum*, vol. ii. No. 1295; and Melanchthon to H. Baumgartner, August 11, 1535, *Corpus Reformatorum*, vol. ii. No. 1297.

[2] The Elector of Saxony to Francis I., August 18, 1535, *Corpus Reformatorum*, vol. ii. No. 1303.

[3] The Elector of Saxony to Dr. Brueck, August 19, 1535, *Corpus Reformatorum*, vol. ii. No. 1304.

[4] Dr. Brueck to the Elector, September 18, 1535, *Corpus Reformatorum*, vol. ii. No. 1328.

colloquy with the Wittenberg divines, and a promise
that on the return of the elector the proposals of
Henry should be carefully considered.[1]   As to
Henry's offer to join the league of Schmalkalden,
John Frederic cautiously replied that, in so grave a
matter, the other members of the league must
be consulted.[2] They would meet in December, and
then Barnes and the English ambassadors who were
to follow him might make their proposals.

After the elector's departure Barnes conferred with
the Protestant theologians, but their mood seemed
to him by no means satisfactory.   Most of the
Wittenberg divines were distinctly hostile to Henry.
They did not soon recover from the shock caused by
the execution of More, and Melanchthon had to defend
himself for having dedicated his *Loci Communes*
to a sovereign capable of such an outrage.[3]   Barnes
failed to convince them of the soundness of Henry's
opinions about the divorce, and, half in despair, he
left Jena for Leipzig, where he proposed to dispute
with Cochlæus, a divine of the old school who had
fiercely attacked the king.[4]

It had now become evident that no northern

[1] The Elector of Saxony to Henry VIII., September 28, 1535,
Corpus Reformatorum, vol. ii. No. 1330.

[2] The Elector of Saxony's answer to Barnes, *Corpus Reformatorum*, vol. ii. No. 1329.

[3] Melanchthon to Camerarius, December 24, 1535, *Corpus Reformatorum*, vol. ii. No. 1381: "Mori casu afficior, nec me
negotiis illis admiscebo.   In dedicatione nondum illa audieramus,
et ego amico cuidam volui consulere."

[4] Dr. Brueck to the elector, November 15, 1535, *Corpus Reformatorum*, vol. ii. No. 1355.

league of any kind could be formed, and that the CHAP. XII.
idea of providing an equivalent for the French *Henry's*
alliance would have to be given up. For the *isolation.*
moment Henry stood quite alone. His isolation,
however, was not necessarily dangerous; it would
become so only if Charles V. were persuaded to help
the English malcontents with men and munitions of
war. The lords who had entered into correspondence
with Chapuis knew this quite as well as the king,
and they urged the ambassador to advise Charles to
send them help. After the execution of the
Carthusians they became even more pressing, and
Lord Bray wrote to Chapuis, entreating him not to *May,*
let the opportunity pass.[1] *1535.*

But Charles V. was fully occupied with his expedition against Tunis, and it would be impossible for
him to exercise proper control over an important
undertaking in a distant country. He decided,
therefore, to leave the matter in the hands of Mary,
Queen of Hungary, who governed the Low Countries.
Queen Mary was a very energetic and courageous
woman, but she shrank from the responsibility of
supporting a rebellion in England. The Low Countries
were by no means quiet. Muenster, which was but
a few miles from the frontier, still held out; the
Anabaptists in Holland, encouraged by the successful resistance of their brethren in Germany, gave
considerable trouble; and risings might occur at any
moment. Besides, an expedition to England might
provoke a war with France, and, in the absence of

[1] E. Chapuis to Charles V., May 8, 1535, Vienna Archives,
P.C. 229½, i. fol. 76.

CHAP. XII.   her brother, Mary could not venture to run the risk
            of exciting so dangerous a conflict.

Expedi-   It was on the absence of Charles V. that Cromwell
tion of
Charles V. had reckoned when he began his crusade against the
to Tunis.   adherents of the papacy. The expedition to Tunis
            was hazardous, and it was generally predicted that
            the emperor would be obliged to abandon his pur-
            pose.[1] If he came back without having succeeded, he
            would probably be attacked by Francis, and negotia-
            tions in which this was assumed were carried on
            between the French and English courts.[2] The
            English malcontents, despairing of help from Charles,
            might then, by flattery, gifts, and promises, be won
            over to Henry's cause ; and at the head of a united
            nation he would find little difficulty in withstanding
            his foes.

            Cherishing such anticipations as these, Henry,
            Anne, and Cromwell, although aware of the extent of
            the conspiracy and of the insecurity of the French
            alliance, did not for some time feel greatly alarmed.
            But a few weeks after the death of Fisher and More,
            circumstances forced them to acknowledge that they
            had vastly underrated the perils to which they might
            be exposed through the emperor's ill-will.

Fall of   On the 24th of June the troops besieging Muenster
Muenster.
June 24,   surprised one of the towers, and, after a bloody fight,
1535.   obtained possession of the town.[1] Holland, therefore,

            [1] G. da Casale to Cromwell, July 27, 1535, *State Papers*,
            vol. vii. p. 618.
            [2] Articles and Instructions to the Duke of Norfolk, *State
            Papers*, vol. vii. p. 608.
            [3] L. v. Ranke, *Deutsche Geschichte*, vol. iii. p. 400.

had no longer anything to fear from the Anabaptists ; and Queen Mary of Hungary would be more able, and might be more willing, to assist the English malcontents.

But more alarming intelligence was soon to follow. On the 23rd of June the emperor began the siege of the Goletta, the principal harbour of Tunis. The works were very strong, the garrison fought bravely, and Khairredin annoyed the besiegers by frequent attacks, so that the enemies of Charles became more and more confident that the expedition would be a total failure. He was resolved, however, to succeed. Never having commanded in person before, he was bent on showing that the blood of Maximilian had not degenerated in him. On the 14th of July a general assault was delivered, and after desperate fighting the place was taken. The whole arsenal of Khairredin, a great many galleys, hundreds of cannon, and large stores of ammunition and victuals fell into the hands of the victors.

Success of Charles in Tunis.
June 23, 1535.

July 14, 1535.

A decided success having been obtained, Charles's generals advised him simply to fortify the Goletta, and to be satisfied with what he had achieved ; but he thought otherwise. Khairredin was still hovering in the neighbourhood, and, had the imperial army left, he would have reappeared and laid siege to the harbour which had been taken from him. Besides, at Tunis there were from 18,000 to 20,000 Christian slaves, whom Charles wished to liberate. So he decided upon an advance, and early on the 20th of July he marched out towards Tunis. Slowly his men toiled through the burning desert which separated

July 20, 1535.

CHAP. XII.

the Goletta from the capital. Towards noon, tired and thirsty, they came in view of some olive groves, where they expected to find water to quench their thirst ; but between them and the object of their desire lay the enemy. They formed in order of battle, and advanced against Khairredin's army. A furious charge of the Moorish horse broke on the pikes of the landsknechts. After the Mohammedan horse had been driven back, the whole Christian army rushed at the Turkish and Moorish infantry, and, carrying everything before it, secured a complete victory. A great many Turks were slain, all their cannon were taken, and the imperial army could encamp around the wells it had so valiantly conquered. That same night the Christian captives in the citadel of Tunis, fearing that Khairredin, in case of a siege, would kill them all, broke their chains, rose against their warders, overpowered them, and closed the gates of the fortress. Khairredin, unable to obtain admittance, had to fly with a few thousand Turks to Algiers, while Charles entered the town of Tunis, reinstated the former Moorish king, Muley Hassan, and decided to keep the Goletta for himself.[1] The object of the expedition had been attained, and the emperor would go back to Europe with a high reputation for military ability and luck, and with more power than ever.

July 21, 1535.

About the middle of August Henry heard of the taking of the Goletta, and he could console himself

[1] *Papiers d'Etat de Granvelle*, vol. ii. pp. 361-386 ; and Diary of Charles V., by Mr. d'Herbays, MSS. Biblioteca Naçional, Madrid.

only by hoping that Charles would not be able to chap. xii.
follow up his advantage.[1] But a fortnight later a *Reception*
courier from France brought the news of Charles's *of the*
complete success. Henry, at first, could not believe *Henry.*
it; but Cromwell, having read the despatches, had *August,*
to confirm the disagreeable tidings.[2] The letters *September,*
were received in the presence of a servant whom *1535.*
Chapuis had sent to ask some favour for the princess;
and the imperial ambassador wrote to Granvelle that
both the king and his minister had looked "like
dogs that had tumbled out of a window." Cromwell,
who had at a glance seen the terrible import of the
news, was most crestfallen; he could scarcely find
breath to mutter a few hypocritical congratulations
on the event. On the following days neither Henry
nor Anne could hide their vexation and apprehension.[3]

In France the peace party was greatly strengthened *Francis*
by the taking of Tunis. ·Francis had looked forward *decides*
with so much confidence to the failure of the expe- *for peace*
dition that he had intended, after the emperor's *with*
return, to fall upon him, and to obtain by force of *Charles.*
arms Milan, Asti, and the other coveted possessions
in Italy. Henry had been asked to contribute towards the expenses of the war, and to close his

[1] Chapuis to Charles V., August 25, 1535, Vienna Archives,
P.C. 229½, i. fol. 121.

[2] Chapuis to Charles V., September 6, 1535, Vienna Archives,
P.C. 229½, i. fol. 123.

[3] Chapuis to N. de Granvelle, September 13, 1535, Vienna
Archives, P.C. 229½, iii. fol. 23 : "Le dict roy . . . et Cremuel
. . . ont estes estonne de la bonne nouvelle comme chiens tum-
bants de fenestres et mesme Cremuel lequel a male peyne pouvoit
parler."

harbours to the fleets of Charles coming and going between Spain and the Low Countries. At Calais negotiations had been carried on about the aid Henry was to give, and his ministers had been instructed to make fair promises in a general way.[1]

Now all was changed. Charles had become the hero of Christendom ; and to quarrel with him, when his adherents and his army were flushed with victory, might prove disastrous. In a war declared just after the emperor had rendered so signal a service, Francis might have to encounter the united strength of Germany. For the moment, an attack upon Charles V. was not to be thought of.

New policy of Francis towards England. Forced to resign his purpose of entering upon a new struggle with the emperor, Francis felt inclined to change his policy towards England. Hitherto his object in dealing with Henry had been to obtain promises of help in the event of war. Now it occurred to him that he would have more to gain by bringing about a marriage between the dauphin and Mary. If this match could be arranged, Francis did not doubt that the emperor, out of regard for his cousin, would accede to it ; and he hoped that Henry might be induced to make his peace with Rome. Mary would then be the acknowledged heir to the English throne, and after the death of Henry and Francis, their children would reign over both France and England. The accession of power obtained in this way would be far greater than any advantage that could be secured by the most successful war.

[1] Instruction to the Commissioners at Calais, *State Papers*, vol. vii. p. 608.

An opportunity of acting upon this policy soon presented itself. After the execution of Fisher and More, Paul III. issued several briefs, setting forth the enormities committed by Henry, and requiring Christian princes to hold no further intercourse with *July 26, 1535.* him and his realms.[1] One of these briefs was addressed to Francis. As a rule, such documents were coolly received at the French court ; but this time it was decided that a special ambassador should be sent to England to let Henry know of the brief, and to explain the position of Francis with regard to it.[2] The person chosen for the errand was the former ambassador-resident, Dinteville, the bailly of Troyes. He left the French court at the end of August, and arrived in England in the beginning of September.

August, 1535.

[1] Baronius, *Annales*, vol. xxxii. p. 366, July 26, 1535.
[2] Jean Breton to Cardinal du Bellay, August 31, 1535, Paris, Bibl. Nat. MSS. Fr. vol. 19,577 ; and A. de Montmorency to Cardinal du Bellay, September 28, 1535, Paris, Bibl. Nat. MSS. Fr. vol. 19,577.

CHAPTER XIII.

THE RESULTS OF HENRY'S POLICY.

Dinte-ville's in-structions.

August, 1535.

THE original instructions given by Francis to the bailly of Troyes seem to have been lost, but we still possess a few letters about his mission, a supplementary instruction sent to him after he had left court, and a long memorandum drawn up by Morette, Antoine de Castelnau, and Dinteville himself, which he took home and sent to court. From these papers it appears that Dinteville was first of all to communicate to Henry the contents of the brief addressed to Francis on the 26th of July.[1] Having done this, he was to represent that Francis, if he stood by Henry, would be attacked by the emperor and his allies, that he would have to prepare for this emergency, and that he would expect subsidies from his good brother of England. Requests for pecuniary aid had hitherto been preferred in a tentative way:

[1] J. Breton de Villandry to Cardinal du Bellay, August 31, 1535, Paris, Bibl. Nat. MSS. Fr. vol. 19,577: "Le Roy a depesche Monsr le bailly de Troyes pour aller en angleterre pour laffaire du brief que Nre St Pere escripvit dernierement au Roy touchant le faict dudict Roy dangleterre;" and A. de Montmorency to Cardinal du Bellay, September 28, 1535, Paris, Bibl. Nat. MSS. Fr. vol. 19,577.

no specified sum had been demanded ; Henry had
only been asked what he might be inclined to grant.
But times had changed, and the tone of Francis had
changed with them. Dinteville was instructed to
insist that if Francis, for any reason whatever, chose
to make war upon the emperor and to attempt the
conquest of Milan, Asti, and Genoa, Henry must
consider himself bound to bear one-third of the
expenses incurred for the French army.[1]

Dinteville was directed not only to press these
demands on Henry and his ministers, but to ascertain
as far as possible what were the feelings of the
English people and to report in general on the state
of the country. On his arrival in England, therefore,
about the beginning of September, he tried to gather
all the information he could ; and the report he took
home a month later gives a gloomy picture indeed of
the misery and discontent of the nation.

Henry's policy had exerted a disastrous influence *English*
on the foreign trade of England. When the king *trade*
ruined by
publicly acknowledged Anne as his wife, an immedi- *Henry's*
ate rupture with the emperor was apprehended. The *policy.*
London merchants went to Chapuis, and anxiously
inquired whether he was going to leave ; they naturally feared that in case of war the goods which they
had in the Low Countries and in Spain would be
seized, and that any ship they might send out
would be captured.[2] Chapuis remained at his post

[1] Francis I. to J. de Dinteville, August 29, 1535, Paris, Bibl.
Nat. MSS. Dupuis, vol. 547, fol. 307.
[2] E. Chapuis to Charles V., April 15, 1533, Vienna Archives,
P.C. 228, i. fol. 41.

CHAP. XIII. and war was not proclaimed, but traders in the city hesitated to undertake any large commercial enterprise. And they were right ; for, although there were no open hostilities, the authorities in Flanders and in Spain were in a very unfriendly mood. In 1534 and 1535 the situation became even more complicated. Adherents of the pope were irritated by the schism between England and the Holy See ; and an angry feeling spread from Flanders and Spain to France and Italy. At the very time when Francis was professing the greatest friendship for Henry, English merchants in France were being daily insulted and robbed, and they could obtain no redress.[1] Lawyers on the continent began even to ask whether Englishmen, in consequence of the rebellion of their king and the papal censures, had not ceased to belong to the Christian republic, and had not forfeited all rights conferred by the *jus gentium* and the imperial laws.[2] Many English merchants in Flanders, Spain, and France, alarmed by the temper which had been evoked among the people around them, sold their wares and returned to England. In the summer of 1535 very few of them remained in France, and shipowners at home were afraid to send their vessels to French ports. Special safe-conducts had to be taken out for those who wished to cross the Channel, and this, of course, hampered all transactions and made them less

August,
1535.

[1] J. Coke to Cromwell, May 12, 1534, R.O. Henry VIII. Box Q ; and Reports from France, October 24 and 25, 1534, R.O. Henry VIII. Box Q, Nos. 84 and 85.

[2] Allegations of Robyn Carre, Gairdner, *Letters and Papers,* vol. vii. p. 625.

profitable.[1] Merchants got no interest on their money,
and mariners were thrown out of employment.

Had Henry acted prudently, it might have been
possible for his subjects to find new outlets for their
energy in those countries in which papal censures were
not respected ; but by persisting in his alliance with
Wullenwever he had irritated the opposite party,
which on the Baltic and on the German Ocean was now
triumphing over the friends of England. Gustavus
Vasa is said to have openly boasted that he was only
beginning the game against Henry ;[2] and when, in
retaliation for the capture of the English ships,
Henry caused the goods of the Dantzig merchants
to be seized, these merchants assured Chapuis that
they did not care, for they meant to take out letters
of reprisal by which they would get from English
merchants and vessels more than their property in
London had been worth.[3] Even the fishing fleet which
went to Iceland and Newfoundland could not be
despatched without risk. Iceland was a Danish
colony, and if Christian III. was not conciliated,
English fishermen would meet with scant courtesy
from his officials.

[1] E. Chapuis to N. de Granvelle, August 3 and September 25,
1535, Vienna Archives, P.C. 229½, iii. fols. 22 and 25.

[2] E. Chapuis to Charles V., October 13, 1535, Vienna Archives,
P.C. 229½, i. fol. 130.

[3] E. Chapuis to Charles V., November 21, 1535, Vienna
Archives, P.C. 229½, i. fol. 137 : "Les marchandisez de ceulx
de Danzic sont tousiours icy en sequestre ; partie de ceulx a qui
sont lesdictes marchandises mont dit quilz navoient garde de
sollicite la relaxation dudict sequestre soy tenant pour certains
quilz trouveront assez moyens destre reccmpensez au double et
du principal et des interetz."

CHAP. XIII.   The circumstances which compelled English merchants on the continent to return to their own
country and to abandon a profitable trade, had a
corresponding influence on foreign traders in England.   They feared that they might be made to
pay for the injury done to Englishmen abroad,
and the latest proceedings of Henry confirmed
them in this opinion.   Accordingly they no longer
imported foreign wares, but were rather occupied in
withdrawing the capital they had invested in English
commerce.   A good many of them, having sold all
they had, left the country altogether, while those who
remained reduced their transactions as much as
possible.   The Venetian secretary was already in-
quiring whether his countrymen would be allowed to
export wool from Spain, that Venice might be independent of England ;[1] and the fleet which had
hitherto come regularly to Southampton to import
wine from Candia, and to export wool and tin, stayed
away.   The English government was rather alarmed
by this demonstration, and tried to allay the distrust
of the Venetian merchants.   A fine they had incurred
was partly remitted, and they were assured that they
might freely export wool and kerseys.[2]   But they
remained supicious, and made no use of the permission
granted.

The bad   During the summer of 1535 the weather had been
harvest.   so bad that the harvest was very small, the yield of

[1] E. Chapuis to Charles V., August 11, 1534, Vienna Archives,
P.C. 229, i. fol. 128.
[2] E. Chapuis to Granvelle, December 13, 1535, Vienna
Archives, P.C. 229½, ii. fol. 69.

corn being less than half of that of average years.[1] The people had observed, Chapuis says, that it had rained ever since the execution of the Carthusians; and the bad weather was ascribed to divine vengeance for the misdeeds of the king.[2] It was in vain that the royal preachers were commissioned to say that God chastises those he loves; the people remained obdurate and angry.[3]

In former times, whenever the harvest in England had failed, the Hanseatic merchants had been large importers of grain; but after the ill-treatment they had suffered in London they sought for other markets, and thus one of the easiest sources of supply was closed.[4] England became dependent for its food on France and on the Low Countries; and both Chapuis and the French ambassadors advised their masters to forbid the export of corn, hoping in this way to be able to bring pressure to bear on Henry and to wring concessions from him.[5]

Such was the condition of England when Dinteville, in the beginning of September, arrived at the court of Henry near Winchester. Seeing how matters stood he adopted a rather high tone, and insisted on all the demands Francis had ordered him to make.

The demands of Francis refused. September, 1535.

[1] Memorandum of the French ambassadors, Paris, Bibl. Nat. MSS. Dupuis, vol. 547, fol. 200.

[2] E. Chapuis to Charles V., October 13, 1535, *loc. cit.*

[3] E. Chapuis to N. de Granvelle, November 1, 1535, Vienna Archives, P.C. 229½, iii. fol. 28.

[4] E. Chapuis to Charles V., October 13, 1535, *loc. cit.*

[5] Memorandum of French ambassadors, *loc. cit.*; and E. Chapuis to N. de Granvelle, November 1, 1535, *loc. cit.*

CHAP. XIII. But even if Henry had been disposed to grant every
request of the French, he would not have been able
to pay such subsidies as Dinteville had been instructed to ask for. If the French really attacked
the emperor, their expenses would not be less than
£100,000 a month, so that the King of England,
had he yielded to Francis, might have had to find
£33,333 a month. This would have been far beyond
his resources, for the whole ordinary royal income
even in fairly prosperous times was not more than
£140,000 per annum. Henry was obliged, therefore,
to refuse the demands of Francis, and all he
would promise was that he would not claim the
instalment of the French pensions which had become
due.[1] Angry words passed between the king and
his ministers on the one hand, and the French

October,
1535.
ambassadors on the other ; and after a short stay at
court the bailly asked leave to return to France.

The
proposed
marriage
of Mary
and the
dauphin.
Before leaving England, Dinteville begged that he
and his colleagues might be allowed to visit the king's
daughters, his real object being to learn, if possible,
from the Princess Mary herself how she felt inclined
towards a marriage with the dauphin. Permission
could not well be refused, and the three Frenchmen
with their train proceeded towards Eltham, where
Mary and Elizabeth were staying. One of the
gentlemen of the king's chamber had been ordered
to accompany the ambassadors, and to see to their
comfort and honourable treatment. This person was
no sooner alone with them than he informed them

[1] Duke of Suffolk to Mr. de Saint Martin, September 25,
1535, R.O. Henry VIII. Box S.

that he had received secret instructions from Anne
to watch their movements; and they afterwards
reported to their government that, so far as the
queen and the princess were concerned, Henry could
not trust even his personal servants, nearly all of
whom were favourable to Catherine and Mary.[1]

On arriving at Eltham the ambassadors were shown
into the presence of Elizabeth, but they were not
allowed to see Mary. They were of course greatly
annoyed at this, but they were somewhat consoled by
all they heard at Eltham, and after their return to
London. They were told that Mary had greatly
wished to see them, but that Lady Shelton had shut
her up in her room, and had caused all the windows
of it to be nailed down.[2] Mary, it was said, had
raged and stormed until the gentleman who had
accompanied Dinteville had gone in and told her that
it was the king's pleasure she should remain secluded.[3]

[1] Memorandum of the French ambassadors, *loc. cit.*

[2] E. Chapuis to Charles V., October 13, 1535, *loc. cit.* : "Sire
les ambassadeurs et bailli ont este visiter la petite bastarde de
ce Roy, de quoy faire les ambassadeurs avoint a ce quilz me
dirent touts deux souvent este requis et instes de la concubine
dudict Roy, et quilz avoint tousiours differe jusqua la venue
dudict baillif, lequel avoit este doppinion dy aller, pensant que
en quelque sorte ils entreverroint la princesse, questoit la chose
du monde quilz desiroient austant, et sans lespoir de laquelle ils
ny feussent allez. Mais que leur defortune navoit point permis
quils la veissent, et ce a cause quelle avoit este non seullement,
comme ils disoint, serree dans sa chambre, mais aussi furent
cloues les fenestres par ou elle pouroit estre veue."

[3] Memorandum of the French ambassadors, *loc. cit.* : "Lautre
part Vous scavez le tumulte qui fut entre sa gouvernante et elle,
quant nous feusmes veoir sa petite seur, et quil nous a este dict
quelle fust mise comme par force dans sa chambre, pour quelle

About this matter the French ambassadors were not well-informed. The truth was that as soon as they had manifested an intention to go to Eltham, instructions had been sent to Lady Shelton to prevent Mary from seeing or conversing with any of them; and Lady Shelton had immediately told the princess that she would have to keep her room while the ambassadors were there. Mary was rather indignant, and sent a message to Chapuis to ask whether she was to obey or not. Chapuis counselled submission, and she acted on his advice, amusing herself while the Frenchmen were in the house by playing on the virginals.[1]

The French ambassadors, however, were convinced not only that Mary had desired to see them, but that she would not dislike a marriage with the dauphin. According to an Englishman with whom they conversed, and who referred to one of Mary's servants as his authority, the princess had said many a time that the dauphin was her husband;[2] and when Lady

ne parlast a nous et quil ne feust possible de la rapaiser et contenir dedans sa chambre que le gentilhomme qui nous menoit ne luy eust premierement asseure, que le Roy son pere luy avoit commande de luy·dire quelle ne se monstra point cependant que nous serions la."

[1] E. Chapuis to Charles V., October 13, 1535, *loc. cit.*: "Ce que ne crois ains que suivant ce que luy avoit escript, veuillant sur ce avoir mon advis, elle se tint tout vouluntierement en sa chambre, jouant de lespinette pour dissimuler lennuyt dicelle visitacion."

[2] Report of the French ambassadors, *loc. cit.*: "Item vous scavez que ung homme nous a asseure que une des femmes de la dicte princesse, luy avoit racompte, que plusieurs fois elle luy avoit oui dire que mon dict Sieur le Dauphin estoit son mari . . ."

Shelton and other servants of Anne had told her
that he had married the daughter of the emperor,
she had replied that it was not true, and that they
only said so to deprive her of all hope, and to make
her forego her rights.[1]   Another Englishman had
suggested that Mary would be prepared to express
her wishes in writing.[2]

The English nation seemed to the ambassadors to
approve of the proposed marriage.   When Dinteville
and his colleagues arrived, and it was supposed that
they had come to denounce to Henry the censures of
the Church and to ask that the marriage of the dauphin
and the Princess Mary should be concluded, they were
heartily received by the common people, by the
gentlemen at court, and even by the king's servants.
As soon as it was known that this was not the object
of their mission, they excited less enthusiasm.[3]   When

[1] Report of the French ambassadors, *loc. cit.* : "Quant sa
gouvernante et autres dames que la Royne qui est a present
a commises pour sa garde luy disoient que mon dit Sieur le
Dauphin estoit marie avec la fille de lempereur, leur respondit
quelle ne le croyait pas, veu quil ne peut avoir deux femmes
et quil ne peut ignorer quelle ne soit sa femme, et que jamais
elle nen perdra lesperance, et quelle scavoit bien quon faisoit
courre ce bruict pour luy en ouster, et par ce moyen luy faire
quitter son droict."

[2] *Ibid.* : "Semblablement Vous scavez que ung sest faict fort
de luy faire mettre par escript sa volonte, affin que les choses ne
soient fondees legerement."

[3] *Ibid.* : "Outre plus Mr. vous noublierez dire sur vostre
venue et que cela feust espards parmy le menu peuple on disoit
que Vous veniez pour denuncer au Roy les excommuniements et
pour demander madame la princesse pour Mr. le Dauphin, dont
le peuple estoit si trescontant quil ne cessoit de faire priere pour
Vous, comme plusieurs vous ont asseure estre vray. Pareillement

they returned from Eltham to spend a few days in
London, they were again warmly greeted : the people,
thinking they had seen the princess, cheered them as
they passed, and wished them good speed.[1] The
desperation of the country had become so great, the
ambassadors wrote, that those who would formerly
have been most opposed to the marriage of Mary with
a foreign prince unwilling to reside permanently in
England, now ardently desired the union. For if
Mary were to marry a prince of lower degree than the
dauphin, she might lose her right to the crown or
obtain it only after a violent struggle, whereas, if she
married the son of Francis, resistance would be
impossible, and her claim would be universally
admitted.[2]

Dinteville and his colleagues were not altogether
wrong. The English people had almost abandoned
the hope of receiving help from the emperor, and in
their perplexity were ready to turn to France for

Vous scavez le bon receuil que les propres gentilshommes de ceux
du Roy vous faisoient, qui estoient meilleur, que depuis quils ont
sceu que vostre charge ne touchoit rien de cela."

[1] Report of the French ambassadors, *loc. cit.* : "Item que lon
nous dict ainsi que nous feusmes arrivez a Londres que le
peuple faisoit priere pour nous ayant entendu que nous estions
alle veoir madame la princesse."

[2] *Ibid.* : "Item le trouble a este si grand et la desesperation
dudict peuple si grande, que ou le temps passe il ne trouvoit bon
quelle fust mariee audict sieur Daulphin, pour le desir quilz ont
davoir un Roy en Angleterre, qui se tint au pays, a present ils
ne desirent rien plus que cela, disant que si moindre que luy
vient a lepouser elle demourera desheritee oubien faudra quelle
aye son droict par guerre et avec grandes incommoditez de tout
le peuple."

assistance against the tyranny of the king. The
warnings of Chapuis had come true.

The extreme unpopularity of Anne and of her
kinsfolk and friends did not escape the notice of the
ambassadors. The common people, they reported,
were extremely angry against Anne, abusing her in
no measured terms for the danger and distress into
which she had brought the country.[1] The upper
classes were nearly all equally bitter, some on account
of the changes in religion, others for fear of war and
of ruin to trade, others, and by far the greater number,
from loyalty to Catherine and Mary.[2] Englishmen
had no wish to see Elizabeth on the throne, with
Anne Boleyn and Lord Rochford as her guardians and
as regents during a long minority.

Anne herself was fully conscious of the difficulties
of her position. To one of the gentlemen who accompanied Dinteville she granted a private audience, and
he reported to Marguerite of Navarre the substance of
their conversation. Anne said that the two things
she most desired on earth were to have a son and to
meet Queen Marguerite once more. She seemed ill at
ease and harassed, and the eagerness with which she

[1] Report of the French ambassadors, *loc. cit.*: "Item aussy
que le peuple menu prevoyant toutes ces choses est fort
anime contre la Royne, jusques a en dire mille maux et
improperes."

[2] *Ibid.*: "Item que tout le peuple est merveilleusement mal
contant, les uns, et quasi tous hormis les parens de la Royne qui
est a present, pour raison des dictes dames, les autres pour la
subversion de la religion, les autres craignans la guerre et voyans
que lentrecours de marchandise cessera tant dedans le royaume
que dehors."

CHAP. XIII. wished to be recommended to Marguerite showed how
much she wanted sympathy and help.[1]

In proof of the great popularity of Mary the
ambassador mentioned the following curious fact.
When Mary had left Greenwich to go to Eltham, a
great many women, in spite of their husbands, had
flocked to see her pass, and had cheered her, calling
out that, notwithstanding all laws to the contrary,

Lady Rochford and Anne. April, 1535. she was still their princess. Several of them, being
of higher rank than the rest, had been arrested, and,
as they had proved obstinate, had been sent to the
Tower.[2] On the margin of that part of the report in
which this circumstance is recorded we find the words
(written by Dinteville himself) : " Note, my Lord
Rochford and my Lord William." [3] The ambassador
clearly meant that Lady Rochford, Anne's sister-in-
law, and Lady William Howard were among those
who had cheered Mary. We know from Chapuis that

[1] —— to Marguerite de Navarre, September 15 (1535), Paris,
Bibl. Nat. MSS. Fr. vol. 3,014, fol. 98. This letter has been
ascribed by Mr. J. Stevenson, in his *Calendar of State Papers*,
to a much later period, and he asserts that the Queen of England
spoken of is Mary Tudor. The whole context shows that this is
not the case. The letter is certainly not addressed to Jeanne
d'Albret (who succeeded Marguerite) ; and besides, the court of
Philip and Mary never was at Winchester in September.

[2] Memorandum of the French ambassadors, *loc. cit.*: " Item,
dernierement quant elle fust remuee de Grenewich, une grande
trouppe de femmes, tant bourgeoyses que autres (au desceu de
leurs maris) luy furent au devant, en pleurant et criant, que
nonobstant tout ce quavoit este faict, elle estoit Princesse, et en
furent mises les plus grandes en la tour, tousiours persistant en
leur opinion."

[3] *Ibid.*: " Nota. Millor de Rochefort et Millor de Guillaume."

Lady Rochford had in the preceding autumn been CHAP. XIII.
sent from court, but the imperial ambassador ascribed
her disgrace to intrigues on behalf of, not in opposition to, Anne. Had Lady Rochford's absence
from court produced a change ? That may have been
so, for it is said that towards the end of the year she
was on bad terms with her husband. Lady William
Howard was certainly hostile to Anne, and she and
Lady Rochford were great friends. Dinteville may
therefore have been right.

Considering the difficulties of the government, the *Scheme*
temper of the nation, and the supposed inclination of *for the*
Mary, the French ambassadors came to the conclusion *Henry.*
that a marriage between the dauphin and the
princess might be brought about more easily than
had been expected. They proposed that Paul III.
should be told of the offers which had been made to
Francis by Henry on condition that Francis would
throw off his allegiance to the Holy See, and
make war on the emperor. The pope should be
warned, they suggested, that if war broke out it
might be necessary to accept these offers, and that
then he would lose his revenues from France as he
had lost his revenues from England. The ambassadors believed that to prevent so unholy an alliance
Paul III. would ask the emperor himself to propose
the marriage, and that Charles, for the sake of his
aunt and his cousin, might be persuaded to do so.[1] If

---

[1] Memorandum of the French ambassadors, *loc. cit.* : " Si le
pape estoit adverty des traictes que le Roy dangleterre pretend
faire avecque le Roy, il entrera en doubte de perdre largent de
France comme il a faict celluy dangleterre si guerre se meust,

he consented, Henry would of course be immediately informed of the fact, and the French king might tell Henry that war would be unavoidable unless the proposal were accepted. Anne would oppose the marriage, but Henry would be afraid to offend both the king and the emperor. Besides, Anne's influence was on the wane ; the king had again changed his mistress.[1]

Henry offended by the French ambassadors.

Feeling sure that Henry would have to give way, the French ambassadors were not at all careful to hide their opinions and their wishes. They permitted their servants to talk openly of the advantages which would arise from the marriage of the dauphin and the princess,[2] and some indignation was caused by this freedom of discourse, for Henry was certain that if he consented to the marriage he would soon have a very precarious hold on the loyalty of his subjects. Perceiving the danger, he was angry with his former

et il moyenneroit bien envers lempereur quil prieroit le Roy entendre au mariage que dessus et croy que le dict empereur y ayderoit pour lamour quil porte a sa niepce."

[1] Memorandum of the French ambassadors, *loc. cit.* : "Item si le dict Empereur vient a prier de ce que dessus, il pourra lors adviser de faire entendre au Roy dangleterre lintention de lempereur et luy persuader de le consentir pour eviter toutes guerres, veu que le dict Sieur ne denie point quelle ne soit sa fille et quil scait bien que le mariaige en est faict.

"Et si le dict Sieur Roy dangleterre ne le trouvoit bon a cause de la persuasion que sa femme luy pourroit faire au contraire, si craindra il bien de mettre contre soy le Roy et lempereur pour la seule affection quil porte a sa dicte femme, qui est beaucoup moindre quelle na este, et diminue tous les jours veu quil y a nouvelles amours comme Vous scavez."

[2] E. Chapuis to Charles V., June 5, 1535, Vienna Archives, P.C. 229½, i. fol. 89.

friends for trying to increase it and to profit by his CHAP XIII
difficulties.

Cromwell also was extremely angry with the *Cromwell and the French.*
French. At heart he was rather favourable to Mary,
and of late his relations with Anne had not always
been very good ; but as he had no wish to see England
become a dependency of France, he resisted the
proposed match and stood loyally by Henry and Anne
against the peril which was threatening them. With
the French ambassadors he had been for some time on
bad terms. On the 29th of June the Bishop of Tarbes *June 29, 1535.*
and Morette had invited him to dinner, but he had
rudely refused, saying that he knew what they wanted
to tell him, and that he did not wish to hear it.[1]
Shortly afterwards he had an angry discussion with *July, 1535.*
the ambassadors, whom he treated with considerable
insolence ; and when they resented his arrogance, he
used his influence to prevent the bishop from being
lodged, as most of his predecessors had been, at the
king's cost at Bridewell.[2]

The English ministers, being in ill humour with the *Chapuis and the English ministers. July, 1535.*
French, tried to convey the impression that their
relations with the emperor were improving. A new
ambassador, Richard Pate, had been appointed to
reside with Charles V. ; and Cromwell and his
colleagues went about talking of the honour with
which he had been received at the imperial court.[3]

[1] E. Chapuis to Charles V., June 30, 1535, Vienna Archives,
P.C. 229½, i. fol. 103.

[2] E. Chapuis to Charles V., July 11, 1535, Vienna Archives,
P.C. 229½, i. fol. 105.

[3] E. Chapuis to N. de Granvelle, July 11, 1535, Vienna
Archives, P.C. 229½, iii. fol. 17.

CHAP. XIII. Henry himself considerably altered his tone, no longer speaking of the ingratitude of Charles, but, on the contrary, praising him.[1] Towards Chapuis the English ministers made a great show of cordiality. They offered him all kinds of little favours, and frequently sent for him to discuss the most unimportant matters, hoping to make the English public and the French ambassadors believe that important negotiations were going on.

Chapuis was not to be duped so easily. He would not have been unwilling to make the French feel uneasy, and to sow distrust between them and the English; but he did not wish the public to suppose that he or his master in the slightest degree approved *August,* of Henry's proceedings. When he received from the 1535. king the honour of being allowed to hunt in the royal parks—and this was considered a great favour— he quietly declared that he would make use of the privilege only if the Princess Mary were treated less harshly.[2] And so in other cases; it was always necessary to bribe him to accept any small courtesy from the king or from Cromwell, and the price he asked was often so high that it could not be granted.

The proposals made by the English ministers for the purpose of regaining the friendship of the emperor were considered by Chapuis quite unacceptable. The negotiation which Sir John Wallop

[1] E. Chapuis to Charles V., July 11, 1535, Vienna Archives, P.C. 229½, i. fol. 105.

[2] E. Chapuis to Charles V., August 3, 1535, Vienna Archives, P.C. 229½, i. fol. 119.

had begun with Viscount Hanart in Paris had led to no result, for Henry would not consent to treat Catherine and Mary with royal honours, as the emperor desired;[1] and by the execution of the Carthusians, of Fisher, and of More, he had shown how he intended to behave towards the friends of the queen and the princess. Cromwell had suggested that a marriage might be concluded between Philip, the son of the emperor, and the little Lady Elizabeth ; but, brazen-faced as he was, even Cromwell dared not press this scheme, and Chapuis contemptuously ignored all references to it.[2] He remained coldly distant, waiting for an occasion when he might advise his master to act for Catherine and Mary with vigour.

The French were not less anxious than Cromwell to please Chapuis. Morette, during the last few weeks of his embassy, affected the greatest cordiality towards him ; Morette's successor, the Bishop of Tarbes, did the same ; and Dinteville, during his short stay in London, conferred with the imperial ambassador, and spoke to him in a most friendly manner.[3]

[1] Sir John Wallop to J. Hanart, May 17, 1535, Vienna Archives, P.C. 229½, ii. fol. 39.

[2] E. Chapuis to Charles V., March 7, 1535, Vienna Archives, P.C. 229½, i. fol. 46 : "Sire sur ce il (Cromwell) mentra a parler de mariage du prince despaigne avec ceste bastarde quilz appellent princesse, mays voyant la myne quen tenois il nen dit que deux parolles, et sans ce que luy disse riens il en fit la responce quil croyoit bien que Vostre Maieste ny vouldroit entendre pour respect de la princesse sa cousine ;" and E. Chapuis to N. de Granvelle, February 17, 1536, Vienna Archives, P.C. 230, ii. fol. 5.

[3] E. Chapuis to N. de Granvelle, July 11, 1535, *loc. cit.* ; and E. Chapuis to Charles V., October 13, 1535, *loc. cit.*

On the continent, as well as in England, efforts
were made to influence imperial policy in favour of
August   France.   In the month of August Queen Leonor of
16, 1535.
France had gone to the northern frontier to meet her
sister Mary, Queen of Hungary. Chabot accompanied
the French queen, and during the few days the two
sisters spent together he had a private conversation
with the Queen of Hungary, and spoke to her about
the marriage of the Princess Mary of England with
one of the sons of Francis. These overtures were
duly reported to the emperor, and the negotiation,
which had come to a standstill, was resumed.[1]

Paul III.   At Rome there were many symptoms of approach-
prepares   ing trouble for Henry. The pope was deeply irritated
for the
punish-   against him, and was preparing a bull of excommuni-
ment of   cation and deprivation. The French cardinals and
Henry.
ambassadors had ceased to oppose this extreme
measure ; they only insisted that the bull should
contain no reflections on the conduct of their king,
September, and that it should in no way tend to put him in
1535.
a disadvantageous position with respect to the
emperor.[2]

---

[1] Account of, the negotiation of Pier Luigi Farnese with
Charles V., November, 1535, Vienna Archives, P.C. 229½, ii.
fol. 60 ; and Charles V. to J. Hanart, October 23, 1535, *Papiers
d'état de Granvelle*, vol. ii. p. 387.

[2] Cardinal du Bellay to ——, Paris, Bibl. Nat. MSS. Fr.
vol. 5,499, fol. 212 : "Quant au faict dangleterre troys Cardinaulx
ont charge de y veoir et aux premiers jours faire leur rapport en
consistoire de ce quilz y auront trouve affin quil y soit oppine de
ce qui se y doibt faire pour procedder a lencontre du Roy ;" and
Cardinal du Bellay and Denonville to Francis I., September 3,
1535, Paris, Bibl. Nat. MSS. Fr. vol. 5,499, fol. 217*b* : "Et en
tant Sire, que touche laffaire dangleterre dont il Vous plaist nous

Paul III. was not only preparing spiritual censures,
he was trying to provide means for the execution of
his sentence.   In response to a secret appeal, Francis
had agreed to help in carrying out the sentence of
deprivation, if Charles would also send a contingent ;
and Paul III. had despatched his son, Pier Luigi
Farnese, to Sicily, where the emperor had arrived, to
bring about an understanding.   Charles V., having a
deep-rooted distrust of any offer proceeding from
Francis, had replied that the French king only meant
to inveigle him into some false step, and that the pope
ought to obtain an authentic written promise from
which it would be impossible for Francis to draw back.
If such a promise were given, Charles would be ready
to do his part.[1]   The pope was not disheartened ; and
it seemed highly probable that his secret negotiations
would have results very disagreeable for the King of
England.

The French party at the English court was so
discredited that Anne had bitter quarrels with her
uncle, the Duke of Norfolk, and, about Christmas,

*Hostility
to France
at the
English
court.*

faire mention par Vos lettres la chose nest passe plus avant et
ne sen est parle depuis que moi du Bellay Vous ay dernierement
escript quon avoit ordonne aux deputez de se faire prests pour
faire leur rapport en consistoire . . . et maidoit beaucoup pour
mes defenses la demonstration que Vous feistes durant pappe
Clement quand Vous menvoyastes icy et la faulte qui y fust
faicte telle et si grande que le dicte pappe confessa que en aviez
tant faict quil se contantait desormais que quoique feist le dict
Roy dangleterre Vous ne Vous empeschissiez pour le Sainct Siege
contre luy ne aussy pour luy contre le Sainct Siege . . . Aussi
que icelluy Sainct Siege debvra considerer de ne Vous rechercher
de chose qui Vous soit trop pernitieuse et contre la rayson."
[1] Account of the negotiation of Pier Luigi Farnese, *loc. cit.*

CHAP. XIII. 1534, abused him in unmeasured terms. The Duke
left her presence in anger, and in the hall spoke
against her with indecent violence.[1] Shortly afterwards he retired from the court, thus relieving
Cromwell of all fear of serious opposition in the royal
council.[2] But Anne was not yet satisfied, and seized
every opportunity to bring her uncle into disgrace.[3]

In October 1535 the Bishop of Tarbes openly complained of Cromwell's insolence, and declined to call
upon him. The bishop told Chapuis that he had sent a
message to this effect to the secretary himself.[4] So
serious a quarrel rendered diplomatic intercourse
difficult, and the chances of an open rupture with
France began to be generally discussed. The Duke
of Norfolk, who intended to send his second son to
France, asked Cromwell whether the friendship with
October, Francis had come to an end; and the reply seems to
1535.   have induced him to keep the young man at home.[5]

Financial   International relations being so unsatisfactory, the
difficulties. country became more and more discontented, and
Cromwell could not venture to act with his wonted
energy and fearlessness. The taxes which had been
granted by parliament he was unable to levy, for fear
of exasperating the people;[6] yet the royal coffers

[1] E. Chapuis to Charles V., January 1, 1535, Vienna Archives,
P.C. 229¼, i. fol. 34.

[2] E. Chapuis to Charles V., February 25, 1535, *loc. cit.*

[3] E. Chapuis to Charles V., July 11, 1535, *loc. cit.*

[4] E. Chapuis to Charles V., November 1, 1535, Vienna
Archives, P.C. 229½, i. fol. 115.

[5] Norfolk to Cromwell, September 9, 1535, R.O. Henry VIII.,
Box R, No. 137.

[6] E. Chapuis to Charles V., November 1, 1535, *loc. cit.*

were empty, not only because the French pensions
were withheld, but because, owing to the bad harvest,
the farmers on the royal domains could not pay their
rents.   The result was that the salaries of officials
were not paid, and that the whole machinery of administration began to go out of gear.   The government was already despoiling small convents, the heads
of houses being brought by bribes, threats, and insults to acquiesce in the dissolution of their communities.   But the lands and other possessions
obtained in this way brought in only a small immediate return in ready money or in things that could
be at once exchanged for ready money; and the advantages of confiscation, such as they were, were dearly
purchased at the cost of much popular irritation.

Altogether, Henry's position was not at this time   *Henry's*
an enviable one.   When he looked around him, he   *troubles.*
saw his people thoroughly disaffected, the pope
exasperated and striving to raise against him as
many enemies as possible, the King of France negotiating with the emperor for the purpose of dethron-
ing him, the Protestant princes of Germany offended
and deeply suspicious, and the fleets of Sweden,
Denmark, and Prussia capturing and pillaging his
ships.

Henry did not underrate his difficulties, nor did he   *Henry*
hide from himself that most of them had sprung from   *again*
                                                      thinks of
the policy necessitated by his union with Anne.   He *discarding*
fondly believed that the hatred of his subjects was   *Anne.*
mainly directed against her, and that if she were not
in his way he might still triumph over his enemies.
As he thought of this, the idea of discarding Anne

CHAP. XIII. rose before his mind even more vividly than it had
done at the beginning of the year; and the idea was
certainly not rendered less attractive by the fact that
Anne, worn out by constant exertion and anxiety, had
lost her good looks.[1] Even to Margaret Shelton, who
had so recently touched his fancy, he was already
becoming indifferent. During the summer he had gone
on progress through the south-western counties; and
on the 10th of September the court had been at
Wolfhall, in Wiltshire, the seat of Sir John Seamer or
Seymour, father of Mistress Jane Seymour, a former
attendant of Queen Catherine. Whether it was on
this occasion that Henry began to pay attention to
his future queen is not certain, but a few weeks later
the French ambassadors reported that the king had a
new love.

*Catherine
in the way.*   Although Henry might be heartily tired of Anne,
he remembered the advice given him in February
when he had first spoken of discarding her.   He
must either keep her or take Catherine back.   Was
this the only conceivable alternative ?   No ; Catherine
might die ; and if she were dead, Henry would not
only be rid of his most energetic opponent, the
woman to whose influence the resistance of Mary
seemed chiefly due, he would be free to separate his
fortunes from those of Anne.

For the last two years Henry and his ministers

[1] Dr. Ortiz to the Empress, September 1, 1535, British Museum,
Add. MSS. 28,588, fol. 12 : " Ayer . . . partio de aqui un cama-
rero del Rey de Inglaterra llamado Tomas Petiple el qual . . .
dice que . . . todos llaman a la Ana Reyna la qual dice que
esta muy fea y que todo el pueblo esta como atonido y espantado
que no saben de que parte a de venir el juizio de Dios sobre ellos."

had spoken of the death of Catherine as an event that would soon happen. One day Gregorio da Casale told Chapuis that Henry had said she had the dropsy and in a short time would die of it. Chapuis remarked that the queen had never suffered from anything like dropsy; and he vehemently suspected that the prediction of her approaching death meant that she was to be poisoned.[1] The friends of Catherine and Mary had been warned that Anne wished to poison her rivals. Dr. Ortiz had been told in Rome by the auditor Simonetta that this was her purpose.[2] The Earl of Northumberland, who at the time was still on friendly terms with Anne, made a similar communication to a gentleman at court, who reported it to Chapuis.[3] Pope Clement VII., after he had delivered sentence in March, 1534, had expressed a fear that the result might be the death of the queen.[4]

*Catherine's
death
foretold.*

January,
1534.

September
1533.
February,
1534.

March,
1534.

[1] E. Chapuis to Charles V., January 17, 1534, Vienna Archives, P.C. 229, i. fol. 8: "Et oultre lespoir quil a sur ses subjectz il a aussi grant . . . sur la mort de la Royne laquelle il dict encoires de nouveaulx a lambassadeur de France ne pouvoir vivre longuement a cause quelle est ydropique de laquelle maladie elle ne fust oncques attaincte. Dont est a doubter, comme jay cydevant escript a Vostre Maieste quilz sement telles choses pour luy faire venir une ydropisie artificielle dont dieu la veuille preserver. Et ma faict advertir Gregoire de Cassal desdictz propos du Roy audict ambassadeur de France et ma faict dire quil pensoit avant que partir dyci de renuncer au service de ce Roy et dresse la banniere blanche."

[2] Dr. Ortiz to Charles V., September 9, 1533, British Museum, Add. MSS. 28,586, fol. 1.

[3] E. Chapuis to Charles V., February 11, 1534, Vienna Archives, P.C. 229, i. fol. 32.

[4] Dr. Ortiz to Charles V., March 24, 1534, British Museum, Add. MSS. 28,586, fol. 191.

CHAP. XIII.

Anne desires the death of Catherine and Mary

Anne herself spoke in a violent strain. In the summer of 1534 she plainly said that she intended to kill Mary during Henry's absence from England ; and in March, 1535, when she regained her ascendency, she was reported to have suborned a man to pretend that God had revealed to him that while the princess dowager and the Lady Mary lived Queen Anne would bear no children to the king. About the same time she denounced the two ladies as rebels and traitors who merited death ;[1] and after the execution of Fisher and More she directly urged

July, 1535.

Henry to inflict the same penalty on Catherine and Mary, saying that they deserved death even more than those who had just been beheaded.[2] The hatred she had conceived for them blinded her to her own real interests.

Cromwell on the death of Catherine and Mary. August, 1534.

Cromwell did not hate the queen and the princess ; but he thought that if they were out of the way he would be able to compose the differences between Henry and Charles, and to avert the danger of a foreign invasion. And he made no secret of his feelings. In August, 1534, he said to one of the

---

[1] E. Chapuis to N. de Granvelle, March 23, 1535, Vienna Archives, P.C. 229½, iii. fol. 1 : "Ces jours la concubine a suborne ung que dit avoir eu revelacion de dieu que estoit impossible quelle conceust enfans pendant que les dictes dames seroint en vie. Je doubte quelle laura faict parler au Roy et ces jours elle la envoye a Cremuel. Elle ne cesse de lautre couste de dire quelles sont rebelles et traictresses meritant la mort."

[2] E. Chapuis to Charles V., July 25, 1535, Vienna Archives, P.C. 229½, i. fol. 107 : "Elle ne cesse de cryer apres ledict Roy quil ne faict bien ny prudemment soufrir vivre lesdictes royne et princesse que meritoint beaulcop plus la mort que ceulx quavoient este executer."

lords that the Low Countries were too much afraid of CHAP. XIII.
losing their commerce to allow the emperor to make
war upon England. "But even if this were not the
case," he added, "the death of Catherine and Mary
would prevent any rupture, for then there would be
no occasion for a quarrel."[1] In March, 1535, he *March,*
asked Chapuis what evil or danger would arise from *1535.*
the death of the princess, even if it excited the
indignation of the people, and what cause the emperor
would have to be offended by it.[2] The ambassador
gave an angry reply, having no wish to hear dark
speeches which might lead to even darker deeds.
But a few weeks afterwards Cromwell spoke again
in the same sense, declaring that Mary was at the *April,*
root of all the king's perplexities. "And," he added, *1535.*
"I pray God——." Here he stopped, but, as Chapuis
remarked, it was not necessary to finish the sentence;
his meaning was clear enough.[3]

Henry had also begun to talk in a rather ominous *Henry's*
way. Mary having fallen ill, he went to Greenwich, *worst*
where she was then staying; and in the presence of *enemy.*

[1] E. Chapuis to Charles V., August 29, 1534, Vienna Archives,
P.C. 229, i. No. 53: "Et quant cela ne seroit la mort de la
Royne et de la princesse amortiroit tout car cela estant yl ne
resteroit aulcune querelle."

[2] E. Chapuis to Charles V., March 23, 1535, Vienna Archives,
P.C. 229½, i. fol. 59: "Me replicquant de nouveaul quel domaige
ne dangier seroit que la dicte princesse feust morte oyres que le
peuple en murmurast et quelle raison auroit V^re M^te en faire cas."

[3] E. Chapuis to Charles V., April 17, 1535, Vienna Archives,
P.C. 229½, i. fol. 68. Cromwell said: "Que la princesse estoit
celle que mettoit la difficulte et que troubloit les affaires et que
pleust a Dieu—il ne ousa dire plus avant mays aussy ny estoit il
besoing."

all the servants he loudly ordered Lady Shelton to tell her ward that she was his worst enemy, and that on her account he was on bad terms with most of the princes of Christendom. Chapuis interpreted this message as an encouragement to those who might feel inclined to poison the princess.[1]

*Chapuis
tries to
protect
Mary.*

During the latter half of 1533 and during the whole of 1534, Chapuis credited Anne and her friends with the most infamous designs. For the protection of Mary against certain dangers at which he occasionally hinted in his letters to the emperor, and to Granvelle and his son, he could trust only to the virtue and firmness of Mary herself.[2] But for her protection against attempts to poison her he took active measures. For some time he wished that she should reside with her mother, but this was refused,

---

[1] E. Chapuis to Charles V., March 23, 1535, Vienna Archives, P.C. 229½, i. fol. 59 : " Ains luy feist signiffier par sa gouvernante quil navoit pire enemys au monde quelle et quelle estoit cause quil estoit mal de la pluspart des princes chrestiens, et ce declairoit le dict Roy publiquement quest bien pour donner cueur et ardiesse a ceulx que luy vouldroient machiner quelque chose."

[2] E. Chapuis to Charles V., December 16, 1533, Vienna Archives, P.C. 228, i. fol. 143 : " La princesse, laquelle, comme il est a doubter et croire, veullent faire mourrir ou de deul ou daultre sorte ou faire renoncer son droict ou marier bassement ou la fere tresbucher en lascivuite pour avoir occasion de lexereder et faire tout aultre mauvais traictement ; " and E. Chapuis to N. de Granvelle, January 17, 1534, Vienna Archives, P.C. 229, ii. fol. 6 : " Monsgr lon ma dit que ce Roy vouloit faire dyvorcer le comte de Nortambellan davec sa femme et luy donner la princesse. Je crois bien que sil estoit sans femme que le Roy luy bailleroit vollentiers ladicte princesse pour les respectz que Vous escripray une autre fois, ce sont choses estranges mais actendu les precedentes il ne sen fault esbayr ."

and in the end it seemed to him best that they should chap. xiii.
not live together; for if Mary stayed with her mother
her enemies might poison her without exciting suspicion, whereas if she was with Lady Shelton they could
not harm her without immediately causing a popular
outcry.[1] Having arrived at this conviction, Chapuis
tried to help the princess by influencing her guardian.
He sent Lady Shelton little presents with complimentary messages, but at the same time gave her to
understand that she herself would be in the greatest
danger if the princess died while entrusted to her
charge. In the spring of 1535 Doctor William Butt, *February,*
the royal physician, was ordered to attend the *1535.*
princess; and he assisted the ambassador by telling
Lady Shelton that it was commonly reported in
London that she had poisoned Mary. The poor
lady was not a little frightened, and whenever Mary
was ill cried bitterly and was in the utmost anxiety.[2]

[1] E. Chapuis to Charles V., February 11, 1534, Vienna
Archives, P.C. 229, i. fol. 32: "Javoye aussi pense pour aultre
remede que la princesse (apres avoir faict solempnes et suffisantes
protestacions de la force que luy est faicte et du dangier apparent
ou elle estoit) quelle ouffert au Roy destre contente de non estre
appelle princesse pourveu quelle feust en liberte daller resider
avec la Royne sa mere. Mais se faisant il seroit paradventure
dangier que la dicte Anne prit alors plus dardyment de executer
sa maulvaise voulente craignant la reconciliation avec le pere et
penseroit que a lheure a moindre soupcon elle pourroit ce faire
soubz umbre damytie que maintenant ou la hayne et inimitie est
ouverte . . ."

[2] E. Chapuis to Charles V., February 25, 1535, Vienna
Archives, P.C. 229½, i. fol. 13. Chapuis spoke to Cromwell:
"Louhant que ceste moderne gouvernante en deust avoir la
charge que me semble le plus seur, car la luy ostant de la main
il y auroit dangier que lon ne luy donnast quelque venin lent,

Catherine did not seem to be in the same imminent danger as her daughter. With a few of her own servants and a large staff of royal officials, she had remained at Bugden until the spring of 1534, when she had been conveyed to Kimbolton, near Huntingdon. She had been several times annoyed by commissioners calling upon her to swear to the new Acts and threatening her with the penalties for high treason; but in the autumn of 1534 she had enjoyed a short time of quiet. When, however, the young lady who had worked in her favour lost the good graces of the king, she was again treated as harshly as before, and in the summer and the autumn of 1535 she bitterly complained of the cruelty of her oppressors.[1]

The only servants of Catherine at Kimbolton, besides her female attendants, were George de Atequa, Bishop of Llandaff, her confessor; Miguel de Lasco, her physician; Juan de Soto, her apothecary; Philip Grenacre, de Soto's assistant; and Francisco Phelipe, her groom of the chamber. The royal servants,

---

ce, pendant quelle demeurra entre ses mains, je pense quelle ne vouldroit faire, ne permettre telle chose pour la suspicion quest desia contre elle. Il y a longtemps que luy ai faict dire par tierce main le mal que luy pourroit survenir mesadvenant de la dicte princesse, et ay aussy tenu main que le medecin du Roy luy a dit que ces jours le bruict estoit tout commung par Londres quelle avoit empoisonne la dicte princesse que la mise en une merveilleuse craincte de sorte quelle ne faict que plorer quant elle veoit la dicte princesse ainsy indisposee."

[1] Sir E. Chamberlain and Sir E. Bedingfield to Cromwell, March 22, 1535, R.O. Henry VIII., Treasury papers, No. 3907; and Sir William Fitzwilliam to Cromwell, Pocock, *Records*, vol. ii. No. cccliv.

under the command of Sir Edward Chamberlain and
Sir Edmund Bedingfield were far more numerous.
They acted as the garrison of the castle, as the
queen's gaolers, and as spies upon her conduct and
upon that of her attendants. She could not leave
the house without permission; and when permission
was granted, she had to accept the company of royal
officers, who prevented her from communicating with
the people. Visitors were not admitted except by
special order from the king or from Cromwell, and
her letters had to be smuggled in and out by her
Spanish servants.

In the summer of 1534 Chapuis had asked *Chapuis*
Cromwell for a warrant to see the queen;[1] and *wishes to see*
having waited for some time without obtaining a *Catherine.*
reply, he had set out with a large train for Kimbolton. *July 17, 1534.*
While he was on the road, a royal messenger passed
him, riding post haste; and shortly afterwards
he received a message from Chamberlain and Bedingfield that by the king's orders he would neither
be admitted to the castle nor allowed to speak with
the queen. After some discussion the ambassador
returned to London, but not before a part of his
retinue had gone close to Kimbolton, where they
spoke with Catherine's attendants, some of whom
were standing on the battlements, while others
looked out of the windows.[2]

By such protests and demonstrations Chapuis hoped

[1] E. Chapuis to Charles V., July 16, 1534, Vienna Archives
P.C. 229, i. fol. 123.
[2] E. Chapuis to Charles V., July 27, 1534, Vienna Archives,
P.C. 229, fol. 124.

to counteract the sinister advice given to the king, and as time went on and the two ladies were neither poisoned nor brought to trial, he became less anxious. He was told that the king had no wish to hurt either of them, but intended to keep them as hostages for his own safety; and Chapuis believed what he was told, and ceased to pay much attention to floating rumours on the subject. Early in November, 1535, his confidence was rudely disturbed.

CHAPTER XIV.

THE DEATH OF CATHERINE.

On the 6th of November the imperial ambassador received a message from the Marchioness of Exeter, the devoted adherent of Catherine, to the effect that " the king had lately told his most trusted counsellors that he would no longer remain in the trouble, fear, and suspicion in which he had so long remained on account of the queen and princess, and that at the next parliament they must rid him of them ; swearing great oaths that he would not wait any longer to provide for this."[1] Some of the royal counsellors—perhaps secretly favourable to Mary—were alarmed by his violence, and could not suppress their tears. Henry brutally exclaimed that " this was not a matter about which to cry or make wry faces, for were he to lose

Ominous threats. November, 1535.

---

[1] E. Chapuis to Charles V., November 6, 1535, P.C. 229½, i. fol. 119 : " Sire tout a cest instant la marquise de excestre **ma** envoye dire que ce Roy a dernierement dict a ces plus privez conseillers quil ne vouloit plus demeurer es fascheries, crainctes et pensemens quil avoit de longtemps este a cause des Royne et princesse et quil [*quilz*] regardassent a ce prouchain parlement len faire quicte ; jurant bien a certes et tres obstinement quil nactendroit plus longuement de y pourveoir."

his crown for it he would persevere in his purpose." [1]
A fortnight later, always according to the same
authority, Henry declared that "he would contrive
that Mary should soon want neither new year's gifts
nor society, and that she should be an example to
show the whole world that nobody was to disobey the
law. He would prove the truth of the prophecy
about himself, that at the beginning of his reign he
would be as gentle as a lamb, but at the end more
fierce than a lion." [2]

The marchioness added that all this was as true as
the Gospel.[3] And Chapuis, knowing her character and
the means she had for obtaining trustworthy information, placed entire faith in what she said. He wrote
that the concubine would never rest until she got quit
of "these poor good ladies," and that for this end she

---

[1] E. Chapuis to Charles V., November 21, 1535, Vienna
Archives, P.C. 229½, i. fol. 137 : "Me fesant dire davantage
icelluy personnaige que voyant ce Roy aucuns de ceulx auxquels
il tenoit les susdicts propos larmoyer, il se print a ·dire quil ny
convenoit ne larmes ne grymasses car oyres quil deust perdre sa
courrone il ne layroit de mettre én effect et experience ce que
dessus."

[2] E. Chapuis to N. de Granvelle, November 21, 1535, Vienna
Archives, P.C. 229½, iii. fol. 30 : "Ce Roy puis quatre ou cinq
jours devisant de la princesse avec quelcung deust dire que bien-
tost il pourvoyroit quelle nauroit besoing ny de train ne de compaignie et quelle seroit dexemple pour monstrer a tout le monde
que nul ne devoit desobeir aux loix et quil vouloit veriffier ce que
avoit este predict de luy assavoir que a lentree de son regne il
seroit doulx comme ung agneaul et a la fin il seroit pire que
lyon."

[3] E. Chapuis to Charles V., November 6, 1535, loc. cit. : "Et
ce ma mande dire la marquise pour chose de croyre veritable
comme evangile."

was making use of every device she could imagine.[1]
" The concubine, who has for some time conspired
and wished for the death of the said ladies, and who
thinks of nothing so much as of how she may have
them despatched, is the person who manages, orders,
and governs everything, and whom the king does
not dare to oppose." [2]   At the urgent request of the
marchioness, Chapuis wrote to ask the emperor to
save his aunt and cousin by immediate action.[3]

Although seriously alarmed, Chapuis did not at this
time suspect any attempt to poison either Catherine or
Mary. His idea was that the king would try to
force a bill of attainder through parliament, and
thus, by making the members of both houses accomplices in his offence, deprive them of all hope of the
emperor's forgiveness and compel them to support
subsequent proceedings.[4]   As parliament was not to

[1] E. Chapuis to Antoine Perrenot, November 6, 1535, Vienna
Archives, P.C. 229½, iii. fol. 29 : " Il fault tenir pour chose plus
que vraye ce que jescripz a sa maieste et croyre que ceste dyablesse
de concubine ne cessera jusques elle ait une fin et soit quictes de
ces pouvres bonnes dames a quoy elle travaille par tous les moyens
quelle peult imaginer."

[2] E. Chapuis to Charles V., November 21, 1535, loc. cit. : " Sire
ce sont choses par trop estranges execrables et pource mal aisees
a croyre, mais considerant ce que yci est passe et passe journellement, la continuacion est longtemps de telles menasses ; et
davantaige la concubine que pieca a conjure et conspire la mort
des dictes dames et que ne pense a rien tant qua les faire des-
pescher est celle que mande commande et gouverne le tout et a
laquelle le dict Roy ne scauroit contredire."

[3] E. Chapuis to Charles V., November 6 and 21, 1535, loc. cit.

[4] E. Chapuis to Charles V., November 21, 1535, loc. cit. : " Le
cas est fort dangereux et fort ·a doubter il voudra comme jay
desia autrefois escript a Vostre Maieste faire participant voyre

CHAP. XIV. meet until after the new year, the ambassador thought
there would be time to provide against this danger.

Illness of   But when, on the 3rd of December, 1535, Chapuis
Catherine.
December   called on Cromwell to ask that some money due to
3, 1535.   Catherine might be paid, he was told that a messenger
had just been sent to the king to announce the
dangerous illness of Catherine. The ambassador,
greatly distressed, at once begged that he might be
permitted to see the queen, and in the meantime to
despatch one of his servants to Kimbolton. The
latter request was granted by Cromwell, who signed
the necessary passport, but as to the proposed visit of
Chapuis, he said that it would be necessary to consult
the king.[1]

Her   When the ambassador was leaving Cromwell's house
recovery.   a letter from de Lasco, Catherine's physician, was
handed to him, and by this he was somewhat reassured. De Lasco said that with God's help Catherine

aucteurs de tel meschiefs ceulx de son parlemant et estats du
Royaulme afin que par ce moyen perdant lespoir de la clemence
et misericorde de Vostre Maieste trestous fussent plus determines
a se deffendre quant il en seroit besoing."

[1] E. Chapuis to Charles V., December 13, 1535, Vienna
Archives, P.C. 229½, i. fol. 114 : " Sire estant il y a environ dix
jours alle trouver Mre Crumuel tant pour le solliciter du
payement de certains arreraiges de la Royne, que aussy entendre
quelques nouvelles icelluy Crumuel me dit quil ne faysoit
quachever de depescher ung homme pour advertyr le Roy son
M^{re} de lindisposicion de la Royne qu se trouvoit tres malade ;
que furent les premieres nouvelles quen avoye ouyez. Je luy
demandey licence pour laller et mander visiter. Yl mottroya
incontinent que y puisse envoyer des miens et depescha sur ce
lettres, quant a mon aller quil en parleroit audt Sr Roy, et a son
retour de la court me resouldroit de lintencion et voulente dud.
Sr Roy."

would recover, and he advised Chapuis not to insist
on receiving permission to visit her. The news from
Kimbolton continuing to be favourable, Chapuis acted
on the doctor's advice : and he was the less inclined
to press his request because Cromwell, who had
promised to let him know the king's will, did not
again allude to the matter.[1]

The queen had suffered from violent pains in the
stomach, flatulence, vomiting, and general weakness ;
but the symptoms had soon passed away, and in a
week she had seemed to be perfectly well again.[2]
She herself did not apprehend immediate death from
natural causes : she only feared that she might
be the victim of some open act such as the king's
violent speech had foreshadowed. On the 13th *December*
of December she wrote to Chapuis and Charles. 13, 1535.
To Chapuis she said that she wished to be taken to
some healthier place than Kimbolton, and she asked
him to obtain for her the payment of the money due
to her, as she wanted to make some presents to her
attendants at Christmas.[3] Charles V. she entreated
to interfere in her favour and in that of her daughter,
now in their hour of need. In this letter her

[1] E. Chapuis to Charles V., December 13, 1535, Vienna
Archives, P.C. 229½, i. fol. 114 : " Ainsi que je sortois dudict
Crumuel jay recu une lectre du medecin de la dicte Royne disant
que a layde de dieu ce ne seroit rien de sa maladie . . . . graces
a dieu elle est tousiours depuis esmendee et soy treuve bien
maintenant."

[2] E. Chapuis to Charles V., January 9, 1536, Vienna Archives,
P.C. 230, i. fol. 3 : " Cestoit une douleur desthomac si aspre et
violente quelle ne pouvoit rien retenir dans le corps."

[3] E. Chapuis to Charles V., December 18, 1535, Vienna
Archives, P.C. 229½, i. fol. 141.

CHAP. XIV. handwriting is as firm as it ever was, and her tone
is that of a person who expects to live many a year.[1]

In accordance with Catherine's wishes, Chapuis saw
Cromwell on the 17th, and spoke of the matters
about which she had written to him ; but the secretary
evaded his requests. Nor was reference made to the
decision of the king with regard to the desire of
Chapuis to visit Kimbolton. Cromwell was evidently
reluctant to introduce the subject ; and as Catherine's
health was restored, and there were political questions
which seemed to be of more urgent importance, the
ambassador still thought it might be inexpedient to
press his application.[2]

*December
27, 1535.*
Christmas passed without any disquieting tidings.
On the 27th Chapuis received a message that the king,
who was at Eltham, wished to speak to him ; and on
the following day it was arranged that he was to have

*December
29, 1535.*
audience on the 2nd of January. But on the 29th
a messenger arrived from Kimbolton at Baynard's
Castle, where Chapuis resided, bringing two letters,
one from Catherine's physician to the ambassador,

*Catherine
ill again.*
another from the apothecary, Philip Grenacre, to
Montesa, the ambassador's steward. Grenacre wrote

*December
26, 1535.*
that the queen was ill again and worse than ever.
For the last two days she had been tormented by

[1] Catherine to Charles V., December 13, 1535, Vienna Archives,
P.C. 229½, ii. fol. 68.

[2] E. Chapuis to Charles V., December 18, 1535, Vienna
Archives, P.C. 229½, i. fol. 141 : "Sire, inste de la Royne madame
Vostre tante je fuz encoires hier faire rencharge a Monsgr le
Secre Cremuel sur le changement de logis de la d. Royne, et pour
luy faire avancer pour ses festes ce peu de reste de ses arreraiges
dont cy devant ay escript a V.^{re} M^{te}."

violent pains in the stomach, and by constant hic-
cuping, and she had been unable to retain any
nourishment whatever, either solid or liquid. She
had scarcely slept an hour and a half during the
whole time, and had lost all strength.[1] The doctor
thought Catherine would not be able to keep up, and
asked Chapuis to come as quickly as possible.[2] The
ambassador, very much alarmed, immediately sent a
messenger to court to renew his request for permission
to visit the queen. Cromwell replied that permission *December*
would be granted, but that in the meantime the king *29, 1535.*
desired to confer with Chapuis about some most
important matters. The ambassador was therefore
requested to be at Greenwich next day at one o'clock
in the afternoon. The king would come from Eltham
to meet him.

Although annoyed at the delay, Chapuis was *Chapuis*
obliged to do as the king proposed ; so on the morning *has an*
audience
of the 30th of December he took his boat and went *of Henry.*
down the river to Greenwich Stairs. He was received *December*
30, 1535.
with more than usual courtesy and attention. Sir
Thomas Cheyne stood at the stairs to welcome him,
and led him to the royal presence. They found the
king in the tiltyard, surrounded by a host of courtiers.
Henry greeted Chapuis with great affability, and
after a little while, throwing his arm round the
ambassador's neck, walked up and down with him for

[1] Philip Grenacre to Montesa, British Museum, Add. MSS.
25,114, fol. 117 : "Et sella a cause de unne tres grande doleur
de son estomak avec ung soubglon que ung dict nicquet que le
tient contignualment."

[2] E. Chapuis to Charles V., December 30, 1535, Vienna
Archives, P.C. 229½, i. fol. 151.

CHAP. XIV. some time.   By and by they went to the king's
chamber, and Henry, ordering everybody away, began
to talk politics.   As Chapuis had expected, there was
no very pressing business to be discussed.   The
French, Henry said, offered him their alliance, and if
the emperor remained hostile he would be driven to
accept it.   He began to speak of Cromwell's suggestion that Elizabeth should become the wife of
Philip of Spain, and Chapuis, wishing to keep him in
good humour, did not positively reject the proposal.[1]
Henry went on complaining of the emperor's ingratitude, as he called it, and told the wildest tales about
all he had done for Charles, who had requited his
kindness by using force at Rome to obtain the papal
sentence against him.   He wound up by saying that
Madame—so he called Catherine—would not live

---

[1] E. Chapuis to Charles V., December 30, 1535, Vienna
Archives, P.C. 229½, i. fol. 151 ; and E. Chapuis to N. de Granvelle, February 17, 1536, Vienna Archives, P.C. 230, ii. fol. 5 :
" Monseigneur jay cydevant oblye descripre comme ces festes de
noel disant a ce Roy que mesbayssays que de tout le temps que
maistre Crumuell et moy avons eu propoz sur la nouvelle intelligence na oncques ouvert nul party, il maffirma plusieurs foys
que si, voyre plus que raysounable, et que en ce Cremuel sestoit
advance plus que ne devoit, et luy demandant la specification
dudict party, ou de honte ou je ne scay pourquoy a pene me
scavoit le dict Roy achever de dire que cestoit du mariaige de
sa petite fille, a quoy luy respondit quil estoit vray que le dict
Cremuel men avoit parle, sed verecunde et tymide ac si porrigeret
assem elephanto de sorte que ne le tenoyt pour estre dict mais
puisque luy mesme lavoit declare quen rescriproye a toutes aven-
tures avec le surplus des nouveaulx propoz quil mavoit tenu et
ne me semble en rien luy rejecter le dict party pour non le
desperer de navoir moyen de reconsiliacion et amytie avec Sa
Maieste et quil feust contrainct traicter avec les francais."

long, and that after her death the emperor would
have no pretext for interference in the affairs of
England, and would be an entire loser by all he had
done in this business. Chapuis immediately replied
that the queen's death would not profit Henry, and
that the papal sentence had been unavoidable.[1]

After this Chapuis took his leave of the king, who
granted him permission to go to Kimbolton, and
ordered Stephen Vaughan to lead him thither.[2] But
before he had reached his boat, he was recalled by the
Duke of Suffolk; and Henry asserted that he had
just received a message that the queen was *in
extremis*, so that Chapuis would scarcely find her
still alive. He showed no sorrow, but rather satisfaction, saying that it would put an end to the
difficulties which existed between Charles and him.[3]

Mary had asked that if the queen became very

[1] E. Chapuis to Charles V., December 30, 1535, *loc. cit.* : "Sire
a la fin le dict Sr Roy me vint a dire quil pensoit que la Royne
quil ne nomma que madame ne le feroit icy longement et que
venant a morir V. M. naura cause de se empescher des affaires
de ce royaulme et se pourra tenir par le bec des poursuites faictes
en ce negoce. Je luy dit que la mort de lad. Royne ne pouvoit
en rien prouffiter, et que en tous advenements la sentence estoit
necessaire."

[2] E. Chapuis to Charles V., January 9, 1536, *loc. cit.* : and Sir
Edward Chamberlain and Sir Edmund Bedingfield to Cromwell,
January 5, 1536, British Museum, Cotton MSS. Otho C. x.
fol. 215.

[3] E. Chapuis to Charles V., December 30, 1535, *loc. cit.* : "Sire
estant party dud. Sr Roy il me feist rappeller par le duc de Suffocq
pour me dire que en cest instant luy estoint venues nouvelles que
la Royne estoit en extreme et que a peyne la trouveraije en vie,
disant davantaige que cela seroit hoster lempeschement que
mestoient les scrupules dentre V. M. et luy."

CHAP. XIV. ill, Chapuis should obtain leave for her to go and see
her mother.   On hearing the bad news, the ambassador complied with Mary's request, but the king
flatly refused.   Chapuis insisted, and Henry, in order
to get rid of him, said he would think about it and
take the advice of his counsellors.   More than this
the ambassador could not persuade him to concede.[1]

Chapuis at Kimbolton.   Chapuis returned to town as quickly as possible,
wrote a short letter to the emperor, and mounted
horse to proceed to Kimbolton.   But it was already
late, and that day he could not proceed very far.
January 1, 1536.   Next day—St. Sylvester's day—he spent on the road,
and it was only on the morning of the first of
January that he arrived at the gates of the castle.[2]
No difficulties were made ; Chapuis and his retinue
were allowed to enter, and he conferred at once with
the principal attendants of Catherine as to seeing her.
It was arranged that the first audience should be in
presence of the royal officers, whom the queen had
not seen for more than a year, and of Stephen
Vaughan.   Immediately after dinner they were all
ushered into the queen's room, where Chapuis, paying
her royal honours, kissed her hand.   In answer to the

---

[1] E. Chapuis to Charles V., December 30, 1535, *loc. cit.* :
" Je luy demanday licence que la princesse puist aller veoir la
Royne sa mere ce quil refusa de prime face et luy ayant fait
quelques remonstrances yl dit que bien yl y penseroit et auroit
adviz. Lad. princesse avoit este dadvis que feisse telle requeste."

[2] E. Chapuis to Charles V., January 9, 1536, Vienna Archives,
P.C. 230, i. fol. 3.   Chapuis says that having stayed four days
at Kimbolton he took leave of the queen on Tuesday.   He must
therefore have arrived on Saturday morning, the first of January,
not on the second, as Chamberlain and Bedingfield wrote.

ambassador's compliments, Catherine thanked him for
all the trouble he had taken on her behalf, and for
having come to see her. His visit, she thought,
would do her much good, and even if it did not do
so it would be a consolation to her to die in his arms,
and not to leave life like a brute.[1] Chapuis tried to
cheer her, telling her that the king had agreed to let
her choose hereafter the house she should live in, and
to pay her the money due to her. Thinking that in
the circumstances it might be permissible to use a
pious fraud, he added that the king was very sorry
for her illness.[2] After this he made a set speech
which had been previously concerted between him
and the queen through her officers. He asked her
to make an effort to recover, if for no other reason,
because on her life depended the union and quiet of
Christendom. This he explained to her at some
length, in the hope that Vaughan, who understood
Spanish, might report the conversation in the proper
quarters, and that it might suggest to Henry the
necessity of taking more care for the preservation of
her life.[3]

[1] E. Chapuis to Charles V., January 9, 1536, Vienna Archives,
P.C. 230, i. fol. 3. " Et du moins quand il plairoit a dieu la
prandre a sa part ce luy seroit consoulacion de pouvoir mourir
entre mes braz et non point la desemparer comme une beste."

[2] *Ibid.* : "Aussy pour sa plus grande consolation que le d. Sr.
Roy estoit tres desplaisant de son indisposicion."

[3] E. Chapuis to Charles V., January 9, 1536, *loc. cit.* : " Sur
ce luy suppliay vouloir prendre cueur et sefforcer pour guerir et
sy elle ne le vouloit faire pour aultre quelle considerast que de sa
salut et vie dependoit ung tres grand bien pour lunion et
tranquillite de la chrestiennete, pour la persuasion de quoy usay

CHAP. XIV.   The whole audience lasted but a quarter of an hour,
Catherine being too weak for much talk.[1] She told
Chapuis to go and rest after his journey, and she
herself would try to sleep a little, which for the last
six days she had not been able to do for more than
two hours in all. At five in the afternoon Chapuis
was called by Doctor de Lasco, who, with Montesa,
accompanied him to the queen's room.[2] They
stayed nearly two hours, and Catherine, notwithstanding her pains and her weakness, took the
greatest pleasure in the ambassador's company. She
had so long been shut off from all intercourse, except
with her servants, that to talk with a man of the
intelligence, knowledge, and standing of Chapuis was
a real treat for her. She complained of her own and
her daughter's misfortune, and of the delay in
providing a remedy—a delay whereby many had
suffered in their persons and goods, and many souls
had been lost ; and she said that she had herself some
scruples of conscience, since she had been the first
cause of all this by resisting Henry's will.[3] Chapuis

---

plusieurs propoz, comme yl avoit este preadvise par interposite
personne entre la Royne et moy ; et ce affin que mon conducteur
et aucuns en eussent peu faire le rapport ou estoit besoing et que
par tel moyen lon eust plus de regard a la conservacion de sa
vie ;" and Chamberlain and Bedingfield to Cromwell, January 5,
1536, *loc. cit.*

[1] Chamberlain and Bedingfield to Cromwell, January 5, 1536,
loc. cit.

[2] *Ibid.* : and E. Chapuis to Charles V., January 9, 1536,
loc. cit.

[3] E. Chapuis to Charles V., January 9, 1536, *loc. cit.* : " Ses
devises estoient . . . . soy quereller de sa deffortune et de celle

comforted her with the assurance that although the
emperor had hitherto not been able to assist her more
than he had done, things would now go better.
There was a hope that the French would turn against
Henry; and the pope, on account of the death of the
Cardinal of Rochester, was going to proceed *pro
attentatis*. This would be very advantageous for her,
because, whatever course the pope might take, the
king could not hold her responsible for it. With
such talk the visit passed, and Chapuis retired.[1]

While he had been sitting by the queen's bedside
another visitor had arrived. Lady Willoughby, the
mother-in-law of the Duke of Suffolk, by birth a
Spaniard, had formerly been an attendant of Catherine
and had remained her devoted friend. Having heard
of the queen's illness, she had straightway repaired
to Kimbolton without asking for a passport, which
would perhaps have been refused. She arrived at
night at the gates, and being asked for her letters of
admission, said they would come soon. She pretended that she had met with an accident on the
road, and begged for God's sake to be taken in and
to have a place near the fire. The royal officers
dared not in so small a matter disoblige the mother
of a duchess; they allowed her to enter the hall, and,
in the confusion caused by the numerous retinue of

de la princesse sa fille et pareillement de la tardance de remede
des affaires, dont tant de gens de bien avoient soufferts en la
personne et biens et tant de ames sen alloient en perdicion
. . . . se tenant par avant en doubte et scrupule de conscience
pour estre les dicts maulx procede a loccasion de son affaire."

[1] E. Chapuis to Charles V., January 9, 1536, *loc. cit.*

CHAP. XIV. Chapuis, she contrived to escape their vigilance and
entered the queen's rooms, where she remained.[1]

During the next four days Chapuis had daily a
long audience of Catherine. His presence really
seemed to benefit her. She was encouraged by his
arguments, and when he declared that all would
ultimately be set right, she believed him and
began to hope for a speedy settlement of her difficulties. Her health, too, appeared to improve. She
was able to take a little nourishment, and slept better
than during the past week. So on Tuesday, the 4th,
Catherine, Chapuis, and Doctor de Lasco consulted
together, and decided that the ambassador should
leave Kimbolton next morning. De Lasco thought
that she was out of immediate danger, and Chapuis
was anxious not to abuse the privilege which had
been accorded to him, but rather to act in such a way
that he might be allowed to come again. He wanted,
too, to obtain a more suitable residence for Catherine.
On the 30th of December Henry had really promised that she should have a good house, and the
ambassador desired to strike the iron while it was hot.

*January
4, 1536.* On Tuesday night he took leave, and remarked with
pleasure that Catherine was in better spirits; she
laughed two or three times at what he said. Nay,
after the ambassador left her, she sent for one of his
servants, who filled the office of a jester, and listened
for a while to his fancies.[2]

---

[1] Chamberlain and Bedingfield to Cromwell, January 5, 1536,
loc. cit.

[2] E. Chapuis to Charles V., January 9, 1536, *loc. cit.* : " Ainsy
prins mon congie delle le mardy au soir la laissant bien allegre

Next morning Chapuis rose early, and sent one CHAP. XIV. of his valets to inquire how the queen had passed the night. The reply was, that she had slept better than before. The horses, therefore, were saddled and the mules loaded, but before mounting horse Chapuis had some serious talk with de Lasco. He asked the doctor whether he had any suspicion of poison. De Lasco shook his head, and said he feared something of the kind, for after the queen had drunk of a certain Welsh beer she had never been well. " It must be," he added, " some slow and cleverly-composed drug, for I do not perceive the symptoms of ordinary poison." [1] He thought that she might get over it this time. If he saw any immediate danger, he promised that he would at once send a message to Chapuis.

January
5, 1536.

After this consultation Chapuis had a request to make. Being a practical man, he thought of the great lawsuit at Rome, and expressed a wish that if the queen suddenly became worse she should, shortly before her death, solemnly declare that her marriage with Prince Arthur had never been consummated. De Lasco promised that this should be done. [2]

et le mesme soir la veiz rire deux ou troys foys, et environ demy heure que fust party delle elle voulust encoires soy recreer avec ung de mes gens que faict du plaisant."

[1] E. Chapuis to Charles V., January 9, 1536, *loc. cit.* : " Je demanday par plusieurs fois au medecin syl y avoit quelque suspicion de venin, il me dit quil sen doubtoit car depuis quelle avoit beu dune cervoise de galles elle navoit fait bien et quil falloyt que ce fust poyson limitee et artificieuse car il ne voit les signes et apparences de simple venin. . . ."

[2] E. Chapuis to N. de Granvelle, January 21, 1536, Vienna Archives, P.C. 230, i. fol. 21 : " Javoye appointe avec le medecin

Having thus provided for everything, Chapuis departed, and proceeded slowly towards London. At every stage he feared that a messenger would overtake him and call him back, but on the evening of the 8th he reached London without having been *January 8, 1536.* disturbed. Early next day he sent one of his servants to ask Cromwell when he might have audience of the king to thank him for the hospitality he had received at Kimbolton, and to speak about a change of residence for the queen. The servant came back with a short message from the secretary, *Death of Catherine.* announcing that Catherine had died on the 7th at two o'clock in the afternoon.[1]

After Chapuis had left Kimbolton, Catherine had passed the 5th and the 6th of January well enough. Her pains had not returned, and she had been able to sleep, and to eat a little. During *January 6, 1536.* the afternoon of the 6th she sat up in her bed, combed her hair, and plaited it round her head. At the customary time she went to sleep, but an hour after midnight she called for her attendants and inquired *January 7, 1536.* what o'clock it was. A short time afterwards she repeated the question, and being asked why she did so, she said that she wished to hear mass and to receive the Sacrament. The Bishop of Llandaff was called,

de la Royne, que survenant quelque danger en elle il se souvint et tinsse main quelle affirmat in extremis quelle navoyt oncques este cogneue du prince artus."

[1] E. Chapuis to Charles V., January 9, 1536, *loc. cit.*: " Crumuel . . . ma envoye dire les tres griefves tres douleureuses et tres lamentables nouvelles du trespaz de la feue bonne tres vertueuse et tres saincte Royne que feust vendredi lendemain des roys environ les deux heures apres midy."

and he, startled by her anxiety, offered to say mass
at once before the canonical hour. But the queen
refused, citing the decrees which forbade it. When
four o'clock had struck, the office began, and the
queen communicated with the greatest fervour, remaining afterwards in prayer. Turning to her
servants, she asked them to pray for her soul, and
that God might forgive the king her husband all the
wrong he had done her, and inspire him to return to
the right path and give him good counsel.[1]

After a while she called de Lasco and dictated two
letters, one to the ambassador of her nephew the
emperor, another to the king her husband, asking him
to give certain sums and trinkets to persons she named.
The letter to Henry she signed, " Katherine, Queene
of England"; and she gave orders that it should be

---

[1] E. Chapuis to Charles V., January 21, 1536, Vienna Archives,
P.C. 230, i. fol. 7 : " Le jour des Roys . . . sur le soir elle seulle
sans ayde de personne se peignant lya ses cheveulx et saccoustra
la teste ; et le lendemain environ une heure apres minuit elle
commenca a demander quelle heure sestoit et si le jour approuchoit
et de ce senquist elle plusieurs foys dempuis, et non pour aultre
comme a la fin elle desclayra synon pour pouvoir ouyr messe et
recepvoir le sainct sacrement. Et combien que levesque de
Landafs son confesseur se offrye a dire messe avants les quatres
heures, elle ne le voulust permettre, allegant plusieurs raysons et
auctorites en latin pourquoy il ne se debvoit faire.   Venant le
jour elle ouyst sa messe et receu son sainct sacrement avec une
ferveur et devotion quil nest possible de plus et dempuis continua
dire plusieurs belles oraysons, et pryer les assistans quilz voulsis-
sent pryer et faire pryer pour le salut de son ame et que Dieu
voulsist perdonner au Roy son mary le tord et sans rayson quil
luy avoit faict et que sa divine bonte le voulsist inspirer au droit
chemin et luy donner bon conseil."

CHAP. XIV. forwarded to Chapuis.[1] At ten o'clock she desired
to receive extreme unction. But she considered
that she ought not to die in private " like a brute,"
as she had said ; so, for want of better men,
Bedingfield and Chamberlain were called in to see
her die.[2] Atequa said the office and administered
the Sacrament, she herself saying the responses.[3]
After this she remained in prayer until two o'clock,
when she expired. Her courage never forsook her ;
she died, as she had lived, without fear.

However callous his office might have made him,
Chapuis had a strong affection for the woman whose
cause he had defended so long, and in his letters he
gave free expression to the grief with which he had
received the tidings of her death. The English
people seem also to have heard of the event with
regret. Catherine, as I have already said, had always
been popular ; and as the rival of Anne Boleyn, who
was generally hated, she was the hope of those who
Rejoicings wished the schism to be healed. But at court, in the
at court. small circle which surrounded the king and Anne

---

[1] *Ibid.*, and Account of Catherine's Burial sent by Chapuis,
Vienna Archives, P.C. 230, iv. fol. 1 : " Pource quellast a ceste
heure la ordonne faire une escripture a son nom adressant au Roy
comme a son mary et a lambassadeur de la Maieste de lempereur
son nepveux laquelle elle souscripvit et signa par telles mots :
Katherine Royne dangleterre ; " and Catherine to Henry, VIII.
British Museum, Cotton MSS., Otho C. X. fols. 216, 217.

[2] Bedingfield and Chamberlain to Cromwell, January 7, 1536,
State Papers, vol. i. p. 452.

[3] E. Chapuis to Charles V., January 21, 1536, *loc. cit.* : " En
apres elle receu lextreme unction respondant elle mesme a tout
loffice tres bien et tres devotement."

Boleyn, the feeling was different. The news was
reported to Henry on Saturday, and he took little care
to hide his pleasure. He praised God who had
delivered them from all fear of war; adding that the
time had come when he would be able to lead the
French better than he had done hitherto, because,
fearing that he might form an alliance with the
emperor now that the cause of dissension had been
removed, they would do all he wanted.[1] The Earl of
Wiltshire and Lord Rochford were equally loud and
coarse in the display of their joy. The only pity
was, they exclaimed, that the Lady Mary was not
keeping her mother company.[2]

Next day the king appeared in the gayest of
dresses, all in yellow, with a white feather in his cap.
Little Elizabeth, who was at court, was on that day
taken to mass with extraordinary pomp, trumpets
blowing before her and numerous servants following.
In the afternoon a ball was given at court, at which
the king was present. He was in the highest of
spirits, and by and by sent for Elizabeth, whom he
carried round the room in his arms, showing her to

---

[1] E. Chapuis to Charles V., January 21, 1536, *loc. cit.*: "Le
Roy le samedi quil eust la nouvelle il dit louhe soit Dieu quy nous
a libere de toute suspicion de guerre et que le temps estoit venu
quil conduyroit mieulx les francois que jusques icy car doubtant
quil ne se ralye avec Vostre Maieste puisque la cause que troubloit
lamytie estoit estainte ils feroint tout ce quil vouldroit."

[2] *Ibid.*: "Sire il nest a penser la joye que ce Roy et les
faulteurs de ce concubinage ont monstre de la mort de la dite
bonne Royne specialement le comte de Vulcher et son fils que
deurent dire que estoit dommaige que la princesse ne luy tinsse
compaignie."

the courtiers. Balls and jousts succeeded one another, and the court rang with gaiety.[1] On the 24th of January, however, the king happened to fall from his horse; and although he was not hurt, he was somewhat sobered by the accident, and the following days were spent more quietly.

These strange rejoicings could not but shock every one who had any sense of decency; and one consequence of them was that all kinds of rumours began to spread. Some declared that the queen had died of a broken heart, caused by the ill-treatment to which she had been subjected. According to others, she had been poisoned.[2] The poison, it was said, had been sent from Italy by Gregorio da Casale, and brought to England by his cousin Gurone, and Casale had received a pension of eight ducats a day for it. To these and other details Chapuis attached little importance;[3] but as to the

---

[1] E. Chapuis to Charles V., January 21, 1536, *loc. cit.* : "Le jour suibvant que fust le dymanche ce Roy fust tout accoustre de jaune de pied en cap ce ne fust la plume blanche quil avoit au bonnet, et fust la petite bastarde conduitte a la messe avec trumpettes et autres grans triumphes. Lapres dine le Roy se trouva en la sale ou dancoient les dames et la comme transporte de joye fist plusieurs choses a la fin il fust querre sa petite bastarde et la pourtant entre ses bras yl lalloit monstrant a lung puis a lautre. Les jours ensuyvant depuis il en a use correspondentement et si a couru quelques lances a grinuyc."

[2] *Ibid.* : " Plusieurs deulx confessent voire sement que le regret est cause de sa mort et ce pour exclure la suspicion du surplus " . . . "il n'est a croyre . . . lindignacion quilz ont contre le Roy luy donnant la coulpe de sa mort laquelle partie imagine avoir ete par venin et les autres par regret. . . ."

[3] E. Chapuis to N. de Granvelle, January 29, 1536, Vienna Archives, P.C. 230, ii. fol. 2 : " Plusieurs suspeconnent que si la

main fact, he firmly believed that Catherine had
been poisoned at the instigation of the king and of
Anne.[1]

Was Catherine poisoned, or did she die from
natural causes? That is the question we have to
answer. Chapuis expected the truth to be established
by the examination of the body. "Should they
open her," he wrote on the 9th to Charles, "the
traces will be seen."[2] But the ambassador was to be
disappointed. The body of Catherine was of course
opened in order to be embalmed, but it was done in
such a way as to prevent any clue to the cause of her
death being found. Catherine died at two o'clock in
the afternoon. Chamberlain and Bedingfield at once
decided that the body should be embalmed by the
chandler of the house, and that it should be immediately afterwards enclosed in lead. "The which,"
they wrote to Cromwell, "must needs shortly be
done, for that may not tarry."[3] At ten o'clock in

Royne est morte de poyson que Gregaire de Casal layt envoye
par ung sien parent modeneys nomme gorron . . . et que ceulx
cy pour avoir poison plus lente et que ne donnoit indice de soy
lavoient envoye querre la; ce que ne puis croire bonnement car
la chose seroit en trop grand dangier detre divulgee."

[1] E. Chapuis to Charles V., January 21, 1536, *loc. cit.*: "Sire
ce Roy et la concubine, impacient de plus longue tardance voyant
mesmement que en Rome lon procedoyt a certes et que y allant
Vostre Maieste les provisions se renforceroint, ils ont voulu
vuyder le proces de la bonne Royne comme yl est apparent par ce
que Vostre Maieste verra cy apres."

[2] E. Chapuis to Charles V., January 9, 1536, *loc. cit.*: "Sil
viennent a louvrir lon en verra les indices."

[3] Chamberlain and Bedingfield to Cromwell, January 7, 1536,
State Papers, i. p. 452.

the evening, the royal officers drove everybody out of the room in which the corpse was lying, and the chandler and two assistants were called in and left alone to do their work. Doctor de Lasco wished to be present, but his request was not granted. Permission was also withheld from the Bishop of Llandaff, who was required by the customs of the Church to remain with the body.[1]

January 8, 1536. Next morning, the work being done, the chandler told the bishop that he had found all the internal organs as healthy and normal as possible, with the exception of the heart, which was quite black and hideous to look at. He washed it, but it did not change colour ; then he cut it open, and the inside was the same. Moreover, a black, round body stuck to the outside of the heart. All this the chandler asked the bishop to keep strictly secret, for his life would be in danger if it became known that he had spoken.[2]

---

[1] E. Chapuis to Charles V., January 21, 1536, *loc. cit.* : "La bonne Royne expira deux heures apres midi et dedans huict heures apres elle feust ouverte par le commandement de ceulx quen avoient la charge de la part de ce Roy et ne fust permis que le confesseur ne medecin de la Royne y assista ne personne du monde, synon le feseur de chandelles de la mayson et ung sien serviteur et ung compaignon lesquels louvrirent."

[2] *Ibid.* : "Lequel sortant de faire la dicte ouverture vint a declairer au dict evesque de Landaf confesseur de la dicte Royne, mais en grand secret comme chose ou yl luy alloit la vie, quil avoit trouve le corps de la dicte Royne et tous les membres interieulx tant sains et nets quil nestoit possible de plus excepte le cueur lequel estoit tout neoir et hideux a veoir, et que voyant que ores que il le avoit tres fort laveen trois eaue il ne changeoit point de couleur, il le fendit par le milieu et trouva le dedant de la mesme couleur laquelle aussy peu se voulsist changer pour

But the good bishop told the doctor; and when, a few days later, a servant whom Chapuis had sent to Kimbolton inquired whether there was any suspicion of poison, the doctor answered that there could be no doubt of it after what the chandler had said, and that even without his evidence the fact had been rendered clear enough by the course and symptoms of the illness.[1]

Doctor de Lasco was somewhat biassed, and his opinion must be received with considerable caution. The chandler also seems to have had a suspicion before he opened the body, otherwise he would scarcely have paid so much attention to its condition. Besides, he was not a surgeon, nor even a barber, although he had opened several bodies before.[2] The symptoms of the illness as they are described are not incompatible with the theory of death by poison; but they do not necessarily lead to this conclusion. We must, therefore, take other circumstances into account before the case can be decided.

We have seen that in the beginning of November the king manifested an intention to have an act of attainder brought in at the next session of parlia-

laver que feit, et dit aussy que trouva certaine chose noire toute ronde questoit tres fort attache au dehors dudict cueur."

[1] E. Chapuis to Charles V., January 21, 1536, *loc. cit.* : " Interrogeant mon homme le medecin si la Royne estoit morte de poison il luy respondist que la chose estoit trop verifiee par ce que en avoit este dit a levesque confesseur, et quant cela neust este descouvert la chose estoit assez clair considerant le discours qualite et accidens de la maladie."

[2] *Ibid:* " Et oires quq ce ne soint berbiers ne sirurgiens touttefois ils ont souvent faict tel office, aumoings le principal . . ."

ment. He spoke very violently about it, and those who knew his obstinacy seem to have been of opinion that he would carry out his purpose. Now, it is quite certain that the introduction of a bill of attainder would have been the signal for instant revolt. In such circumstances even Chapuis would have favoured an insurrection, and the conspirators, driven to extremity, would have acted unanimously and enthusiastically. If Catherine had been left at Kimbolton and Mary at Hatfield or Hunsdon, an attempt would have been made to carry these two places, and it would most probably have been successful, for the royal garrisons were by no means trustworthy. Had Henry, wishing to have the ladies in his power before submitting the bill of attainder to parliament, brought them to the Tower, the rebellion would have broken out all the sooner, for his aim would then have been manifest ; and, Kingston being secretly in favour of the queen and the princess, the Tower would almost certainly have been thrown open to their supporters. As the king had hardly any real adherents, and as he could not rely on the few troops he possessed, the conspirators could scarcely have failed to triumph even without assistance from the Low Countries.

It was impossible for the trusty and well-beloved councillors of Henry to approve of a proposal which was likely to lead to such a result as this. They could not but suspect that if there was to be civil war the more obnoxious of them would fall as victims to the popular fury, and that the rest, besides losing all power, might have to disgorge their ill-acquired wealth. For their own sakes Henry's threats must have filled them with alarm ; and, as it happened, their personal interests coincided with the public weal. A successful insurrection would have been most disastrous to the commonwealth.

Three courses would have been open to the victorious insurgents. The first and mildest course would have been to drive away or kill Anne Boleyn and her adherents, to oblige the king to recognise Catherine as his wife and Mary as heir to the crown, to force him to give up the royal supremacy and to submit to the pope, and to take security for the fulfilment of all these conditions by requiring the appointment of a council entirely composed of the leaders of the insurrection. But this would have been extremely dangerous for the peers. Henry was so vain that he would never have forgotten his humiliation, so vindictive that he would never have forgiven those who had brought it upon him, so false that he would not have allowed himself to be bound by any promises or oaths which might have interfered with his vengeance. Sooner or later he would have tried to recover absolute power, and if he had succeeded, not one of those who had opposed him would have been safe. This course, therefore, would not have suited the insurgents at all.

The second course would have been to dethrone Henry, either by the authority of parliament, or in fulfilment of the papal sentence, or in obedience to the imperial over-lord, and to set up Mary in his place. But it was doubtful whether Mary would give her consent to so perilous an undertaking ; and even if she did so, it was not less doubtful whether she would always be willing and able to withstand her father's intrigues. If she were made queen, Henry would never cease to resist her authority, and by conspiracy and civil war he might in the end regain his throne.

The third course would necessarily have been taken. During the conflict Henry would somehow have died, and Mary would have succeeded him as his lawful heir. It would not have been the first time that an English king had been murdered to make place for his child. Edward II. had been dethroned and murdered by the adherents of his son, and the reign of Edward III. had been one of splendour and of at least outward success. There would have been great differences, however, in the two cases. First of all, morals had changed, and what had been possible in the fourteenth might have proved impossible in the sixteenth century. Moreover, when the bloody deed was done in favour of Prince Edward, he was a mere boy and far away; he could scarcely be held responsible. But Mary was nearly twenty; and it would be impossible for her to escape censure if a crime were committed for her benefit. Edward III. was a man of considerable ability and with an undisputed title to the crown. Mary was a woman of very small ability, full of prejudices and scruples, slow of resolve, unused to action, and with a title to the crown which was by no means very clear. I have no doubt that if Mary had succeeded under conditions similar to those under which Edward III. ascended the throne, she would in a few years have been as unpopular as Henry

had ever been, and as she actually became at a later
period. There would have been fresh rebellions with
their train of misery and bloodshed, and the condition
of the English people would have been even more
wretched than it had been before her accession.

Salus populi suprema lex esto. In King Henry's
time this famous saying had not been uttered, but
the rule it sets forth had long been the standard of
public morals for practical English statesmen. In a
case in which the welfare of the nation coincided for
once with the welfare of ministers, the rule obtained a
force which must have been quite irresistible. When
the royal councillors heard Henry's angry vow, when
they became aware that he really meant it, when they
rapidly weighed the consequences, they must have
come to the conclusion that it would be necessary to
use every means in their power to avert the catastrophe they foresaw. And there was but one way in
which Henry could be prevented from doing what he
proposed. Catherine at least must be dead before
the assembling of parliament. A single death of an
old and unhappy woman might save many thousands
of lives, those of the trusty and well-beloved included.
Cromwell and Audeley, Wiltshire and Rochford, and
many others undoubtedly viewed the matter in this
light. Cromwell, we know, had already spoken like
Caiaphas, and there is every reason to believe that he
felt as he spoke.

Early in November Henry uttered the ominous
words reported by Lady Exeter. Four weeks later
Catherine fell ill under circumstances which were at
least suspicious. She recovered, fell ill again, and

CHAP. XIV. died.   The danger was past, the king was free, the

councillors were safe.   Was there no connection
between the words of the king and the death of
his wife ?   The world thought there was, and Chapuis
directly accused the king and Anne Boleyn of having
murdered the queen.[1]

Suspicious circumstances after Catherine's death.   The events which followed Catherine's death seem
to be inexplicable if she died in the ordinary course
of nature.   The government acted again and again as
if it knew that a murder had been committed.
The indecent haste made at Kimbolton to have
Catherine's body embalmed as quickly and as secretly
as possible, certainly looks very suspicious.   Why was
the body to be immediately enclosed in lead ?   It was
winter, and Catherine had not died of any disease by
which the decomposition of the body was hastened.
And why was Doctor de Lasco prevented from being
present at the opening ?

January, 1536.   After much solicitation Chapuis obtained permission
for Doctor de Lasco and Juan de Soto to see Lady
Mary for the purpose of giving her an account of
her mother's death.   It is significant that when they
arrived at the house where Mary was kept a prisoner
they were refused admittance and peremptorily ordered
back.[2]

February, 1536.   Doctor de Lasco, who was still a Spanish subject,
considering himself of no farther use in England,

---

[1] E. Chapuis to Charles V., January 21, 1536, *loc. cit.*

[2] E. Chapuis to Charles V., January 29, 1536, Vienna
Archives, P.C. 230, i. fol. 22 : " Je suis esbay oyres que ce Roy
meust permis y envoyer les susdicts que lon leur a permis entrer
aussy peu que mes gens ; lon la garde de parler au monde mais
elle sen revanche bien. . . ."

wished to return to his native country. He applied
for leave to go, but it was refused. He once more
pressed his request, and was met by an offer of
employment in the royal service. This the doctor
declined, but he could not obtain the necessary
passport.[1] The Bishop of Llandaff, also by birth a
Spaniard, seeing this reluctance to let the late
servants of Catherine depart, began to fear that he
might have to live in a country where the papal
supremacy was denied, and tried to leave in disguise.
But Cromwell's spies watched him; and he was
caught and sent to the Tower.[2] What reason could

---

[1] E. Chapuis to Charles V., March 7, 1536, Vienna Archives,
P.C. 229½, i. fol. 20: "Ce Roy doubte que le medecin de la dicte
feue royne vuille desloger dicy et tache le plus quil peult pour y
obvier de retirer le dict medecin a son service ou du moings
lentretenir yci quelque temps; et pour traicter dudict affaire
cremuel ma a ce matin envoye prier luy envoyer ledict medecin,
auquel il a faict plusieurs remonstrances pour accepter ledict
service du roy son maistre, et luy respondant icelluy medecin que
acceptant si soubdainement ledict service ce seroit donner
occasion au monde de mal penser et mal dire . . . ledictCremuel
replicqua . . . que cependant le dict Sr Roy feroit donner
secretement bon traictement audict medecin lequel toutesfois ne
sest voulu resoldre, remectant le tout a mon advis."

[2] *Ibid*: "Sire levesque de Landaf confesseur de la feue Royne
dangleterre . . . . se deslibera le propre jour de la date de mes
dernieres lectres que furent du XXVe du passe de vuyder
secretement de ce royaulme et sen retirer pour quelque temps en
flandres ou en aragon dont yl est natifs ayant premierement este
devers Vre Mte et devers Sa Ste mais il porgecta et dressa si mal
et si symplement son cas, quil fust descouvert et constitue
prisonnier dans la tour de ceste cite et ne scait lon encoires
quelle issues auront ses affaires, du moings je pense quilz ne
le permectront sortir de ce Royaulme pour craincte quil ne sollicite
ou dise quelque chose contre eulx."

CHAP XIV. there be for retaining these men except the dread
that once out of England they might tell an ugly
tale?

*Accusa-
tions
against
Anne
Boleyn.
May 2,
1536.*
On the second of May following, Anne Boleyn was
arrested. That same evening, when the Duke of
Richmond, Henry's bastard son, was saying good
night to his father, the king burst into tears. "The
duke and his sister, the Lady Mary," exclaimed Henry,
"might thank God for having escaped the hands of that
damned poisonous wretch who had conspired their
death."[1] And shortly afterwards, at the trial of Anne,
the royal officers laid it to the charge of the prisoner

*May 15,
1536.*
that she was strongly suspected of having caused the
late princess dowager to be poisoned, and of having
intended to do the same by the Lady Mary.[2] A
scapegoat having been found, Henry's ministers did
not deny that Catherine had been murdered.

With so formidable a mass of evidence it cannot
but seem likely that Catherine met with foul play.
If such was the case, the poison was probably ad-

---

[1] E. Chapuis to Charles V., May 19, 1536, Vienna Archives,
P.C. 230, i. fol. 82 : "Sire le mesme soir que la dicte concubyne
feust menee a la tour allant le duc de Richemont donner le
bonsoir au Roy et luy demander la benediction a la coustume
dangleterre, le dict Roy se print a larmoyer, disant que luy et sa
sueur, enctendant la princesse, estoient bien tenus a dieu davoir
eschapper les mains dicelle mauldicte et veneficque putain quavoit
delibere les faire empoisonner ; dont fault il dire que le dict Roy
en scavoit quelque chose."

[2] *Ibid* : "Ce principallement dont elle fust chargee, estoit
. . . . quelle avoit receu et donnee certaines medailles au dict
Noris que se pouvoint ainsi interpreter quelle avoyt faict
empoysonner la feue Royne et machine de fayre le mesme a la
princesse."

ministered twice in small doses, at the end of
November and shortly after Christmas. Poisoning
by repeated low doses was thought by the great
toxicologists of the sixteenth century to be preferable
to every other method. Usually the victim did not
die of the direct effect of the poison, but of exhaustion
caused by frequent illnesses ; so that, as a rule, no
traces of the drug were found in the body, and the
course of the disorder did not present those strong
and characteristic symptoms which might otherwise
have appeared. Thus poisoners were able to baffle
the efforts of the most skilful physicians, and in most
cases to prevent the detection of their crime.

If a murder was committed, it is for the present impossible to say who was the actual murderer, or whose
immediate orders he obeyed. The accusation brought
by the royal officers in May against Anne Boleyn may
have been well founded. Chapuis thought her guilty,
and so did others ; but Chapuis equally accused the
king, and from what we know he had good reason to
do so. The behaviour of Henry II. towards Thomas
a Becket was not worse than that of Henry VIII.
towards Catherine, and historians are generally agreed
in saying that Henry II. prompted a murder.

On the king, who made the death of Catherine a *The*
political necessity, rests the responsibility for what *principal*
culprit.
may have been done, not on those who in their own way
fulfilled his command. Anne Boleyn may have contributed to the result, her advice may have strengthened
the king in his opinion, and may have encouraged those
by whom the crime was directly ordered. But the

attempt to throw the whole blame on her shoulders was an attempt to exonerate the principal culprit. Her guilt, whatever it may have been, was less than that of Henry, for she was bound by no tie to the queen, and she did to Catherine what would have been done to her had Catherine possessed the power.

CHAPTER XV.

JANE SEYMOUR.

On receiving the letter of Chamberlain and Beding-field which announced Catherine's death, Cromwell immediately wrote to the Bishop of Winchester and Sir John Wallop, the English ambassadors at the French court. He instructed them to communicate the good news to Francis, and in their negotiations to modify their action in accordance with the new order of things. But before he had time to send off the letter, he received a message from Henry directing him to point out to the ambassadors that, Catherine being dead, there was no longer any reason to appre-hend the hostility of the emperor. This they were to explain to the French, and Francis was to be warned that he might be forestalled by Charles V. if he did not at once accept Henry's proposals. If, notwithstanding this warning, Francis still required the ambassadors to abate their claims, they were to show themselves un-willing to do so.[1] It is quite clear that Henry fully understood how much his position had been bettered

Instruc-tions to English ambassa-dors in France. January 8, 1536.

[1] Cromwell to Gardiner and Wallop, January 8, 1536, British Museum, Add. MSS. vol. 25,114, fol. 126.

by the death of his wife, and how much less he depended on the goodwill of France.

A few days after Dinteville had left England the Bishop of Winchester had been sent to assist and perhaps to watch Sir John Wallop at the French court.[1] The choice was not a happy one, for Gardiner had made himself unpopular with the French by his overbearing temper, and by the part he had taken in the intrigues at Marseilles. Probably he was chosen as much because at home they wished to be rid of him as because he was considered a very fit instrument. At the French court he met with little success. The demands of France were as exorbitant as ever, and Gardiner quickly perceived that there was scarcely any chance of an agreement. But a few days after his arrival news came from Italy which raised a hope that the French would attribute more importance to the friendship of Henry, and that they might be brought to make considerable concessions.

Maximilian Sforza, the Duke of Milan, had died without issue ; and Francis, who had always pretended a title to the duchy, now claimed the succession. He at once asked the emperor to give investiture of the duchy to Henry, Duke of Orleans, his second son. To this Charles demurred, for Henry of Orleans, next to the dauphin, who was of feeble health and unmarried, was at this time heir to the French crown ; and if he were made Duke of Milan, and if his elder brother died childless, the duchy would belong to the King of France, who would thus

---

[1] Gardiner to Cromwell, October 21, 1535, R.O. Henry VIII. box S.

obtain a strong hold over upper and central Italy.
Moreover, Henry of Orleans, in virtue of his wife,
Catherine dei Medici, thought he had some claim to
the Duchy of Urbino, Camerino, and other places in
the Romagna. If he obtained possession of Milan,
he would try to enforce his pretensions; so that the
emperor, instead of securing peace by the concession
demanded of him by Francis, would be involved in
new quarrels and new wars.

But while Charles would not grant Milan to Henry
of Orleans, he was ready to make sacrifices in order
to avoid a war with France. The Tunisian expédition
had been rather expensive; and Khairredin, although
beaten and driven from one of his strongholds, had
been able to retain Algiers, and had reconstituted a
fleet with which he was once more threatening
the shores and islands of Spain and Italy. The
emperor was, therefore, really anxious to maintain
peace with France, and in the hope that a compromise
might be accepted he offered to give the investiture
of Milan to the third son of Francis, the Duke of
Angoulême. Negotiations were begun for the fulfilment of this plan, the pope did his best to mediate,
and the moderate party in France were favourable to
an understanding.[1]

The English ambassadors watched these negotia- *Triumph*
tions with keen interest, and strove to counteract *of the war*
party in
them, making common cause with the admiral of *France.*
France, who was at the head of the war party, and *December,*
1535.
with the Italian refugees, who wished to return to

[1] Memoir by N. de Granvelle, *Papiers d'etat de Granvelle,*
vol. ii. p. 395.

CHAP. XV. their country and estates by the force of French arms. Gardiner and Wallop promised Francis some subsidies if he would invade Italy, and with the help of Chabot they prevailed over the moderate party. As a preliminary for further operations, Francis sent the Count de Saint Pol with a strong force to invade Bresse and Savoy up to the Alps. He assisted the malcontents at Geneva, who had driven out their bishop and the officials of the duke, and he urged the Swiss to overrun the Pays du Vaud. Thus, before the new year, Charles of Savoy was deprived of nearly all his lands on the western side of the Alps.

The Emperor's preparations for war.

The emperor, who fully understood that this was but the beginning of a far more serious war, set himself to prepare for the worst. He tried to gain the pope over by making great offers to his son, Pier Luigi Farnese, and endeavoured to unite the smaller Italian states in a general confederacy for the protection of the Duke of Savoy and the defence of Italy. Best of all, new troops were raised in Germany and Italy to reinforce the army the emperor had brought back from Tunis. In Spain, the Low Countries, and Italy, everything was made ready to repel an attack by the French in the coming spring.

Henry expects to profit by the struggle.

These signs of an approaching storm were observed by Henry with unfeigned delight. He thought that if war broke out Francis would be less overbearing, and thankful for any assistance England might give him, while the emperor would no longer dare to favour the English malcontents. Even if the latter anticipation proved to be mistaken, Henry was persuaded that Charles would be unable to do him any harm.

He was confident that the struggle between his lukewarm friend and his staunch opponent would be an excellent safeguard for his own tranquillity.

Henry altogether misapprehended the influences which were likely to determine Charles's course. Hitherto the emperor had been held back from active interference in favour of Catherine and Mary chiefly by the fear that any attempt of the kind would occasion a rupture with France. If for other reasons he were compelled once more to fight Francis, the principal cause of his hesitation would be removed. No sooner, therefore, did war seem to be unavoidable than he began to think rather seriously about giving the English malcontents the aid they asked for. In December, after the invasion of the territory of the Duke of Savoy by St. Pol, he all but decided to assist the English lords; and an important preliminary step was taken.

The emperor's intentions regarding England

Charles did not rely on the assurances of the malcontents that in case of insurrection Mary would be in no danger. He could not feel quite sure as to Kingston's loyalty to her and to the queen; and he feared a sudden outbreak of rage on the part of the king. Besides, he wished to be able to set up Mary as a pretender against Henry; and it appeared to him necessary that she should be in some place where he could constantly communicate with her. After the death of Fisher and More, Mary had repeatedly urged Chapuis to procure for her the means of flight, but the ambassador, bound by his instructions, did not dare to proceed any further in the matter. Now Charles V. himself took the initiative. The Count de

Measures proposed for Mary's safety.

CHAP. XV. Roeulx, his captain-general in the Low Countries, was commissioned to send a special agent to England to prepare for Mary's flight. If all went well, the princess was to be carried off in February, and in March or April the insurrection was to follow.[1]

February 9, 1536. Shortly after the new year, Roeulx's agent arrived in England, and he and Chapuis carefully considered how Mary could be safely carried away.[2]

The sentence of excommunication. December, 1535. This was only one of many difficulties in which Henry was now entangled. In November Sir Francis Bryan had been sent to help Gardiner and Wallop in their negotiations with the French; and in the beginning of December he had met the court near Pargaix, the country seat of Chabot de Brion. Here, immediately after Bryan's arrival, the three ambassadors were told by the ministers of Francis of some despatches which had just been received from Rome.[3] They contained a copy of the sentence of excommunication and deprivation against Henry VIII. which had been drawn up by order of the pope. It *November 10, 1535.* had been read in the middle of November in consistory, and Cardinal du Bellay, who was at Rome, had forwarded a copy of it to Francis I. The cardinal expressed his belief that there would never be another sentence like it. "We are well aware," he continued, "that it is necessary for you that the sentence should

---

[1] E. Chapuis to Charles V., February 10, 1536, Vienna Archives, P.C. 230, i. fol. 26.

[2] E. Chapuis to Charles V., February 17, 1536, Vienna Archives, P.C. 230, i. fol. 30.

[3] Chabot de Brion to Cardinal du Bellay, December 3 and 10, 1535, Paris, Bibl. Nat. MSS. Fr. vol. 19,577.

be in any case a very severe one, but there are some CHAP. XV.
articles so expressly designed for you that a blind
man would see that they have been inserted for no
other purpose than to compel you to lose either the
pope or the King of England."[1] Du Bellay added
that he and the Bishop of Mâcon would do their
best to gain time until they should hear from Francis,
but that they had little hope of succeeding.

Francis now found himself in a very perplexing *The dilemma of Francis.*
position. If he chose to stand by Henry, he would
drive the pope into the arms of Charles ; and he knew,
of course, that nothing could be more detrimental
to his interests in Italy, which were at this moment
engrossing his attention. On the other hand, if
Francis wished to obtain the good-will of the pope,
he would have to give up his alliance with Henry.
The difficulty was in part explained to the English
ambassadors, who knew not what to do. Bryan
decided that he would not declare his charge to
Francis until he and Gardiner received fresh instructions.[2]

Henry received the news with astonishment and *Henry's anger.*
anger. He had never doubted that the death of

[1] Cardinal du Bellay and Denonville to Francis I., November
22, 1535, Paris, Bibl. Nat. MSS. Fr. vol. 5499, fol. 2446 : "Nous
vous envoyons Sire le double de la dicte sentence conceue ainsi
que dict est, qui este telle que jamais aultre nen approchera. Il
nous semble bien que en quelque evenement que ce soit il faut
pour vous quelle soit fort rigoureuse mais il est a notter quil y a
aulcuns articles qui sont si expressement couchez pour vous, que
ung aveugle verroit quilz ne sont mis a aultre effect que pour
Vous faire perdre par necessite ou le pape ou le roy dangleterre."

[2] Chabot de Brion to Cardinal du Bellay, December 10, 1535,
loc. cit.

CHAP. XV.　Sforza would make the French more desirous of
securing his friendship, and to his dismay he found
that this was not the case. Some contemptuous
expressions used by the admiral of France about his
power greatly enraged him, and he instructed Gardiner
and Wallop strongly to protest against them.[1] He
appears to have been really convinced that he possessed formidable power, and that he ought to have
been taken more seriously into account.

According to his wont, Henry exaggerated his
own importance. He was held in very small esteem,
and every prince who had anything to lose shrank
from an alliance with a king who might be deposed
the day after the treaty was signed. His duplicity
had been so great that nobody would rely on his
assurances or accept his offers without good guarantees.

Even now he was doing what he could to destroy
the last remnant of good-will which the members of
Wullen-　the Schmalkaldic League might feel for him. In the
wever at　beginning of November, after having been arrested,
Roten-
burg.　Juergen Wullenwever had been closely questioned by
the officials of the Archbishop of Bremen as to his
former doings and as to his intentions in leaving
Luebeck and coming to Rotenburg. Of his negotiations with Henry VIII. something was known,
and a great deal more was suspected;[2] but no hint

[1] Henry VIII. to Gardiner and Wallop, January 4, 1536,
British Museum, Add. MSS. vol. 25,114, fol. 119.

[2] Johann von Werden to Duke Albrecht of Prussia, December 4,
1535, G. Waitz, *Luebeck, etc.* vol. iii. p. 470: "Genedyger furst,
ich befynde bey myr awssz mennychfeltygen ursachen, dasz eynen
hemlyche swynde practicke zwyschen dem konynge zu Engelandt
Wollenweffer unnd Merckus Meyer musz seyn geweszen; szo

of his last negotiations with Bonner and Cavendish had been conveyed to the archbishop, to King Christian, or to any of the princes and towns by whose delegates he was about to be examined.

Hoping, probably, that Henry would intercede for him and obtain his release, Wullenwever did not wish to compromise the King of England. He remained silent as to his proceedings at Hamburg, and even on the rack he did not speak of Bonner and Cavendish, but asserted that he had acted on behalf of the Count Palatine Frederic, who pretended a right to the Danish throne.[1]

Henry was less prudent. On hearing of the arrest of Wullenwever, he wrote to the senate and to the Archbishop of Bremen in such violent terms that the latter could not but suspect that there must be very special reasons for his interference. Henry called Wullenwever his beloved friend, declared that he had been arrested against all law and equity, complained that he himself had been badly treated by the archbishop, demanded the release of the prisoner, and threatened reprisals on the persons of all Bremen citizens in England if his request were refused.[2]

Henry intercedes for Wullen-wever. December 15, 1535.

werde ich berycht, wyhe meyn g. h. von Bremen inhnen geret zu peynlycher froge hot stellen lasszen;" and the Bishop of Ermeland to Duke Albrecht of Prussia, December 13, 1535, G. Waitz, *Luebeck unter Juergen Wullenwever*, vol. iii. p. 471.

[1] Examination of J. Wullenwever, December 31, 1535, and January 1, 1536, G. Waitz, *Luebeck unter Juergen Wullenwever*, vol. iii. pp. 475 to 477.

[2] Henry VIII. to Christoph, Archbishop of Bremen, December 15, 1535, Buchholtz, *Geschichte der Regierung Ferdinand I.*, vol. ix. p. 351: "Intelleximus V. R. D. . . . praeter fas et aequum dilectum amicum nostrum Georgium Wolweber a suo

CHAP. XV.   This threat could have no great effect on the mind
———   of the archbishop, who was on very bad terms with
            the burghers over whom he was nominally set.
            Wullenwever remained a prisoner, and was repeatedly
            examined by the officials of the archbishop, and by
            delegates sent by Christian III., by Duke Henry of
            Brunswick, and by the senate of Luebeck.

January   But Henry was not disheartened even by so decided
7, 1536.   a rebuff.   Bonner and Cavendish wrote once more to
            the senate of Bremen, asking them to obtain the
            release of the prisoner and, like the king, threatening
February   them with reprisals.[1]   Henry himself penned a second
10, 1536.   letter to the archbishop, in which he said again that
            Wullenwever had not been guilty of any crime, and
            pretended that his friend, being in prison, was unable
            to defend himself or to prove his innocence.
            Christopher had committed a sacrilege, Henry went
            on, in behaving as he had done ; and he was asked
            to believe that if Wullenwever had really offended

itinere interceptum . . . Modus hic agendi indignior est, quam
suo intimi nostri amici tractare debeant iniquiorque et in-
humanior quam nostra in cives vos benevolentia expectasset.
Caeterum . . . eam impense rogamus ut velit eum e carceribus
statim liberare ; alioquin eandem R. D. V. neutiquam ignorare
volumus, nos hac injuria . . . provocatos parem vicissitudinem
in tot, quot hic adsunt Bremenses cives esse ostensuros . . .
gravissime nos pati tam duras injurias in amicos nros a quocunque inferri."

1 Translation of Bonner and Cavendish's letter to the Senate
of Bremen, January 7, 1536, G. Waitz, *Luebeck unter Juergen
Wullenwever*, vol. iii. p. 473 : "Dieweil doch derselbige furtrefflich
berumbter Mann sein lebenlang nichts dergleichenn verschuldet
hat . . . Dann sein ko. M^t hat beschlossenn solichs an allenn
Bremischen kauffleuten in Enngelandt zu rechen."

against the emperor, Henry, as the great friend of CHAP. XV.
Charles, would punish him most severely. To Henry
the prisoner was to be delivered, and, if Christopher
declined, signal vengeance was to be taken on his
subjects.[1]

The archbishop, exasperated by this arrogant letter, *March*
replied that although it professed to be only a friendly 1, 1536.
representation on behalf of an innocent man, it read
rather like a declaration of war. In this matter
nothing had been done that was contrary to law or
justice, for, as a prince of the empire, the archbishop
had full jurisdiction over all persons in his territory.
He was ready to justify his acts before the emperor
and the electors, to whom Henry might complain if
he chose. Should the King of England proceed
against citizens of Bremen, Christopher would appeal
to the princes of the empire, and sharp retaliatory
measures might follow.[2]

[1] Henry VIII. to the Archbishop of Bremen, February 10,
1536, printed by G. Waitz, vol. iii. pp. 473 and 474, according
to the draft in British Museum, Cotton MSS. Vitellius, B. xxi.
fol. 97, and extracted by Buchholtz, vol. ix. p. 352, from the
original: "Nullum ideo jus in eo detinendo D. V. competit . . .
quin potius ejus partes essent, meminisse synceram ac firmam
inter Cesarem et nos amicitiam esse, eoque jure famulum hunc
nrum criminis causa (quod tam atrociter illi a vobis impingitur)
ad veritatem perspecta, in Cesaris manum et arbitrium multum
quam vos justius nos posse consignare, vel admissi in Cesam.
Mm. (quem ut fratrem amamus) facinorus si reus convincatur,
nos esse de eo supplicium pro culpa exacturos. . . . D.V. . . . in
admissi sacrilegii apertam labem incurrisse patebit . . . nil
quoque nos obstare videmus, quomimus tantam injuriam et in-
dignitatem, quacunque ratione possimus, et in quoscunque id
commodum videbitur, retaliemus."

[2] Christoph of Bremen to Henry VIII., March 1, 1536, Buch

CHAP. XV.   Henry and his ministers seem to have understood
at last that the archbishop was not to be frightened.
The correspondence ceased, and the Bremen citizens
March   were not molested.   Bonner and Cavendish, however
13, 1536.   tried another way.   They addressed a long letter to
the King of Denmark, lecturing him about his duties
as a Christian, and exhorting him to forgive past
offences and not to persecute Wullenwever any
longer.[1]   This production had no more effect than the
preceding letters.   The prisoner was kept in close
confinement at Rotenburg.

Effect of   Henry did far more harm than good to the ex-
Henry's   burgomaster.   His violence increased the suspicions
inter-
cession.   of Wullenwever's enemies, and the prisoner was more
closely questioned as to his dealings with the English

holtz, *Geschichte der Regierung Ferdinand I.*, vol. ix. pp. 352 to 354:
" So schmeckt solch Schreiben mer nach einer betrolichen herben
Absag wider uns und die Unsern . . . so haben wir auch . . .
als ein Fuerst des h. R. Reichs von kays. Maj. unser hohe und nider
Gericht und Regalie krafft derselben einen Uebelthetter recht-
fertigen zu lassen uns wol gepuret . . . den wuerden wir verur-
sacht, solche hochgedachten unsern Obrigkeiten und gemeinen
Stenden des h. R. Reichs anzuzeigen und gleichmessig Anhaltung
Hilff und Beswerde ueber E. k. M. Underthanen und Verwand-
ten zu Waszer unde Lande wo die angetroffen moechten werden,
Uns und den Unsern zu gestatten zu bitten . . ."

[1] Bonner and Cavendish to Christian III. of Denmark,
March 13, 1536, British Museum, Cotton MSS. Vitellius, B. xxi.
fol. 127, printed by G. Waitz, vol. iii. p. 474, but wrongly taken
by him to be a letter to Henry VIII.: " Quid vero turpius,
quam sub titulo publico privatam injuriam et contumeliam ulcisci,
denique que tua sunt querere, non que Jhesu Christi? . . . Nunc
autem oramus et obtestamur tuam Celsitudinem ut hanc effrena-
torum hominum licentiam, quo in bonorum omnium perniciem
grassatur et in proscriptionem evangelii sedulo laborat, tua
auctoritas non compescat modo . . ."

ambassadors. At last (on the 27th of January),
having been racked several times, and seeing that no
help was likely to come, he confessed all that had
passed at Hamburg between him and Bonner and
Cavendish.[1] After this he declared in his dungeon
that even two kings of England would not be able to
save his life.[2]

If the course taken in this matter did no good
to Wullenwever, it did much harm to Henry. It
had been arranged that after the arrival of Fox and
Heath in Saxony, and after the return of the elector
from Vienna, the proposals of Henry should be
considered by the members of the league of Schmalkalden. While the princes and delegates were
sitting, they heard of Wullenwever's arrest and of
Henry's outrageous talk. Peter Schwaben, who was
present as the ambassador of Christian III., bitterly
complained of Henry's dealings with the Luebeck
demagogues; and the assembly, impressed by his
appeal, decided to let the King of England know that
he must no longer oppose the new King of Denmark
or assist those who withstood his lawful authority.[3] A
few days later, in reply to Henry's proposals for a league,
the princes made counter-proposals, which clearly
showed how thoroughly they distrusted him. They

---

[1] Examination of J. Wullenwever, January 27, 1536, G. Waitz,
Luebeck unter Juergen Wullenwever, vol. iii. pp. 490 to 496.

[2] Juergen Wullenwever to Joachim Wullenwever, G. Waitz,
vol. iii. p. 483 : "Du moest dorch den marckgreven hartych
Hynryck styllen, edder ick kame umme den hals, wenne ick ock
twe konnynge von Engelant tho bate hadde."

[3] The Elector of Saxony and the Landgrave of Hessen to
Henry VIII., December 23, 1535, *State Papers*, vol. vii. p. 538.

CHAP. XV. asked that Henry should accept the Augsburg confession, and that he should give them 100,000 crowns
to aid them in defending themselves against the
opponents of their faith. In return they offered him
a barren title of protector of the league and a promise
not to assist his enemies.[1]

Henry was not told the whole truth, for he was
allowed to believe that the Wittenberg theologians
approved of the divorce and of his marriage with
Anne. Even with the facts which were reported to
January, him, however, he was displeased, and in his reply to
1536. his ambassadors he refused to be ordered by others as
to the faith of his realm, although he declared himself
ready to hear what the German theologians might
have to say about further reformation. The title of
protector of the league he did not immediately accept,
but the 100,000 crowns he was willing to deposit for
the defence of the Protestant princes and towns.[2]

Shortly afterwards a second set of instructions
were forwarded to the ambassadors. In these
instructions it is said that Henry " knoweth not that
the Bishop of Rome, the emperor, or any other prince
picketh any quarrel with him, and much less war ;
and although his grace feared some hostility of them,
nevertheless, by the death of a woman, all calumnies
be extincted." He asks that, in case any prince shall
invade his dominions, the members of the Schmalkaldic League shall furnish him with 500 horse or

[1] Proposals of the Elector and Landgrave, December 25, 1535,
Corp. Ref. vol. ii. No. 1383.

[2] Answer to the proposals of the Elector and Landgrave,
Burnet, *Collectanea*, part iii. book iii. No. 45.

with ten ships of war at their own cost for four CHAP. X.
months, and that they shall find him at his expense
2,000 horse and 5,000 foot. Finally, he requires
"that the said confederates will take upon them in
all councils hereafter, and everywhere else, to promote
and defend the opinion of the reverend fathers,
Dr. Martyn, Justus Jonas, Cruciger, Pomeran, and
Melanchthon, in the cause of his grace's marriage."[1]

Meanwhile, apart from Henry's foreign policy, the
prospects of Anne had not been improving. On the
day on which Catherine's death had been reported at
court, she had shown the greatest exultation.[2] She
had come to hate Catherine most cordially, and re-
joiced at the tidings that her detested rival was no
more. For, up to this time, every success Anne had
gained, every distinction she had obtained, had remained
incomplete. She had been proclaimed queen, and
heavy penalties had been threatened against those
who refused her that title. But Catherine had
remained firm, and Henry had not dared to proceed
against her to the full extent of his laws. And Anne
knew full well that by ninety-nine out of every
hundred Englishmen, by nine out of every ten even of
her own servants, she herself was secretly regarded as

Anne rejoices at the death of Catherine.

[1] Answer of the king's ambassadors, Burnet, *Collectanea*,
part iii. book iii. No. 46. This paper is a draft of the answer
which the ambassadors were to make, but which they subsequently
had to alter.

[2] E. Chapuis to Charles V., January 29, 1536, Vienna
Archives, P.C. 230, i. fol. 22: "La concubine de ce Roy nonobstant quelle eust monstre grande joye des nouvelles du trespas
de la bonne Royne pour lesquelles elle avoit donne ung bon
present au messaigier . . ."

a concubine and usurper, while the prisoner at Kimbolton was considered the lawful wife and queen.
Now and then this feeling displayed itself. If wise
men were afraid to speak, fools were bolder. We find
it related that in July the king's jester in open court
called Anne and little Elizabeth opprobrious names.
Henry was so angry that Sir Nicholas Carew hid the
culprit away ; but after a short time the king's wrath
subsided, and the jester reappeared.[1]

Fallen as Catherine was from her former greatness,
she could not be wholly deprived of the honour due
to the daughter of the great Catholic kings, the aunt
of the Kaiser, the kinswoman of nearly every royal
family in Europe. She was still spoken of with
respect ; and Christian princes, even when they were
politically opposed to her, protested against the
manner in which she was treated. Anne, on the
contrary, was reminded every day of the lowness of
her origin, and Henry himself often taunted her with
it. No foreign prince unequivocally recognised her
as the lawful Queen of England. The German
Protestants, following the advice of their theologians,
held that Catherine was Henry's wife. Francis I., the
only king who ever expressed a kind of friendship for
Anne, acknowledged the pope's authority in the
matter of the divorce, and could never be brought
absolutely to admit the validity of her marriage. As

[1] Decipher of a note of Chapuis, Vienna Archives, P.C. 229½,
iii. fol. 20 : "Le roy dangleterre a cuyde tuer son fol quest ung
innocent pour ce quil disoit et parloit bien des Royne et princesse
et disoit Ribalde a la concubine et bastarde a sa fille et a este
banni de court et la recelle le grand escuyer."

to his ministers, we have seen how little respect they
now showed her.

In these circumstances the death of Catherine
seemed at first sight a great gain for the cause of
Anne. Now that she was without a rival, it was
possible to hope that all the opposition offered to
her would die out, and that, having no other queen
to revere, people would generally acknowledge her
claims. But a very little reflexion brought her to a
better appreciation of her position. On the day after
Catherine's death she held a small council with her
brother Rochford and a few of her most tried friends.[1]
The precise result of the conference does not appear,
but it was remarked that Anne's joy quickly subsided.
For the first time, perhaps, she understood why
Henry had so ardently desired the death of his wife.[2]

Anne becomes less sanguine. January 8, 1536.

But Anne Boleyn was not a woman to succumb
without a struggle. She still had a considerable hold
over Henry, who stood in some awe of her intelligence,
her energy, and her courage. If she could contrive
to help him over the worst of his difficulties, she
might regain much of her power, and at least postpone
her fall. Now, one of Henry's chief difficulties arose
from the persistency with which Mary asserted her
rights. By her stubborn resistance to his demands
she encouraged her adherents to oppose him, and in
case of an insurrection her friends might prove very

Anne and Mary.

---

[1] Indictment found at Deptford, May 11, 1536, R.O. Baga
de Segretis, Pouch ix. Membrane 21.

[2] E. Chapuis to Charles V., January 29, 1536, *loc. cit.*:
"Touteffois elle avoit souvent larmoye soy doubtant quil en
oseroit faire delle comme de la bonne Royne."

formidable. Could Mary be brought to yield, the
king would be delivered from a serious danger; the
one person capable of being put forward as a
pretender against him would thereby lose most of her
influence.

A few days after Catherine's death Cromwell said
to a servant of Chapuis that Charles had no reason to
regret an event which would have a good effect on
the relations of the empire and England, and that
henceforward he would communicate more frequently
and more fully with the ambassador. All that was
wanted was, that Mary should be persuaded to submit to the king, and in this respect Chapuis would be
able to do more than anybody else. Chapuis certainly ought to try to influence her, for by doing so
he would not only greatly please the king, but benefit
Mary who, if she gave way, would be treated better
than she had ever been. These suggestions were, of
course, disregarded by the ambassador, and for the
moment he rather avoided Cromwell.[1]

This effort having failed, Anne determined to try
whether she could not accomplish a task which was
beyond the powers of others; believing that if she
succeeded Henry would be less eager to abandon her,
and might even reward her with as much gratitude as
his nature permitted. First of all, she endeavoured
to attain her object by means of what seemed to her
to be very generous offers. Mary was told through
Lady Shelton that if she would act as a dutiful
daughter towards the king, Anne would be to her a
second mother and strive to obtain for her everything

[1] E. Chapuis to Charles V., January 21, 1536, *loc. cit.*

she could desire. And if Mary should afterwards
wish to come to court, she would be held excused
from bearing Anne's train and would always walk by
her side. That is to say, Mary was to take rank
before every other lady at court, Anne herself
excepted ; she was to have all honour shown to her
as at the height of her former fortune.[1] Even
ladies of the blood royal were obliged occasionally
to bear the queen's train, and the princesses were
not always entitled to walk at the queen's side.
The greatness of the offer shows how much Anne
desired to see Mary at her court.

But Anne had misunderstood Mary's character.
Her opposition to the divorce and to the subsequent
Acts was not due only to her regard for her mother,
nor was her resistance after Catherine's death
influenced by worldly considerations. So when Lady
Shelton besought her with tears to submit to the will
of the king, Mary would give no other answer but
that she wished to obey her father in everything that
was not opposed to her honour and conscience.[2] The

---

[1] E. Chapuis to Charles V., January 21, 1536, *loc. cit.* : "La
concubine a ce que ma envoye dire la dicte princesse luy a fait
gecter la premiere amorse et luy a fait dire par sa tante quest
gouvernante de la dicte princesse que si elle vouloit se demettre
de son obstinacion et obeyr comme une bonne fille a la volente
du Roy son pere quelle luy seroit la meilleure amye du monde et
comme une autre mere et procureroit luy faire avoir ce quelle
scauroit demander, et que si elle vouloit venir en court elle
seroit exemptee luy haulser la quehue de sa robe et si la mes-
neroit tousjours a son couste . . ."

[2] *Ibid.* : "Et ne cesse la dicte gouvernante et a chauldes
larmes de prier la dicte princesse davoir regard aux dictes
affaires a quoy na aultre respondu la dicte princesse synon quil

acceptance of the new statutes she considered contrary to both. She stood up not only for her mother's fair fame, but for the authority of the pope and the tenets of the Church of Rome.

Instead of promises, threats were now tried. Anne wrote to Lady Shelton that she was not to take any further trouble with that obstinate and undutiful girl. All that Anne had hitherto done had been out of charity and pity, and she was indifferent whether Mary submitted or not. She merely wanted to save Mary before she herself should give birth to a son, as she shortly expected to do. For after the birth of a prince—she well knew—the king would not hesitate to punish Mary, and no mercy would be shown to her. This letter Lady Shelton, as if by chance, dropped in Mary's oratory ; and the princess, finding it there, read it and took a copy of it, which she sent to Chapuis.[1] Mary was frightened for a moment, but she did not yield, and a message from Chapuis sustained her courage.

Anne was bitterly disappointed to find that the will she had attempted to bend was as inflexible as her own. She was seen to cry, and was extremely harassed and agitated.[3] Almost her only hope now lay in the pregnancy to which she had alluded in her letter to Lady Shelton. The statement was true ; and if she was lucky enough to bear Henry a son,

ny avoit fille au monde que voulsust estre plus obeissante a son pere en ce quelle pourroit faire saulvant son honneur et sa conscience . . ."

[1] Anne Boleyn to Lady Shelton, Vienna Archives, P.C. 230, i. fol. 34.

he might in his joy forget everything else and once
more return under her sway.   But the excitement of
the last few days had told upon her health, which
constant anxiety had been steadily undermining; and   *Anne*
on the 29th of January—the very day on which her   *miscarries.*
rival and victim was buried—she miscarried in the   *January*
fourth month of her pregnancy.[1]   *29, 1536.*

Henry had no compassion for Anne in her trouble.
He went to her bedside, and gruffly told her that he
now saw that God would not give him a son; then,
rising to leave, he said harshly that when she recovered he would speak to her.   The unhappy woman
passionately exclaimed that her miscarriage was not
her fault.   She had been frightened by the way in
which the Duke of Norfolk had told her of the king's
fall from his horse.   Besides, as her love for the king
was far greater than Catherine's had ever been, she
could not bear to see him making love to others.
This imprudent explanation enraged the king, who
did not admit her right to reprove him for his
unfaithfulness.[2]

[1] E. Chapuis to Charles V., February 10, 1536, Vienna Archives,
P.C. 230, i. fol. 26.

[2] *Ibid.* and Chapuis to Charles V., February 24, 1536, Vienna
Archives, P.C. 230, i. fol. 42: "Sire jentends de plusieurs de
ceste court quil y a passe trois mois que ce Roy na parle dix fois
a la concubine et quant elle abortit il ne luy tint guayres aultres
propoz synon quil voyoit bien que dieu ne luy vouloit donner
enfans masles, et en sen allant comme pour despit il luy dit
assez de male grace que aprez quelle seroit releve quil parleroit
a elle et me semble que la dicte concubyne disoit deux choses
estre en cause du dict inconvenient, lune la chute du Roy, lautre
pour ce que lamour quelle luy pourtoit estoit trop plus grande

Anne had alluded to a fact of which the whole court had lately become aware. The king was making love to Mistress Jane Seymour, or Seamer, the daughter of Sir John Seamer of Wolfhall in Wiltshire. In a letter to Antoine Perrenot, the son of the lord keeper Granvelle, she was described by her ally and friend Eustache Chapuis. Writing on the 18th of May, 1536, Chapuis says that the emperor, or my lord the chancellor, may wish to hear something of the new friend of the king. "She is the sister," he continues, "of a certain Edward Semel, who has been in the service of his majesty [the emperor]; she is of middle height, and nobody thinks that she has much beauty. Her complexion is so whitish that she may be called rather pale. She is a little over twenty-five. You may imagine whether, being an English-woman, and having been so long at court, she would not hold it a sin to be still a maid. At which this king will perhaps be rather pleased. . . . for he may marry her on condition that she is a virgin, and when he wants a divorce he will find plenty of witnesses to the contrary. The said Semel is not very intelligent, and is said to be rather haughty. She was formerly in the service of the good queen [Catherine], and seems to bear great good-will and respect to the princess. I am not sure whether later on the honours

plus fervente que celle de la feue Royne, de sorte que le cueur luy rompoit quant elle veoit quil en aimoyt des autres. Duquel propoz le dict Roy a este fort marry et en fait bien le semblant veu que ces jours de feste et bonne chiere yl est yci et laissa lautre a Grinuich la ou autrefois ne la pouvoit habandoner une heure."

heaped on her will not make her change her
mind." [1]

Chapuis added a few remarks which cannot be
decently translated, and Perrenot, while deciphering
the letter, interspersed it with glosses of his own,
which, while they do not speak in favour of the
propriety of the future cardinal, show that he had no
very exalted opinion of Jane's virtue.

The account given by Chapuis to the secretary
seems upon the whole to have been correct. If we
may judge by her portraits, Jane was indeed very
pale, and by no means remarkably handsome. There
is nothing in her career which indicates superior
intelligence ; and although Henry necessarily affected
to believe in her virtue, she was no better than the
other young women of a coarse and dissolute court.

But she had a very great advantage. Nearly the
whole court favoured her, and the most intimate
servants of the king instructed her how to humour
him. The consequence was that she played her game
more skilfully than any of her predecessors (with the
exception of Anne) had done. While trying to
fascinate Henry, and to be as much as possible in his
company, she resisted his wishes, and made a great
profession of high principles.[2] That he believed in
her sincerity is improbable, his opinion of others
being always extremely low. But he was as well
pleased with a decent appearance of virtue as with

[1] E. Chapuis to Antoine Perrenot, May 18, 1536, Vienna
Archives, P.C. 230, ii. fol. 20.

[2] E. Chapuis to Charles V., April 1, 1536, Vienna Archives,
P.C. 230, i. fol. 50.

CHAP. XV. virtue itself, which he had been taught by Catherine
to associate with many disagreeable characteristics.
Jane's influence, therefore, increased, and the whole
party of Anne became seriously alarmed.[1]

*Divided
councils of
the mal-
contents.*
The malcontents were highly pleased; but their
councils were divided. Those who were nearest the
court hoped that, by the aid of Mistress Seymour, they
might effect their purpose without having recourse to
open rebellion. The other party, on the contrary,
thought that their hopes had been too often deceived,
and that the safest plan would be to rise in the spring.
Chapuis, who had not yet received new instructions,
did not wish to commit himself: he favoured neither
the one opinion nor the other, but prepared quietly
for the flight of Mary and for his own safety in case
of a rupture.[2]

*Henry
alienated
from
Anne.*
Before Anne's miscarriage, a few days after
Catherine's death, the king said in strict confidence to
one of his most trusted servants (so Chapuis was
informed by Lord and Lady Exeter) that he had been
driven by sorcery to marry Anne, and that he
thought such a marriage could not be valid. God
himself clearly showed its invalidity by not granting

[1] E. Chapuis to N. de Granvelle, March 18, 1536, Vienna
Archives, P.C. 230, ii. fol. 10 : "Les nouvelles amours de ce roy
avec la demoyselle dont ait cydevant escript vont tousiours en
avant a la grosse raige de la concubyne."

[2] E. Chapuis to Charles V., January 29, 1536, *loc. cit.* ; and
E. Chapuis to Antoine Perrenot, January 29, 1536, Vienna
Archives, P.C. 230, ii. fol. 1 : "Si le cas me preignoit bien
comme ceulx cy sont barbares et diaboliques vous verriez de
terribles exclandres toutesfois le mandant sa maieste lon post-
posera le tout, je dis de mon couste."

him male offspring.[1]   When Anne recovered from her
confinement, Henry continued to treat her with
marked coldness.   She had been accustomed to follow
him wherever he went; now she had to remain at
Greenwich while he spent with his courtiers a merry
shrove-tide in London.[2]   The altered demeanour of
the king towards Anne was generally remarked, and
held to bode no good to her.

Anne's former allies, the French, were now among   *Francis*
her most active enemies.   As soon as Francis I. had   *ceases to*
received du Bellay's letters, containing a copy of the   *uphold*
Henry at
proposed sentence, he had sent off a courier to Rome   *Rome.*
with instructions to his ambassadors.   They were   *December*
3, 1535.
ordered not to interfere in favour of Henry: whether
the sentence against him was issued or not, whether
it was severe or mild, whether it deprived him of his
kingdom or only laid him under spiritual censures,
was all the same to the King of France.   The letter
reached Rome on the evening of the 9th of December,
and was read by du Bellay with mingled wonder and
dismay.   The tone of his reply shows how sorry he

---

[1] E. Chapuis to Charles V., January 29, 1536, *loc. cit.*: " A ce
matin lon mest venu dire de la part de la dame mencionne en
mes lectres du six de novembre et de son mariz quilz estoient
advertiz dung des principaulx de court que ce Roy avoit deu dire
a quelcung par grand secret et comme en confession quil avoit
faict ce mariaige seduict et contrainct de sortileges et que a ceste
cause yl tenoit ce dict mariaige nul et que bien le monstroit dieu
que ne leur permectoit avoir lignee masculine et quil tenoit quil
en pouvoit prendre une autre, ce quil donnoit a entendre avoyt
envie de faire.   La chose mest bien difficile a croyre, oyres
quelle soit venue de bon lieu."

[2] E. Chapuis to Charles V., February 24, 1536, *loc. cit.*

CHAP. XV. was that he could not use the influence of Francis
on behalf of Henry and Anne.[1]

December
10, 1535.   On the day after the courier arrived at Rome a
consistory was held about the English business, and
the pope caused an altered draft of the sentence
to be read to the cardinals. In sending a copy of
this draft to their king du Bellay and Denonville
wrote : " We have followed your orders point by point.
The thing appears to everybody to be badly drawn up
and full of danger for the future, but it is according
to your wishes. We presume you are content that
the sentence should be on the one hand so severe
and on the other so unjust, that you may be able to
make such use of it as your affairs require. If this
be so, your intention has been very well fulfilled." [2]

To the Cardinal of Lorraine and the Cardinal of

---

[1] Cardinal du Bellay to the Cardinals of Lorraine and of
Tournon, December 22, 1535, Paris. Bibl. Nat. MSS. Français,
vol. 5,499, fol. 275-6 : " Lequel Trany estoit pour faire ce que les
serviteurs du Roy luy eussent dict et la pluspart des aultres avec
et jen avois seurete . . . . mais ayant la nuict precedente et a
propoz receu ses lettres du troysieme je suyvy son intention car
nottez que jeusse peu faire tourner le de sur ung coste ou sur
lautre " . . . . " le jour du feu Trivolce sen sceut tres bien
exempter depuis que je luy euz faict responce quil ny alloit de
linterestz du Roy ne pro ne contra."

[2] Cardinal du Bellay and C. de Denonville to Francis 1.,
December 22, 1535, Paris Bibl. Nat. MSS. Français, vol. 5,499,
fols. 269 b : " Le lendemain au matin fut mis sur le bureau
laffaire dangleterre dont nous estions en grande peine. Et en
icelluy y avons suivy vostre intention de poinct en poinct. . . .
La chose semble a chascun mal digeree et de mauvaise consequence, mais elle est selon vostre desseing ; et presuposons bien
que Vous estes content que la sentence soit si aigre dune part et
si injuste de lautre que Vous puissiez Vous en ayder selon ce que

Tournon, du Bellay wrote at greater length, giving
them an account of what had passed in the consistory.
The pope was extremely irritated on finding that in
the opinion of nearly all the cardinals the sentence was
too severe, and that they thought he ought not to
issue it without first citing Henry to appear and show
cause why he should not be excommunicated for having
killed Cardinal Fisher.[1]   Cardinal Schomberg was in
favour of proceeding at once, but he thought the
terms of the bull too severe.[2]   Schomberg, Contarini,
and Gonzaga represented to the pope that times were
changed, that the papal power was somewhat less
than it had been, and that regard ought to be had
to the irritation which such a sentence might produce
among foreign nations.[3] This roused the anger of the
pope.   God, he declared, had placed him above
emperor, kings, and princes, and he fully intended to
make use of his power.[4]   As to the sentence, it was a
perfectly proper one ; it had been drawn up by men

The
sentence
against
Henry
discussed
by the
pope and
the
cardinals.

Vos affaires le requerent. Si ainsi est Vous avez tres bien
Vostre intendit."

[1] Cardinal du Bellay to the Cardinals of Lorraine and of
Tournon, December 22, 1535, Paris, Bibl. Nat. MSS. Français,
vol. 5,499, fol. 275-6 : " Jusques a Capua tous sont dadvis que non
debere Incipi ab executione et que citatio seu monitio (?) deberet
procedere sentenciam maxime quum ageretur de novo et graviore
delicto pro quo nondum Rex fuerat citatus."

[2] *Ibid.* : " Capua mitiga encore plus les paines mais tolust la
citation. . ."

[3] *Ibid* : " Et aux aultres qui estoient Capua, Contarin, et
Mantue pour ce quilz vouloient que, habenda esset Ratio
temporum quum imminuta sit aliquo modo auctoritas sedis
apostolice . . . . . . Censuimus agendum nec provocandas omnes
nationes In nos ob interdicta commertia."

[4] *Ibid.* : " Et sur ce point fut le grand feu de la colere. Et

whose fitness for the task was above suspicion.[1] Some cardinal—probably du Bellay—said the emperor and the King of France ought first to be consulted, but the pope answered that he had consulted them long ago. The emperor had replied that, if the pope did his duty, he would show by executing the sentence to the utmost of his ability that he was the true friend and protector of the Holy See. And the king, to give him his due, after having greatly blamed the abominable misdeeds of the King of England, had promised as much if the emperor kept his word.[2]

Du Bellay was taken aback by this statement, having never heard that any such promise had been made by Francis. But of late he had not been very well informed as to the policy of the king, and, mindful of his instructions, he remained silent.[3]

Schomberg, aided by Campeggio, tried to induce

Dieu scait sil menassa bien et reitera de nespargner empereurs, Roys et princes puisque Dieu la constitue sur eulx."

[1] Cardinal du Bellay to the Cardinals of Lorraine and of Tournon, December 22, 1535, Paris, Bibl. Nat. MSS. Français, vol. 5,499, fol. 275-6 : " Pour conclusion quil falloit quelle se despeschast et incontinent comme bien faicte, bien digeree et bien couchee et en bons termes quoy quon en dist et ne quon laccusast que plusieurs estoient davis de limer le style, et quil y avoit commis viros omni ecceptione majores et sic est finis."

[2] Ibid. : " Pource quaulcuns vouloient quon en advertist premierement le Roy et lempereur il sen courouca et dist lavoir desia faict et que le dict empereur avoit respondu que la ou il seroit icy procedde comme il doibt il monstreroit en lexecution quil est vrai advocat et protecteur de leglise et quil se y mecteroit jusques au bout. Et le Roy, et ne et ipsum frauderet sua laude, apres avoir fort blasme et abominez les meschancetez faict par le Roy dangleterre en avoyt promis aultant que dessuz moyennant que le dict empereur ny faillist de son coste."

[3] Ibid. : " Si cela est vray je ne scais, car Monsr de Mascons

du Bellay to explain the position of the King of
France in this matter. Campeggio urged that in
issuing the sentence the pope ought not to offend
those princes who had some understanding with
Henry, especially the most Christian king. It was
said that the King of France was a great friend of
the King of England, and that they had concluded a
treaty of alliance which both kept secret.[1] Schomberg made a more direct effort to compel du Bellay
to reveal what he knew. He reminded the consistory of the promptitude with which Pope Clement
had acted in a moment of difficulty. Some persons
had made a show of promoting a reconciliation of
Henry with the Church, and had pretended that he
was sending a mandate, when in reality astute men
were being despatched to enter a protest. Clement,
perceiving this, without waiting for the customary
forms, had pronounced sentence, deceiving thereby
those who had hoped to take him in.[2]

At this very direct attack du Bellay fired up. He

ne moy nen sceumes jamais rien entendre de dela quelques instances que nous ayons faictes."
  [1] Cardinal du Bellay to the Cardinals of Lorraine and of
Tournon, December 22, 1535, Paris, Bibl. Nat. MSS. Français
vol. 5,499, fol. 275-6 : " Campiege disoit considerandum esse ne
fœderati principes lederentur presertim Rex Christianissimus,
quem audiebat magnam amicitiam habere cum Rege Anglo et
inter eos aliqua fœdera esse et pacta, qua ipse nesciret qua essent,
ut esse solent inter principes amicos secreta."
  [2] Ibid. : " Capua en persuadant de incontinent donner la
sentence dist : ne nobis, inquit, accidat ut accidisset Clementi
nisi mature providisset. Clam quum essent qui ostenderent velle
Illum Reconciliare ecclesie et fingeretur mittendum mandatum,
interim huc mitebat clam viros astutos qui facerent protestationes
quod previdens Clemens subitum nec expectatis terminis pro-

first ironically thanked Campeggio for the care with which he watched over the interests of Francis. Then he launched into a long discourse, defending his own action and that of his king. He had begun to speak of the meeting of Marseilles, and was saying that all would have been satisfactorily arranged but for the Bishop of Winchester, when the pope broke in—" And nevertheless," he exclaimed, " that very scoundrel, that accursed man, is even now ambassador with the most Christian king."[1] Du Bellay went on to say that at Calais Francis had withdrawn from the negotiations about the marriage of Angoulême and Elizabeth, which would have made the young duke the future King of England, because Henry insisted on certain articles in the treaty that might ultimately have brought about some danger of discord between the Holy See and France.[2] " No," interrupted the pope, " your king broke off because the King of England wanted to have the Duke of Angoulême as a hostage. That I know perfectly well." The cardinal, according to his own account, replied with no more nuntiavit sententiam, illis deceptis qui his artibus eum volebant fallere. Voila ses motz."

[1] Cardinal du Bellay to the Cardinals of Lorraine and of Tournon, December 22, 1535, Paris, Bibl. Nat. MSS. Français, vol. 5,499, fol. 275-6 : "Et tamen, dist le pape perseverant en sa collere ou furie en tous propoz et contre chacun, ille idem nebulo ille maledictus vir etiam nunc est orator apud regem christianissimum."

[2] *Ibid.* : " Concluant que le Roy avoit laisse a saproprier pour son filz de ung tel Royaulme que celuy dangleterre pour le respect du Sainct Siege pour aultant quaux conditions proposes par le dict Roy dangleterre il y avoit ung article qui de degre en degre a la fin engendroit par indirect quelque dangier de discorde a ladvenir entre ledict Sainct Siege et la France."

moderation than was necessary, and he and the pope
seem to have had a violent quarrel.[1] At last Cardinal
de Cupis, who on that day acted as dean of the
college, managed to quiet the pope.[2] Du Bellay, on
his part, gave up further opposition, and agreed that
the pope might issue the bull without submitting it
once more to the college of cardinals.[3]

The matter remained in suspense for a few weeks,
for Paul III. himself, however incensed against Henry,
could not but feel some misgivings as to the effect
the bull might produce. No public step, therefore,
had been taken when the news of Catherine's death
arrived. This suggested to the pope a possibility of
new combinations; and as he thoroughly mistrusted
du Bellay and du Bellay's friend, Denonville, he sent
for the French secretary, Nicolas Raince, and opened
his mind to him. He simply wished Francis to offer
the hand of his daughter Madeleine to Henry. For the

[1] Cardinal du Bellay to the Cardinals of Lorraine and Tournon,
December 22, 1534, Paris, Bibl. Nat. MSS. Français, vol. 5,499,
fol. 275-6: "Mais la nostre Sainct pere me vint rompre la parolle
disant que le Roy avoit laisse de traicter pour ce que le Roy
dangleterre voulait le duc dangoulesme pour ostage me replicquant
par plusieurs foys et en collere quil le scavoit bien et eust
vouluntiers dict mieulx que moy. A quoy je use en mes
responces dhumilite non plus grande que je debvoye."

[2] *Ibid.* : " Trany faisant le doyen mist peine de le rappaiser de
sorte que pour ce coup nous ne feusmes poinct envoyez au
chasteau Sainct Ange."

[3] Cardinal du Bellay and Denonville to Francis I., December
22, 1535, *loc. cit.* : "Jay faict soubz main que la dicte sentence
afin destre moins valide ne fust plus remise au consistoire et a
nostre Sainct pere arreste en soy quelle passera oultre non en la
forme que je Vous disoy premierement mays en celle que je Vous
envoye le double cotte."

sake of so great a match, Henry might be prepared to
A match
suggested
by
Paul III.
January,
1536.
March,
1536. discard Anne and to return to communion with Rome.[1]
Raince seems to have reported the matter to his
friends at the French court, and in subsequent letters
we find hints that Francis really took up the matter
and felt his ground in England, or at least gave out
that he was doing so.[2]

The fact was, Francis now thoroughly understood
that it was necessary to make a choice; that if he
continued to stand by Henry and Anne he would
entirely lose the good-will of the pope. And as
Henry did not offer him any great advantages, the
choice was soon made. The death of Catherine only
confirmed Francis in his purpose, for Henry, feeling
more secure, became much less tractable. The object
of the new policy of the French king was to bring
about an understanding with the emperor; and he
formally undertook to forsake the King of England
if Charles would satisfy his demands with regard to
Italy. Du Bellay, who was considered too violent
and too friendly to Henry and Anne, was recalled
from Rome;[3] and after his departure the French

---

[1] Nicolas Raince to Cardinal du Bellay, May 23, 1536, Paris,
Bibl. Nat. MSS. Français, vol. 19,577.

[2] N. Raince to Cardinal du Bellay, April 3, 1536, Paris, Bibl.
Nat. MSS. Français, vol. 19,577; and E. Chapuis to Charles V.,
April 1, 1536, *loc. cit.*

[3] Viscount Hanart to the Empress, March 10, 1536, British
Museum, Add. MSS. 28,588, fol. 226: "Anoche despues de
venido de la corte questa a VI leguas de aqui en el delfinado supe
que el cardinal de paris es venido en posta de Roma dice el vulgo
en esta villa que *viene . . . por miedo de sus malas platicas . . . en
perjuycio* de Vras Majestades."

agents with the pope, so far from opposing the issuing
of the sentence, seem (about the end of March) to
have urged the pope publicly to excommunicate the
former ally of their master.   Francis, having ceased
to look for any considerable assistance from Henry,
wished to have the sentence published, that Charles
might be prevented from concluding an alliance with
England.[1]

After the failure of Anne's attempt to subdue
Mary, the princess had not been further molested,
and in some minor points Cromwell had granted the
requests made in her name by Chapuis.   Nevertheless,
feeling uneasy about her safety, the ambassador
went on with his preparations for her flight.   But
towards the end of February he received a message
to the effect that Cromwell desired to have a secret
interview with him at St. Austin's church.   On the
24th Chapuis complied with this request, and the
secretary, after complaining of some news he had
received from France, began to speak of a closer
alliance between Charles and Henry, and urged
Chapuis to propose conditions.[2]   At first the ambassador was somewhat reticent, but after some time he
hinted at four conditions which might form a basis for
negotiation.   What answer would be given, he inquired, if Charles asked, first, that Henry should submit to the pope and acknowledge the power of the
Holy See ? secondly, that the Princess Mary should be
declared legitimate and reinstated in her former rank ?

[1] Charles V. to E. Chapuis, April 13, 1536, Vienna Archives,
P.C. 230, iii. fol. 19.
[2] E. Chapuis to Charles V., February 24, 1536.

thirdly, that the King of England should furnish help
against the Turks? and fourthly, that an offensive and
defensive alliance should be concluded between Charles
and Henry against everybody who might wrong
or attack either?[1]   Cromwell quickly replied that
as to the two latter points there would be no difficulty
whatever; the king wished for such an alliance, and
was ready to help to fight the Turk.   As to the Lady
Mary, this certainly was the proper time to arrange her
affairs; and he felt sure it would be done to Charles's
satisfaction.[2] The first demand presented the only
real difficulty. "Might not the question," he suggested, "be referred to commissioners?"   Chapuis
met this proposal with an absolute refusal; he would
not hear of the matter being referred even to a council
called by the emperor.   Henry must admit the pope's

---

[1] E. Chapuis to Charles V., February 24, 1536: "Je luy
vins a dire de moimesme que pour retourner a renovacion
de intelligence et amitie dont il mavoit parle, si Vostre
Maieste comme prince tres catholique et protecteur de leglise
requeroit prealablement le Roy son maistre de soy remettre
en lobeissance apostolique et reconcilier a lunion de leglise et
pareillement si demandoit Vostre Maieste la princesse estre
declaree legitime et reintegre en son estat et tiercement si Vostre
Maieste requeroit le Roy dangleterre dentrer en lighe contre le
turcq pour y faire entrer la Germanie qua pieca ouffert une tresgrande ayde pour icelle entreprinse pourveu que les autres princes
y entrevinssent et quartement si Vostre Maieste le requerroit
de lighe generale offensive et deffensive contre ceulx que pourroient tenir et avoir tort de lung ou de lautre, quest ce que le dit
Roy son maistre vouldroit respondre et faire sur le tout."

[2] Ibid.: "Au regard de la princesse que maintenant estoit la
propre et opportune sayson dentendre a pourveoir de remedier
aux affaires de la dicte princesse au contantement de Vostre
Maieste et que la porte en estoit ouverte."

authority. Afterwards the points in dispute, with the consent of both parties, might be submitted to a council to be called by the pope. Cromwell did not entirely reject these conditions ; he only remarked that it would be best to begin the negotiations about some minor matter that would lead in the end to the principal question. He thought the emperor might send Chapuis full powers to treat of a reconciliation and alliance.

The French he continued to condemn in strong terms ; and in doing so he used an expression which could not but arrest the attention of the ambassador. He said that the conduct of Francis was resented not only by him and his friends but by the chief of those who were in receipt of French pensions—Norfolk, Suffolk, and Fitzwilliam—nay, even, he added, by the other party and faction. The reference was to Lord Wiltshire ; and the obvious intention of Cromwell was to show that he no longer desired to be associated with the adherents of Anne.[1] He ended by asking Chapuis to be of good cheer with regard both to the rights of the Lady Mary and to all other matters still undecided. Let him remember the wonders that had been accomplished since Cromwell had had the direction of the royal affairs.[2]

Chapuis immediately wrote a detailed account of

[1] E. Chapuis to Charles V., February 24, 1536 : "Et aussy ceulx questoient comme il disoit de lautre part et faction cest assavoir le comte de Vulcher."

[2] *Ibid.* : "Que au surplus eusse bon expoir et que considerasse les merveilles quil avoit yci faictes depuis quil avoit eu le gouvernement des affaires du Roy son maistre."

the conversation to his master, and, pointing out the advantages that might be derived from a reconciliation with England, he asked for further instructions and, if a reconciliation was to be effected, for the necessary powers. The direct route to Italy being unsafe, the courier to whom this despatch was entrusted was obliged to take a roundabout way, and, as the roads at that time of the year were bad, his *March* 29, journey lasted no less than five weeks. At last, on 1536. the 29th of March, he overtook the emperor at Gaeta on his way to Rome.[1]

[1] E. Chapuis to Charles V., February 24, 1536 : Indorsement : "Receues le 29ᵉᵐᵉ de Mars a Gayette."

CHAPTER XVI.

CHARLES V. AND ANNE.

Instruc-tions to Chapuis. February 29, 1536.

On the 28th of February, 1536, Charles V. received a packet containing three letters from Chapuis, dated the 18th of December, the 30th of December, and the 9th of January. He immediately sent the ambassador new instructions. Chapuis was to take up the proposals for a reconciliation and for a closer alliance which had been made by Henry on the 30th of December ; the pretext being that since the queen was dead it might be unnecessary to adopt further measures with regard to the sentence, or to remit the matter to a council, if only Mary were fairly treated. Henry was to be advised that the best way of dealing with the princess would be to arrange for her some honourable marriage. These instructions were not seriously meant, for the emperor, seeing Henry so obstinate about Anne, thought that a good under-standing was in the meantime impossible. But he considered it expedient to seem to be carrying on negotiations. King Francis would hear of them, his insolence would be somewhat checked, and he might even be brought, if he were made sufficiently angry with Henry, to treat with Charles to the advantage of Mary. In any case time would be gained, and when Charles had beaten the French he would be better able to dictate his conditions as to the princess and as to English affairs in general.[1]

New instructions. March 28, 1536. The letter written by Chapuis on the 24th of February changed the emperor's opinion ; and on the day on which he received it new and more detailed instructions were sent to the ambassador. They were highly characteristic of the emperor and of his advisers. Charles had been a staunch friend of Catherine, and even after her death he never admitted that the divorce was legal. In this respect he acted in a perfectly honourable manner, postponing his interest to what he considered right and due to his aunt. But, on the other hand, although he believed that Catherine had been poisoned, although he knew that she had been persecuted at Anne's request, he either thought of her wrongs with perfect composure, or concealed his indignation to suit the exigencies of his policy. He himself, as he had already proved, and as he proved still more decisively at a later period, was so ready to plan and order murders, that he may have felt it would be slightly absurd to resent a murder committed by an adversary. His new instructions to Chapuis were, therefore, a model of cool and able statecraft, as statecraft was understood in the sixteenth century.

As to the four points raised by the ambassador, the difficulties of the first did not seem to the emperor to

---

[1] Charles V. to E. Chapuis, February 29, 1536, Vienna Archives, P.C. 230, iv. fol. 5 ; and Lanz, *Correspondenz Kaiser Karls V.*, vol. ii. p. 212.

be very great. It related to the sentence of divorce
and to the refusal of the annates. If the claims of
the princess were respected, the complications connected with the sentence might be avoided; and
regarding the annates Charles would do his utmost at
the court of Rome to settle the dispute to Henry's
satisfaction. Chapuis was to urge that the princess
should be expressly declared legitimate, and to point
out that this might be done in virtue of the *bona fides
parentum.* If Henry would not concede so much, he
ought at least to let the matter remain in suspense,
and to make no declaration to the contrary. On the
other hand, Mary ought to abandon the hostile tone
she had adopted, and should not ask the emperor to
support her claims by force or to do more than he had
done already. "As long as the king lives," the
emperor wrote, "the said princess cannot pretend to
anything more, nor can we or any other of her relatives proceed much further by asking for other things
in her favour. It matters not what the wrong done
to her late mother may have been. For she cannot
in good conscience insist upon avenging this wrong
on her father or consent to its being done by others,
even if the life of her mother has been, as is suspected, shortened by foul means. If the sentence
about the divorce be executed in order that the king
may forsake his concubine, he may marry somebody
else, while it is quite clear that from the said concubine he can have no progeny that can hereafter
dispute the right of the princess to the succession."[1]

[1] Charles V. to E. Chapuis, March 28, 1536, Vienna Archives,
P.C. 230, iv. fol. 12: "Vivant le dit Roy dangleterre la dicte

CHAP. XVI.   As clear and logical as possible. If at Henry's
death the choice of the nation lay between Mary and
Elizabeth, the former would be pretty sure to succeed.
And as Anne's marriage was invalid, any son she
might have would be illegitimate, and Mary would
still have a right to the crown.   It was, therefore, to
the advantage of Mary and indirectly of Charles that
her father should retain his mistress, and in the
opinion of the emperor this consideration was more
important than any other. So we find the son of
Juana la Loca preaching filial respect, the murderer
of Vogelsberger and so many others inculcating the
duty of forgiving all offences.

But Charles thought that Mary might not be able
to control her feelings ; perhaps, too, he feared that
Henry and Anne, to make quite sure, would prefer to
poison her.   He added, therefore, that if possible a
husband should be found for her out of England.
The Infante Dom Luis of Portugal—brother of the
empress — would be a very suitable match.   The
concubine and her adherents, said Charles, would
be unreasonable if they objected to such a marriage,

princesse ne peult pretendre davantaige ni a aultre action ny
nous et autres ses parents pouvons passer plus avant quant a
requerir dadvantage en sa faveur quoy quil soit des injures faictes
a sa feue mere dont elle ne peut persister en bonne conscience a
la vendicacion contre son dict pere ne encoires consentir quil se
fist quant oires la vie de sa dicte feue mere fut este advancee
sinistrement comme lon sen doubte et si lon veut poursuivre
lexecucion de la sentence dudict divorce affin que le dict Sr Roy
delaisse sa concubyne il se pourra marier marier (*sic*) a aultre
ou il est tout certain et evident que de lad. concubine il ne peut
avoir lignee que empesche le droit de succescion de lad. princesse.''

for the Portuguese were peaceful neighbours. " But," CHAP. XVI.
he continued, " should the concubine not be satisfied
with the proposal either that Mary should be legiti-
mated, or that the matter should be left in suspense
—a proposal which, after all, she and all her adherents
ought to welcome as a means of escape from the
fear and danger in which they now continually are—
and should she claim more for her daughter, or for
the children she may still have, the negotiation must
not for that be broken off. Her ultimate object must
be found out. And after you have made to her such
observations as you think may serve, you shall say
that you will write to us about it, unless indeed the
thing be too exorbitant." [1]

Granvelle here added a few words on the draft of
the letter to the effect that Chapuis was in this
matter to ask for Cromwell's help. He was to communicate the above. If there was anything the
concubine or her adherents were not to know, a
certain sign would be made. And the sign appears
before a paragraph setting forth that if Henry had

---

[1] Charles V. to E. Chapuis, March 28, 1536, Vienna Archives,
P.C. 230, iv. fol. 12 : " Et pourtant quant oires la d^te concubine ne
se vouldroit contenter de lung ou lautre des moyens avantdits de la
declaration ou suspencion que touteffois elle et touts ses adherens
devront tenir pour tres grand bien pour soy quicter de la crainte
et dangier ou continuellement ils sont et oultre ce voulsist
requerir et pretendre plus pour sa fille et au dicts enfans quelle
pourra avoir, ne fault point tant en faire rompre la pratique,
mais assentir du tout ce aussy a quoy elle sarrestera, et aprez
luy avoir remonstre ce que verrez servir aux propoz Vous remectre
a nous en avertir si [non] que la chose soit par troup ex-
horbitante . . ."

CHAP. XVI. already decided to discard Anne and to take somebody else, Chapuis was not to offer too much
opposition, unless the king wanted to marry
a Frenchwoman.[1]

This despatch shows how far Charles was ready to
go. For years he had been the bitterest enemy of
Anne. Now his ambassador was ordered to treat
with her, to negotiate with her a kind of truce,
almost an alliance. So strong were the terms of the
first draft of the letter that Granvelle, fearing Chapuis
might defend Anne even against Henry himself,
warned him that this was to be done only under
certain conditions.

The explanation of all these concessions was indicated in the last two points noted in the instructions.
Charles wanted aid against the Turk, and he wanted
an alliance against Francis ; at least, Henry was to
defend the Low Countries or to give a good sum of
money for the war. The emperor would have found
it quite compatible with his religion to pocket the
proceeds of the sale of the abbey lands ; and had
Anne been able to obtain for him so great a favour,
he would have thanked her for it by smoothing over
her difficulties.

The courier who carried this reply did not travel
more rapidly than the one who had brought the letter
of Chapuis. The consequence was that the ambassador did not receive his new instructions before the

---

[1] Charles V. to E. Chapuis, March 28, 1536, Vienna Archives,
P.C. 230, iv. fol. 12 : " En vous aydant dudict Crumuell . . .
et sil y a chose que doige estre tenue secrete ou dissimulee a
la dicte concubine ou ses adherens il sen usera selon ce +."

15th of April.[1] In the meantime a good deal had
happened to change the situation.

The influence of Jane Seymour had greatly
increased. By the end of February her brother
Edward Seymour had been made a gentleman of the
king's privy chamber.[2] In the middle of March,
when Jane was with the court at Greenwich, Henry
sent her from London a letter and a purse full of
sovereigns. This gave her an opportunity of making
a fine show of virtue. She took the king's letter,
kissed it in token of respect and devotion, but
returned it unopened ; then, falling on her knees, she
charged the gentleman who had brought it to do the
same to the king, and to beseech him in her name to
remember that she was a gentlewoman sprung from
a good and honourable stock, free from any taint
whatever. She had no greater treasure in this
world than her honour ; not even fear of death
would make her forget it. She would not take the
purse, but said that if the king wanted to make her
a present, let it be when God should send her some
good and honest husband.[3] The gentleman, who

*Henry
and Jane
Seymour.
February,
1536.
March,
1536.*

---

[1] E. Chapuis to Charles V., April 21, 1536, Vienna Archives,
P.C. 230, i. fol. 58.

[2] E. Chapuis to N. de Granvelle, March 18, 1536, *loc. cit.*

[3] E. Chapuis to Charles V., April 1, 1536, *loc. cit.* : "Sire tout
a cest instant la marquise ma envoye dire ce que desia mavoit
affirme maistre heliot ascavoir que ses jours passez estant ce Roy
en ceste ville, et la demoyselle maistresse semel laquelle yl sert
a grynuitz yl luy envoya une bourse pleine de souverains ensemble une lectre et que la dicte demoyselle ayant baise la lectre
la retourna au messagier sans la vouloir ouvrir et se gectant a
genoulx elle supplia au dict messagier vouloir supplier au Roy

seems to have been a friend of Jane, returned to
Henry with the purse and the letter, and delivered
the lady's message. The king was by no means
displeased; the next time he saw her he greatly
praised the modest and prudent answer she had sent
him. She had acted most virtuously, he said; and
to give her full proof that the love he bore her was
honest, henceforward he would not speak to her
except in the presence of some of her relatives.
That the good king might suffer no loss by his
scrupulous delicacy, Cromwell had to give up a room
he occupied in the palace. In this room, which had
the advantage of being accessible by a secret passage,
Sir Edward Seymour and his wife were lodged, and
there Jane received her lover.[1]

Henry was probably not aware that the highly
moral speeches of Jane were not even of her own

de sa part vouloir considerer par sa prudence quelle estoit gentil-
feme issue de bons et hounorables parens sans nul reproche et
quelle navoit plus grande richesse en ce monde que son honneur,
lequel pour mille mors elle ne vouldroit blesser et que syl luy
vouloit faire quelque present dargent elle luy supplioit que ce
fust quand dieu luy enverroit quelque bon party de mariaige."

[1] E. Chapuis to Charles V., April 1, 1536, *loc. cit.*: "Sire
icelle marquise ma envoye dire que par ce lamour et fantaisie dicelluy Roy sestoit augmente vers la dicte demoiselle
merveilleusement et quil luy avoit dit quelle en avoit use tres
vertueusement et que pour luy donner a cognoistre quil ne
laymoit synon damour honneste il ne deliberoit desormais de
parler avec elle synon en presence de quelqun de ses parens et a
ceste cause le dict Roy a faict desloger maistre cremuel dune
chambre a laquelle le dict Seigneur Roy peut aller par certaines
galleries sans estre veu ne appercu, et illec a losge laisne frere de
la dicte damoyselle avec sa femme pour illec faire venir la dite
demoyselle . . ."

invention, but that she was taught by his attendants
how to behave. Sir Nicholas Carew, Sir Thomas Eliot
and other intimate servants of the king warned her
not to yield to Henry unless he married her, and
Jane was wise enough to follow their advice. At a   *Intrigue*
given moment, they further urged, she was to tell the   *against*
  Anne.
king that the whole nation held his marriage with
Anne in abomination, and that nobody considered it
valid. All around there were to be people who would
confirm what she said, if the king ordered them on
their allegiance to tell him the truth. For this
purpose the help of Chapuis was desired; and the
Marchioness of Exeter, who kept the ambassador well   *April* 1,
informed of all that went on at court, sent him a   1536.
message on the 1st of April imploring him to lend his
aid.[1]

Chapuis, who had not yet received his new instruc-   *Cromwell*
tions, felt rather inclined to grant the request of Lady   *favours*
  the Im-
Exeter. Since the meeting at Austin friars Cromwell   *perialists.*
had shown himself more and more friendly to the
imperial ambassador and to the imperial party. In
the beginning of March he happened to speak to

[1] E. Chapuis to Charles V., April 1, 1536, *loc. cit.*: "Laquelle
est bien endoctrine de la pluspart des privez du Roy qui hayent
la concubyne quelle ne doije en sorte du monde complaire a la
fantaisie du Roy sy nest par tiltre de mariaige de quoy elle
este toute resolue. Il luy est aussy conseille quelle die hardy-
ment au Roy quelle abhominacion a tout ce peuple de ce mariage
et que nul ne le tient pour legitime et au poinct quelle proposera
la dicte affaire yl ny doit avoir que gens attiltres que propos-
eroient le mesmes pourveu que le Roy les contraigne sur le jure-
ment et fidelites quilz luy ont, et desireroit ladicte Marquise que
moy ou quelque autre de la part de Vostre Maieste tint la main
audict affaire . . ."

Doctor de Lasco, whom Henry wanted to place with Mary ; and the doctor observed that when Cromwell pronounced the princess's name he raised his cap —a mark of respect with which he had never before honoured her.[1]   A little cross of gold which Catherine from her death-bed had sent to Mary, had been taken away by the royal officials.   A few days after speaking to de Lasco, Cromwell had it sent back to the princess.[2]

But Cromwell did more than all this.   In the reply which the English ambassadors at the Saxon court were to make to the Schmalkaldic princes, there was, as we have seen, a paragraph requiring the league to defend the opinion of Luther, Melanchthon and Pomeranus in the matter of the divorce.   This paragraph the ambassadors were obliged to suppress, for they knew that the Lutheran theologians had maintained, and continued to maintain, that the marriage with Catherine was valid.[3]   At first the royal ministers tried to keep the matter secret ; but as it soon began to be talked about, the opinion of the Lutheran divines was laid before a number of bishops and doctors that they might draw up a fitting answer.[4]   This was an excellent opportunity for

[1] E. Chapuis to Charles V., March 7, 1536, Vienna Archives, P.C. 229½, i. fol. 20.

[2] E. Chapuis to Charles V., March 18, 1536, *loc. cit.*

[3] Melanchthon to Camerarius, February 5, and March 30, 1536, and Melanchthon to Th. Vitus, February 6, 1536, *Corpus Reformatorum*, vol. iii. Nos. 1396, 1409, and 1397 ; and Opinion of Lutheran divines, Seckendorf, *De Lutheranismo*, p. 112, etc.

[4] E. Chapuis to Charles V., April 1, 1536, *loc. cit.*: " Aussi sont les dicts prelats en besogne pour responde a certaine escrip-

those among them who were adverse to further
innovation ; and the opportunity was not lost.
Members of the reforming party found themselves in a
very unpleasant position, and the result of the conference was decidedly unfavourable to Protestantism.
Cranmer was unable to restore the credit of his
adherents, for he himself was in disgrace with the king.
At the very time when Henry wished to be reconciled
to Charles, the archbishop had chosen to preach most
violently against what he called the usurpations of
the imperial power, the supremacy of which he
angrily denied.[1]

Seeing the tendency of events, Cromwell apparently
began to think in earnest of the possibility of a
reconciliation with Rome. The "malleus monach-
orum," as he has been called, was heard to protest
against the way in which the abbeys were despoiled.
He took the side of the conservative churchmen
against those who had been hitherto considered Anne's
principal supporters ; and he did so with a boldness
and energy which offended both the vacillating king
and Anne.[2] About the end of March the court was

ture faite par luter et ses compaignons laquelle levesque ambassadeur de ce Roy estant avec eux a envoye par laquelle le
dict luter et ses adherents concluent que le premier mariage fut
tolerable et que fut tel ou non sans nul doubte la princesse estoit
legitime et est vray que le dict ambassadeur pour complaire a son
maistre a escript que combien quil pense que les dits luter et
autres saichent lopposite de ce quilz avoient escript touttefois ilz
ne le ousoint dire pour crainte de Vostre Maieste."

[1] E. Chapuis to Charles V., April 1, 1536, *loc. cit.*; and
Cranmer to Cromwell, March 29 and April 20, 1536, R.O.
Cranmer Correspondence, Nos. 44 and 45.

[2] *Ibid.*

full of rumours regarding a serious quarrel between
Anne and the secretary.

At a dinner given by Chapuis to the Marquis of
Exeter, Lady Kildare, and Lord Montague, the latter
told the ambassador of the ill feeling between
Cromwell and Anne, and mentioned a report that
*A
friendly
conference.* Henry was bent on a new marriage.[1] Shortly afterwards Chapuis had an interview with Cromwell, to
whom he bluntly spoke of what he had heard. If it were
true, he said, the secretary ought to prepare for the
coming struggle better than Wolsey had done. Did
the king really wish to make another marriage, it
would be a very good thing, as all his difficulties
might then be overcome. Cromwell demurely replied
that if the fate of Wolsey overtook him, he would try
to bear it patiently. He had been no promoter of
the marriage with Anne ; he had only found the
means by which it could be accomplished when the
king vehemently desired it. As to a new marriage,
the king in former days had certainly rather loved the
fair sex, but Cromwell thought that henceforward he
would live more chastely and not change again. But
he said this in a way which convinced Chapuis that
he meant the contrary ; as he spoke, he put his hand
before his face to conceal a smile. One thing he

---

[1] E. Chapuis to Charles V., April 1, 1536, *loc. cit.*: " Estant
venu ces jours disner avec moy le jeusne Marquis, la veufve
comtesse de Childra, monsieur de Montagu et certains autres
gentilzhommes ledict sieur de Montagu apres plusieurs quere-
monies du desordre des affaires dyci me vint a dire que la
concubyne et Cremuel estoient en picque et quil se bruyoit de
quelque nouvel mariaige pour ce Roy, que conformoit a ce que
mestoit escript de France. . . ."

assured Chapuis of; if the king re-married, he would
not choose his bride in France. During the whole
interview Cromwell was most friendly; and when
they were about to part, he begged Chapuis to accept
a very fine horse as a gift from him.[1]

After this conversation Chapuis felt pretty sure that
Cromwell would no longer maintain the cause of Anne.
The intrigue which had been proposed by Lady Exeter
seemed, therefore, to have every chance of success;
and the ambassador considered whether he ought not
to become the chief mover in the attempt to drive
" the concubine " from the throne. He saw, however,
that the interests of Mary might be imperilled if Henry
were free to marry again. Accordingly, before
deciding finally, he wrote once more to Mary, and,
placing the two sides of the question before her, asked
to be informed what her wishes were.[2] As he had expected, she immediately replied that she did not care
how her own interests might be affected, if her father
could be saved from the sinful life he was leading.
She wished Chapuis to do as Lady Exeter had desired,
and hoped he would succeed. This decided the
ambassador's course. During the following days he

Chapuis and the intrigue against Anne.

---

[1] E. Chapuis to Charles V., April 1, 1536, *loc. cit.*: " Et
ce me disoit sy froydement quil me donnoit suspicion du
contraire, mesmes que le me disant ne saichant quelle contenance
tenir yl sappoya sur la fenestre ou nous estions mectant
la main devant la bouche pour se garder de soubrire ou pour
le couvrir, disant en apres que dune chose se pouvoient bien
assurer les francois que advenant le cas que le dict Roy son
maistre voulsist autre femme quil ne la yroit sercher vers
eulx. . . ."

[2] *Ibid.*

had several interviews with Cromwell and with the leading conspirators, and some arrangements had been made when the despatches from Charles arrived.[1]

Chapuis receives his new instructions. April 15, 1536. April 16, 1536.

On receipt of the emperor's letters Chapuis sat down to decipher them at once. As they were rather long he had to work until late at night, but he made a short abstract of such points as he was to communicate, and early next morning he went to Cromwell to request that he might have an audience of the king. The secretary, on hearing what Chapuis had to say, was so pleased that he would have liked to open negotiations without delay. But it was Easter Sunday, and Henry, who always shrank from forming a definite judgment, was glad to have a pretext for putting off the audience. Cromwell had to reply that the ambassador would be received on Tuesday the 18th.

Chapuis at Greenwich. April 18, 1536.

The news that Charles was disposed to be on good terms again with Henry was not kept a strict secret. A good many of the courtiers heard of it, while Anne

---

[1] E. Chapuis to Charles V., May 2, 1536, Vienna Archives, P.C. 230, i. fol. 80 : " Sire je tiens Vostre Maieste assez souvenante de ce quescripvis' a icelle au commencement du mois passe touchant les propoz que je tins a maistre Cremuel sur le divorce de ce Roy davec la concubyne. Surquoy, depuis ayant entendu la volunte de la princesse, selon laquelle comme deslors escripviz entendoye me gouverner laquelle volunte estoit que deusse tenir main audict affaire principalement pour lhonneur et descharge de conscience du Roy son pere, et quelle ne socioit en facon du monde que le dict Roy son pere puist avoir hoirs legittimes que luy hostassent la sucession, ne de toutes les injures faictes ne a elle ne a la feue Royne sa mere lesquellee en lhonneur de dieu elle perdonnoit de tresbon cueur a tout le monde, jay tenu plusieurs moyens pour ayder a leffect tant envers ledict maistre Cremuel que diverses autres personnes que me sembloit convenir. . . ."

and her nearest kinsfolk and friends seem to have been
more particularly informed as to the proposed articles.
Consequently, when Chapuis arrived on Tuesday
morning at Greenwich Palace, he was welcomed by a
throng of joyous courtiers, Lord Rochford, Anne's
brother, being foremost among them. With Rochford
the ambassador had a most friendly conversation, the
young lord making loud protestations of his desire for
an alliance between England and the emperor. Even
then, however, as Chapuis remarked, he spoke as a
strong Lutheran—which, of course, was not to the
taste of the imperial minister.

After a short while Cromwell went to greet Chapuis,
and to ask him in Henry's name whether he would
not see the queen and kiss hands. The king would
be pleased if he did so, but left him entirely free.
Chapuis cleverly answered that it might be better to
wait until he had conferred with the king about the
new proposals; and with this opinion Cromwell
agreed. Henry also, when the secretary reported
to him what Chapuis had said, declared himself
satisfied.[1]

The truth is, if Chapuis had thought that he would
have gratified the king and advanced the interests of
his master by allowing himself to be presented to
Anne as queen, he would gladly have gone. As he

---

[1] E. Chapuis to Charles V., April 21, 1536, Vienna Archives,
P.C. 230, i. fol. 58 : " Avant que le Roy sortit pour aller a la
messe Cremuel me vint demander de la part dudict Roy sy vouloit point aller visiter et baiser la dicte concubine, et que en ce
feroit plaisir a icelluy Roy, touteffois quil sen remectoit a ma
voulente. . . ."

wrote to Granvelle, he would have been ready, had
Henry been tractable, to offer, not a pair of candles,
but a hundred, on the altar either of the devil or of
the she-devil. But he had been warned that she was
in disgrace, and that it would be of no use to pay his
court to her.[1]

Coming out of his apartment to go to mass, Henry
plainly showed that the refusal of Chapuis had not
displeased him. He was most gracious to the ambassador. After this the king went on, and
Rochford again placed himself by the side of Chapuis
to acccompany him to the chapel. There was a great
rush after them, for as Anne was also going to mass
she and Chapuis would be brought face to face ; and
the host of idle courtiers were curious to see how they
would behave to each other. Chapuis was placed
close to the door by which Anne was to enter,
probably in order that he might be quite near her.
It had not been observed that after the opening of
the door he would be concealed behind it. Anne,
however, knowing that he was there, turned round
as she passed. He made her a deep bow, and she
responded with as deep and gracious a salute. Then
she swept on to her place at the king's side.[2] A

[1] E. Chapuis to N. de Granvelle, April 24, 1536, Vienna
Archives, P.C. 230, ii. fol. 16 : "Je reffusay de laller visiter
jusques a ce queusse parle au Roy. Si jeusse veu quelque ap-
parence ou espoir en la responce et propoz du Roy je fusse aller
ouffrir non point deux seullement mais cent chandelles au diable
ou diablesse combien que aussy une autre chose men faisoit
perdre lenvye, assavoir quil me fust dit quelle nestoit fort en
grace du Roy. . . ."

[2] E. Chapuis to Charles V., April 21, 1536, loc. cit. : "Je fuz

good many people who had hoped that Chapuis
would be rude to his former enemy were grievously
vexed, and Mary herself was astonished when she
heard that the ambassador of the emperor had bowed
to "that woman."[1]

After mass Henry went to Anne's rooms, where he
was accustomed to dine. The foreign ambassadors
and most of the courtiers followed him, but Chapuis
—with Rochford always at his side—dined with the
principal noblemen in the chamber of presence.
Anne seems to have been disappointed that Chapuis
did not attend her to her apartments, for she asked
the king why he had not come with the other
ambassadors. Henry, annoyed by the question,
answered that Chapuis had good reasons for staying
away.[2] Nevertheless, Anne was resolved to throw in

conduyt a la messe par le sieur de Rocheffort frere de la concubyne et venant le Roy a loffrande yl y eust grand concours de
gens, et une partie pour veoir quelle mine la concubine et moy
nous tiendrons. Elle en usa assez cortoisement car comme jestoys
derrier la porte par ou elle enstroit elle se retournast du tout
pour me faire la reverence conforme a celle que je luy fiz."

[1] E. Chapuis to N. de Granvelle, April 24, 1536, *loc. cit.*:
"Encoires que je ne baississe ne parlasse a la concubyne touteffois
et la princesse et plusieurs autres bon personnaiges ont eu quelque mal a la teste des mutuelles et par honnestete inevitables
reverences que furent faictes a leglise. . . ."

[2] E. Chapuis to Charles V., April 21, 1536, *loc. cit.*: "Apres
la messe le dict Roy sen alla disner au logis et chambre de la
concubine ou tout le monde laccompaigna excepte moy que fuz
conduit par Rocheffort a la chambre de presence dicelluy Roy
ou disna avec touts les principaulx de la court, et a ce que ma
dict quelque homme de bien la dicte concubyne interrogea le Roy
pourquoy nestoit la entre comme faisoyent les autres ambassa-

her lot with the imperial faction; and after dinner she spoke strongly against Francis. "It was a great shame," she said, "that the King of France treated his uncle the duke of Savoy so badly, and intended to invade Milan in order to prevent further action against the Turks." "It seems," she exclaimed, alluding to the infamous disease of Francis, "that the King of France, tired of life on account of his illness, wants to shorten his days by going to war." [1] These remarks were of course repeated, and they were meant to show that there was an open rupture between her and her former friends.

In the afternoon Henry left Anne's rooms, and taking the ambassador into the recess of a window, prepared to hear his communication. When Chapuis had submitted his proposals, Henry broke out into the most extravagant talk, declaring that he would make no concessions, and boasting in a preposterous way about his greatness and power, and about the benefits he had heaped upon Charles. Chapuis, although irritated by this rodomontade, allowed the king to go on, that he might have his fill of vainglory and slowly quiet down. [2] But Henry would

deurs et que icelluy Roy avoit respondu que ce nestoit sans bon respect."

[1] E. Chapuis to Charles V., April 21, 1536, *loc. cit.*: "Ce neantmoings a ce que ma dict personne que affirme lavoir ouy icelle concubyne apres disne deust dire que cestoit grande honte au Roy de France de ainsy traicter son oncle le duc de Savoye et de vouloir movoir guerre contre Milan pour entrerompre lemprinse contre les Turcqs, et quil sembloit proprement que le dit Roy de France ennuye de sa vye a cause de ses maladies a envye dachever par guerre plus brefvement ses jours."

[2] *Ibid.*; and E. Chapuis to N. de Granvelle, April 21, 1536,

not quiet down; he refused to listen to reason, and
insisted, among other things, that Charles should
acknowledge himself to have been altogether in the
wrong, and should either have the papal sentence
quashed or declare that it had been obtained against
justice by threats.[1]

By and by, the king called Cromwell and the Lord
Chancellor Audeley into the recess, and asked Chapuis
to repeat his message to them. When they had
heard it, the ambassador retired and began to speak
with Sir Edward Seymour, keeping, however, a
watchful eye on the little group at the window. He
could soon perceive that there was an acrimonious
dispute between the king and Cromwell. After a
protracted discussion the secretary called out that he
was so thirsty he could not bear it any longer, and,
snorting and puffing with anger, he left the king and
Audeley, and went to sit on a chest where Henry
could not see him.[2]

After a while Henry left the chancellor; and
Chapuis, perceiving that for the moment nothing
more could be done, made ready to depart. Henry
was a little more gracious when the ambassador came

Vienna Archives, P.C. 230, ii. fol. 14: "Pour le saouler de
gloire et non lirriter. . . ."

[1] E. Chapuis to N. de Granvelle, April 21, 1536, *loc. cit.*

[2] E. Chapuis to Charles V., April 21, 1536, *loc. cit.*: "Et la
y eust de la dispute et courroux assez aigre comme il sembloit
entre le dict Roy et Cremuel, et apres ung grand espace de temps
le dict Cremuel romphant et grondisant se part du conclave de
la fenestre ou estoit le dict Roy prenant excuse que estoit tant
altere quil nen pouvoit plus, comme aussy estoit, et se alla asseoir
sur ung coffre hors de laspect dudict Roy."

to take his leave, but he made no concessions. Chapuis was accompanied by many of the courtiers to the gates, where he mounted his horse. They were rather crestfallen, and some of the councillors said plainly that they were very sorry for what had happened. On the road Chapuis was overtaken by Cromwell, who was also riding back to London; and the secretary did not hide his vexation at the obstinacy and folly of the king. He was in a state of such excitement that when he arrived at his lodgings at Roll's house he had to take to his bed, where he remained for several days.[1]

Antoine de Castelnau, Bishop of Tarbes, the resident French ambassador, soon heard of the negotiations *Henry and the French ambassador. April* 19, 1536. opened by Chapuis; so, curious to know what had been the result, he went on the following day to Greenwich. He saw the Duke of Norfolk, who assured him that, whatever the emperor might offer or propose, the king would not withdraw from the alliance with Francis.[2] Afterwards Castelnau was received by the king, who complained that Francis did not show him sufficient respect, and that a special envoy who should have been sent to him long ago

[1] E. Chapuis to Charles V., April 21, 1536, *loc. cit.*; and E. Chapuis to N. de Granvelle, April 21, 1536, *loc. cit.*

[2] Francis I. to J. de Dinteville and A. de Castelnau, April 29, 1536, Paris, Bibl. Nat. MSS. Dupuis, vol. 547, fol. 303: "Le Roy a tres bien entendu . . . les propoz et langaige que luy tint a son arrivee a Grenuic Mr. de Norfort et lasseurance quil luy donna derechef que quelque praticque ou ouverture que le dict Empereur peust faire ne mettre en avant audit Roy dangleterre les choses ne seroient jamais autres quelles ont este par cydevant et sont de present entre son maistre et le dit sieur Roy. . . ."

had not yet arrived. The bishop tried to soothe his anger, and at last the king told him about the mission of Chapuis. The four propositions of the imperial ambassador had now swollen into five, besides curiously altering their nature. The first referred to the day when Charles V. would enter Rome. Secondly, Charles asked Henry to intercede with the French king in favour of the Duke of Savoy. Thirdly, fearing that Francis might invade Milan, Charles begged Henry to help him if he were so attacked. Fourthly, Henry was entreated to forget all that had passed between him and the emperor on account of Catherine, and to renew the old treaties of friendship and confederation. The fifth proposition set forth a demand for aid against the Turk.[1] Henry pretended that as to Savoy

[1] Francis I. to J. de Dinteville and A. de Castelnau, April 29, 1536, Paris, Bibl. Nat. MSS. Dupuis, vol. 547, fol. 303 : "Et pource diront iceulx Evesque de Tarbe et Bailly de Troyes audit sieur Roy dangleterre comme le Roy a tres bien entendu ce que ledit de Tarbe luy a faict scavoir touchant la lettre que luy avoit dernierement escript ledit Empereur contenant les cinq chefs et articles contenuz et declarez es lettres dudit Evesque. Le premier faisant mencion du jour que devoit entrer icelluy Empereur a Romme, le second du faict de la guerre que le Roy faict au duc de Savoye et la requeste que icelluy Empereur faict au dit sieur Roy dangleterre a ce quil veuille interceder envers le Roy pour icelluy duc de luy rendre et restituer ce qui a este gaigne sur luy. Le tiers quil crainct que le Roy luy veuille faire la guerre a la duche de Milan et layde quil luy demande advenant icelluy cas. Le quart quil veuille oblier ce qui est passe entre eux pour raison de sa feue tante, estant a present cessee loccasion, le priant au surplus pour lever et oster tous les suspecons et racines dinimitie et dissentions de vouloir renouveller les viels traites de leur amitie et confederation, et le dernier quil se delibere de dresser une armee contre le turcq

CHAP. XVI. he had replied in a manner quite favourable to Francis. He warned the bishop that Charles was raising a large army with which to repel the French, and advised the king not to advance any further, but to fortify the conquests he had made, and to await the emperor's attack. Castelnau thanked Henry for the friendly feeling he had exhibited, and immediately after his return to London wrote an account of the audience to his master. He added that at this moment Henry seemed most favourably inclined.[1]

Anne's position. Anne's position was now a very strange one. After years of unrelenting hostility the emperor had proposed the terms of a truce which appeared likely, as the death of Catherine had appeared likely, to be of great advantage to her. If she could have had her way, the offers of Charles would have been accepted; and had she been willing to give up Protestantism, she might then have persuaded Henry to submit to the pope, who would have given absolution to both of them and recognised the validity of their marriage from the time of Catherine's death. But it was too late to hope for these great results. New influences were at work—some of them of Anne's own creation— over which she had no control, and which brought her to the scaffold.

When Henry obstinately refused to submit to the pope, it was not only his vanity which was at play; he was impelled also by greed and by fear of rebellion.

pour la diffension de la chrestiennete, priant icelluy Roy dangle-terre de luy vouloir estre pour cest effect contribuable. . . ."

[1] Francis I. to J. de Dinteville and A. de Castelnau, April 29, 1536, Paris, Bibl. Nat. MSS. Dupuis, vol. 547, fol. 303.

By an act of Parliament passed in March a good many abbeys had been dissolved, and their lands vested in the king.[1] His coffers had thus been filled, and he had been enabled to meet the expenses of government and of an extravagant court without exasperating his people by odious taxes. Submission to Rome meant for him the loss of this agreeable and plentiful source of income; it meant retrenchment and economy—a prospect which had no attractions for him. But it meant even more. A good part of the abbey lands seized by the king's officers had been granted away to his servants and courtiers, or to the lords and gentry in the neighbourhood of the confiscated estates. These favoured persons, and others who expected similar bounties, had a direct interest in opposing a reconciliation with the Holy See, which might have endangered the peaceful possession of what they held and cut off all hope of new spoliation. As long as Henry was firmly resolved not to return to communion with Rome, it may have been excellent policy to give away abbey lands, but his generosity at the expense of the church made it very difficult for him to alter his course.

Among those to whom large grants had been made were the Duke of Norfolk, the Duke of Suffolk, and several other recipients of French pensions. They became the leaders of the party opposed to submission to the pope; and as Cromwell had begun to speak against the destruction of the abbeys, and had resisted further grants, they looked upon him as

---

[1] Statutes of the Realm, 27 Henry VIII. cap. 28.

CHAP. XVI. their great enemy.[1] During the illness which kept
Cromwell at Roll's house, Norfolk ruled supreme at
the council board, and he employed his time very
well. The official party without their chief presented but a poor front; they could not thwart so
powerful a peer. The object of Norfolk now was
to throw Henry into the arms of Francis, to make
reconciliation with Charles and with the Holy See
impossible, and to displace the imperialist first
April 22
1536.
secretary. He succeeded so far that on the 22nd
Henry summoned Castelnau to his presence, and
asked him to go to France and explain the whole
position to Francis, and to obtain the speedy conclusion of a treaty of alliance. As Henry seemed
ready to grant terms most advantageous to Francis,
the bishop consented, and returned to London to
prepare for his journey.[2]

Henry was not, however, without misgivings.
Had he, by rejecting the proposals transmitted by
Chapuis, definitively closed the door to a reconciliation with the emperor? That would be
extremely awkward, for if it were made known the
French would become as arrogant as ever. He was
already half sorry for what he had done. Sending
for de Lasco, about whose future service with Mary
he pretended that he wanted to speak, he closely
questioned the doctor as to the way in which
Chapuis had talked since his audience at Green-

---

[1] E. Chapuis to Charles V., April 1, 1536, *loc. cit.*
[2] E. Chapuis to Charles V., April 29, 1536, Vienna Archives,
P.C. 230, i. fol. 78.

wich. He was evidently afraid of the anger of the

ambassador.[1]

It was in this state of mind that Cromwell found his royal master when after his brief illness he returned to court. The secretary had had time to review quietly the whole situation, and he had arrived at the conclusion that vigorous action on his part had become inevitable. By opposing the further destruction of abbeys, by stoutly advocating the imperial alliance and the concessions necessary to obtain it, he had kindled the anger of Henry, of the greedy courtiers, and of the French faction. His position was threatened, Norfolk was gaining on him, and by some means or other he must strengthen his hold over the king. It would be necessary to teach Henry that he could not afford to dispense with his secretary's services. He would have to be confronted by some difficulty which he could hope to dispose of only with the aid of the powerful and complicated organisation over which Cromwell presided.

At this moment there was a difficulty which, if brought to a crisis, might be made to serve. Henry had been so well worked upon by Jane Seymour and her friends that he ardently wished to be rid of a woman with whom he was no longer in love, and who could not bear him the son he desired. He had already on several occasions spoken of his marriage with Anne as invalid, and of his intention to proceed with another divorce. He had assured Jane Seymour that his love for her was honourable, and had clearly

[1] E. Chapuis to N. de Granvelle, April 24, 1536, Vienna Archives, P.C. 230, ii fol. 16.

CHAP. XVI. shown that he intended to marry her.   But, as usual,
he had not courage to strike the blow with his own
hand; he was waiting for some one to take the
responsibility of the deed.

*Why
Anne was
not
divorced.*
Of course Cromwell might have helped to obtain a
divorce; but he saw that it would be neither in his
own nor in the king's interest to proceed in this
manner.   To have applied for a divorce would have
been to proclaim to the world that Henry, on entering
the holy bonds of matrimony, was careless whether
there were impediments or not; it would have been
to raise a very strong suspicion that the scruples of
conscience he had pleaded the first time, were courtly
enough to reappear whenever he wanted to be rid of
a wife. Henry's reputation would have greatly suffered,
and as he knew this himself, although he chafed at
his fetters, he dared not cast them off.   A second
reason—which more especially affected Cromwell—
was that Anne, if she were simply divorced, would
still remain Marchioness of Pembroke, with a very
considerable fortune, and with some devoted friends.
Rochford had gained experience, and showed no
little ability, and he, acting with his sister, might
form a party which would be most hostile to the
secretary.

Besides, a divorce could have been secured by
Norfolk as easily as by Cromwell.   There would
really have been no difficulty at all.   Cranmer would
not have dreamt of disobeying the royal commands;
he did in fact pronounce the marriage to be void.
Of the other bishops one half were bitterly opposed
to Anne, while most of those whose promotion she

had aided were supple courtiers who would do the CHAP. XVI.
king's bidding. Indeed, we hear of some zealous
servant, who, perceiving what was wanted, went on
the 27th of April to consult Stokesley, the bishop of *April* 27,
London, as to whether the marriage between the king 1536.
and Anne was valid or not. Stokesley, although he
hated Anne and the Boleyns, was too cautious to offer
an opinion. He said that he would reply to such a
question only if it were put by the king himself; and
he added that, should the king intend to ask him, he
would like to know beforehand the kind of answer
that was desired.[1]

For all these reasons it was necessary that Anne *Cromwell*
should be got rid of in a quicker and more violent *plots for*
way. Difficulties and dangers were to be invented, *the ruin of*
that Cromwell might save the king from them. Anne *Anne.*
was to be found guilty of such heinous offences that
she would have no opportunity of avenging her
wrongs. Her friends were to be involved in her fall,
and the event was to be associated with horrors that

---

[1] E. Chapuis to Charles V., April 29, 1536, Vienna Archives,
P.C. 230, i. fol. 78: " Le frere de monsieur de Montaguz me dit
hier en disnant que avant hier que levesque de Londres avoit este
interrogue si ce Roy pourroit habandonner la dicte concubyne et
quil nen avoit point voulu dire son adviz ne le diroit a personne
du monde que au seul Roy et que avant de ce faire yl vouldroit
bien espier la fantaisie dudict Roy vuillant innuyr que le dict
Roy pourroit laisser la dicte concubyne toutteffois connaissant
linconstance et mutabilite de ce Roy il ne se vouldroit mectre en
dangier de la dite concubyne. Ledict evesque a este la principale
cause et instrument du premier divorce dont de bon cueur il sen
repent et de meilleur vouldroit poursuivre cestuy mesme a cause
que la dicte concubyne et toute sa race sont si habominablement
lutheriens."

would strike the imagination of the king and withdraw the attention of the public from the intrigue
at the bottom of the scheme. Calamity was to be
brought upon her, too, in a way that would satisfy
the hatred with which she was regarded by the
nation, and take the ground away under the feet of
the conspirators. Thus Cromwell, as he afterwards
told Chapuis, resolved to plot for the ruin of Anne.[1]

[1] E. Chapuis to Charles V., June 6, 1536, Vienna Archives,
P.C. 230, i. fol. 92: "Et que sur le deplesir et courroux quil
avoit eu sur la responce que le Roy son maistre mavoit donne le
tiers jours de pasques il se meist a fantaisie et conspira le dict
affaire . . ."

CHAPTER XVII.

THE ARREST.

WHETHER Henry was at once informed that Anne was to be killed is not certain. Probably he was only told by Cromwell that he was menaced by grave dangers, and that it would be necessary to appoint commissioners to hold special sessions at which offenders against him might be tried. On the 24th of April, in accordance with these representations, the king signed a commission by which the Lord Chancellor Audeley, the Dukes of Norfolk and Suffolk, the Earl of Oxford, lord high chamberlain, the Earl of Westmoreland, the Earl of Wiltshire, lord privy seal, the Earl of Sussex, Lord Sandys, chamberlain of the household, Sir Thomas Cromwell, chief secretary, Sir William Fitzwilliam, treasurer, Sir William Paulet, comptroller of the household, and the nine judges or any four or more of them were empowered to make inquiry as to every kind of treason, by whomsoever committed, and to hold a special session to try the offenders.[1] That this was virtually a death-warrant

Commissioners appointed. April 24, 1536.

---

[1] R.O. Baga de Segretis, Pouch VIII. Membranes 10 and 14.

for Anne, Henry must have known, or at least suspected ; but his conscience remained quiet : the deed would be done by others.

The commission was not made public ; nor was it communicated to the persons to whom it was addressed. That would have been contrary to all the traditions of the Tudor service. It was kept strictly secret ; and only a few chosen instruments were to be employed until the case should be sufficiently prepared. To make out a case against Anne was now the great object of Cromwell, and he began his task with characteristic energy.

Cromwell recovers his influence. The tacit understanding between Henry and Cromwell which led to the signing of the commission restored the secretary to his former influence. When, therefore the Bishop of Tarbes, ready to leave *April* 25, for France, repaired to court on the 25th of April, 1536. and asked for the articles he was to submit to his master, he found that they had not been drawn up ; and he was kept the whole day at Greenwich, the council sitting and debating until late at night.[1] Although Henry, acting on Cromwell's advice, treated the French coldly, he was not prepared to conciliate the emperor, as he showed clearly enough in a despatch sent at this time to Richard Pate, the English ambassador at the court of Charles V. In giving directions for the composition of this despatch —for it was evidently in substance the work of the king—Henry seems to have resolved to have once more what Chapuis had called, a week before, " his fill of glory." He asserted that through his influence

[1] E. Chapuis to Charles V., April 29, 1536, *loc. cit.*

Charles had been made King of Spain and Emperor ;
he rejected and complained of all the conditions
Charles had proposed for a reconciliation ; he protested that he would not be dictated to ; and finally,
in a ciphered paragraph at the end, he instructed
Pate to ascertain the most favourable terms the emperor might be brought to offer.[1] It was an extremely
foolish letter, but Cromwell allowed it to pass, well
knowing that a complete change in the state of affairs
would shortly render it inoperative.   In return for this
concession to the king's vanity, he was allowed to add
to the articles agreed upon with Castelnau certain demands which, as he knew, Francis would never grant.
The consequence was that when the bishop, already
somewhat angry at the delay, returned to court on
the 27th and heard what was proposed, he indignantly   *April* 27,
refused to go to France on such an errand.   For the   1536.
moment there was no further danger of a closer
alliance with Francis.[2]

Cromwell was thus in a position to devote himself   *His*
to the work of collecting evidence against Anne.   *efforts to*
The old stories about her antenuptial misconduct   *obtain*
would not of course suffice.   Even with regard to   *evidence*
irregularities of which she had been accused after   *against*
marriage there was a difficulty ; for by the statute   *Anne.*
passed in the autumn of 1534 any statement capable

[1] Henry VIII. to Richard Pate, April 25, 1536, British
Museum, Harleian MSS. vol. 282, fol. 7 ; and *State Papers*,
vol. vii. p. 683. The editors of the *State Papers* and Mr. N.
Pocock ascribe this letter to the year 1537. That it belongs to
the year 1536 is clear from the letter written by Chapuis on the
21st of April.

[2] E. Chapuis to Charles V., April 29, 1536, *loc. cit.*

of being interpreted as a slander upon the king's issue might be accounted treason, so that people were rather loath to repeat what they might have heard to Anne's discredit. Cromwell decided, therefore, to have her movements watched closely, in the hope that she might be caught in some imprudence. As most of her servants were secretly her enemies, he did not doubt that some of them would gladly give information against her, if they could do so without risking their own lives.

On the 23rd there had been an election to a place in the Order of the Garter, rendered vacant by the death of Lord Abergavenny. Sir Nicholas Carew and Lord Rochford had been candidates for it, and in ordinary circumstances the brother-in-law of the king would certainly have carried the day. But it was Sir Nicholas, Anne's open enemy, who had been elected. This incident, although insignificant in itself, was of great service to Cromwell, for those who disliked Anne began to think that it could not be very dangerous to speak against her, when she had not influence enough even to obtain a favour for her brother. On the day after the election her opponents sent a triumphant and cheering message to Mary.[1]

[1] E. Chapuis to Charles V., April 29, 1536, *loc. cit.*: "Le grand escuyer maistre Caro eust le jour Sainct George lordre de la jarettiere et fust subroge au lieu vacant par la mort de monsieur de Burgain, qua este ung grand crevecueur pour le seigneur de Rocheffort que le poursuyvoit mais encoires plus que la concubyne que na eust le credit le faire donner a son dict frere, et ne tiendra audict escuyer que la dicte concubyne quelque cousine quelle luy soit ne soit desarconnee et ne cesse de conseiller maistresse Semel avec autres conspirateurs pour luy faire une venue et ny a point

It seems to have been Anne's own imprudence
which gave Cromwell his first clue. She was ex-
ceedingly vain; and, like her daughter Elizabeth, *Anne's imprudence.*
who inherited many of the qualities of her strange
character, she delighted in the admiration of men,
and fancied that every man who saw her was fascinated
by her charms. Her courtiers soon found out that
the surest road to her favour was either to tell her that
other men were in love with her, or to pretend that
they were in love with her themselves. She was
extremely coarse, and lived at a most dissolute court;
so that the flattery she asked for was offered in no
very modest terms. Lately, her health had been
giving way, and her mirror had been reminding her
that she was getting rather old and losing her good
looks. This caused her to crave more than ever for
adulation; and her increased coquetry gave rise to
scandalous stories, and provided Cromwell with the
kind of charges he wanted. On the 29th of April, at *Mark Smeton.*
Greenwich, Anne found a certain Mark Smeton, a *April 29, 1536.*
groom of the chamber to Henry, and a player on the
lute, standing in the bow of the window of her
chamber of presence. She went up to him, and,
according to her own statement, asked him why he
was so sad. Smeton replied it was no matter; and
she then said, "You may not look to have me speak
to you as I should to a nobleman, because you be an

quatre jours que luy et certains de la chambre ont mande dire a
la princesse quelle feit bonne chiere et que briefvement sa contre-
partie mectroit de leau au vin car ce Roy estoit desia tres
tant tanne et ennuye de la concubyne qui nestoit possible de
plus."

CHAP. XVII. inferior person." "No, no," Smeton replied, "a look
sufficeth me, and so fare-you-well."[1]

Arrest of Smeton. April 30, 1536.

The conversation seems to have been overheard,
and to have been reported by Cromwell's spies.
Smeton's manner, or that of Anne, had excited suspicion; and when, on the following day, the unhappy musician took his way to London, he was
arrested at Stepney and rigorously examined.[2] It is
not known how much Smeton confessed at this first
examination. He may not have admitted that he had
committed adultery with Anne; but he was no hero,
and fear of the rack or the hope of pardon probably led
him to make statements by which she was seriously
compromised and by which other persons were impli-
cated. He was kept in close confinement at a house
in Stepney, but his arrest and examination were not
immediately made known, for Cromwell wanted further
evidence before striking the blow.

Sir Francis Weston.

Among the friends of Anne there was a young
courtier named Sir Francis Weston, the son of Sir
Richard Weston, under-treasurer of the exchequer.
He had first been a royal page, but had risen to the
rank of groom of the privy chamber, and was now
one of the gentlemen of it. For the last eight years,
by reason of his office, he had resided constantly at
court, and he had obtained a good many grants and
pensions. In May, 1530, he had married Anne, the

[1] Sir William Kingston to Cromwell, Cotton MSS., Otho C.
x. fols. 224-26, printed in Singer's edition of Cavendish's *Life of
Wolsey*, p. 456.

[2] Constantyne's Memorial to Cromwell, *Archæologia*, vol. xxiii.
pp. 63-65 ; and Cronica del Rey Enrico otavo de Ingalaterra.

daughter and heiress of Sir Christopher Pykering; and having thus become a man of considerable property, he was created, at the coronation of Anne, a knight of the Bath.

Another of Anne's friends was Henry Noreys, *Henry* also a gentleman of the king's chamber, and the *Noreys.* keeper of his privy purse. Noreys had been for many years a favourite attendant of Henry. He had at once sided with Anne when she had begun her struggle; and he had been among the foremost of those who had worked the ruin of Wolsey. Ever since the death of the cardinal he had belonged to the little group of personal adherents of the Boleyns. He had married a daughter of Lord Dacres of the South; but having been for some time a widower it had occurred to him that he would please both Henry and Anne if he took as his second wife pretty Margaret Shelton, who, although she had lost her hold on Henry's caprice, had remained at court. So a marriage had been arranged between him and Mistress Margaret. But of late he had become somewhat cold, and Anne attributed his estrangement to jealousy, for she had observed that Sir Francis Weston had been paying rather marked attentions to her cousin. Accordingly, on the 23rd of April she had some private talk with Sir Francis, *April* 23, and upbraided him for making love to Margaret and 1536. for not loving his wife. The young man, knowing how great was her appetite for flattery, answered that he loved some one in her house more than either his wife or Margaret Shelton. Anne eagerly asked who it was, and he replied, " It is yourself." She affected

CHAP. XVII. to be angry, and rebuked him for his boldness ; but
the reprimand cannot have been very terrible, for
Weston continued his talk, and told her that Noreys
also came to her chamber more for her sake than for
that of Madge, as Margaret Shelton was called.[1]

April,
1536.   Finding all this very interesting, Anne took occasion to speak to Noreys, hoping perhaps that he
would gratify her with the same kind of compliments
as those which had been paid to her by Weston.
She asked him why he did not marry her cousin, to
which he replied evasively that he would wait for
some time.   Displeased by this cautious answer,
Anne said he was waiting for dead men's shoes, for if
aught came to the king but good, he would look to
have her.   Noreys, being older and more experienced
than Weston, understood how dangerous a game he
was being made to play.   He strongly protested that
he dared not lift his eyes so high ; if he had any such
thoughts, he would his head were cut off.   Anne
then taunted him with what Weston had told her.
She could undo him if she would, she said.   About
this they seem to have had some words, Noreys being
evidently afraid that he might be drawn into a
perilous position.   Perhaps Anne herself began to
feel uneasy, for she ended the conversation by asking
Noreys to contradict any rumours against her honour.
April 30,   This he consented to do, and on Sunday, the last day
1536.   of April, he told Anne's almoner that he would swear
for the queen that she was a good woman.[2]   Cromwell

[1] Sir W. Kingston to Cromwell, May 3, 1536, British Museum,
Cotton MSS., Otho C. x. fol. 225, printed by Singer, p. 451.

[2] Sir W. Kingston to Cromwell, May 3, 1536, *loc. cit.*

apparently heard of this conversation, and concluded
that the time had almost come for making the case
public. Henry was informed of what was about to
be done, that he might be ready to play his part.

The following day being May Day, a tournament
was held at Greenwich, Henry Noreys and Lord
Rochford being among the challengers. The king
and Anne were present, and seemed to be still on
tolerable terms. When the tilting was over, Henry
bade Anne farewell, and, as had lately become his
custom, rode off towards London. On the way he
called Noreys to his side, and telling him he was
suspected of having committed adultery with the
queen, urged him to make full confession. Although
the king held out hopes of pardon, Noreys refused
to say anything against Anne, and protested that
his relations with her had been perfectly innocent.
Henry then rode away, and Noreys was immediately
arrested, and kept, like Smeton, a close prisoner.[1]
He was taken to the Tower by Sir William Fitzwilliam, who, it was afterwards asserted, tried hard
to persuade him to confess that he was guilty.
Whether, as was further stated, Noreys said anything
that compromised Anne is not known, but he certainly
did not confess that he had committed adultery with
her.[2] Having left him at the Tower—to which
Smeton had been brought about the same time—Sir

---

[1] Constantyne to Cromwell, *Archæologia*, vol. xxiii. pp. 63-65;
and *Histoire de Anne de Boullant*, etc.

[2] Sir E. Baynton to Sir W. Fitzwilliam, British Museum,
Cotton MSS., Otho C. x. fol. 209*b*.

William Fitzwilliam went to Greenwich, where the commissioners were to examine Anne herself.

Anne realises her danger. May 1, 1536.

That evening nothing further was done.   Anne was still treated with the outward respect due to a queen, but she knew that her enemies were working against her, and that she was threatened by the greatest dangers.   At ten o'clock at night she heard that Smeton was confined in the Tower, and shortly afterwards it was reported to her that Noreys had been sent there too.   Combining these facts with Henry's growing coldness to herself, and his increasing affection for Jane Seymour, Anne began to fear that she would have to take the same way.[1]   She was absolutely without means of defence.   Henry had gone to Westminster to be out of the way, and she could not bring her personal influence to bear on him.   The few friends she had were equally out of reach, most of them having gone with the king to London ; so she could do nothing but await her doom.   Even flight was impossible, for had she been able to leave the palace and to go on board a ship—to elude the vigilance of the searchers and to cross the sea—she would not have been safe.   Neither Charles nor Francis would have afforded her an asylum ; her flight would have been taken as a clear proof of guilt, and she would have been given up in accordance with the treaties which forbade the various sovereigns to shelter one another's traitors.

Anne before the council. May 2, 1536.

So passed the night.   On the following morning Anne received a message requesting her to appear before the council.   She obeyed, and was then told of

[1] Sir W. Kingston to Cromwell, British Museum, Cotton MSS., Otho C. x. fol. 224*b*.

the powers given to the royal commissioners. She
was also informed that she was suspected of having
committed adultery with three different persons—
Smeton, Noreys, and a third whose name does not
appear—and that the two former had already confessed
the crime. Her remonstrances and protestations had
no effect.[1] She subsequently described the behaviour
of the commissioners as generally rude. The Duke of
Norfolk, who presided, would not listen to her defence;
Sir William Fitzwilliam seemed the whole time to be
absent in mind; Sir William Paulet alone treated her
with courtesy.[2]

At the end of the interrogatories, the royal com- *Anne*
missioners ordered Anne to be arrested, and she was *arrested and taken*
kept in her apartment until the tide would serve to *to the*
take her to the Tower. At two o'clock her barge was *Tower.*
in readiness, and in broad daylight, exposed to the
gaze of the populace who had assembled on the banks
or in boats and barges, she was carried along the river
to the traitors' gate.[3] She was accompanied by the
Duke of Norfolk, Lord Oxford, and Lord Sandys, with
a detachment of the guard.

[1] Sir William Kingston to Cromwell, May 3, 1536, *loc. cit.*

[2] Sir William Kingston to Cromwell, Cotton MSS., Otho C.
x. fol. 224*b*.

[3] E. Chapuis to Charles V., May 2, 1536, Vienna Archives,
P.C. 230, i. fol. 80: "Laffaire . . . est venue beaulcop mieulx
quasy que personne peust penser et a la plus grande ignominie
de la dicte concubyne laquelle par jugement et pugnicion de dieu
a ete amenee de plein jour dois Grynuych a la tour de ceste ville
de Londres ou elle a este conduicte par le duc de Norphoch, les
deux chambellan du Royaulme et de la chambre et luy a lon
laisse tant seullement quatre femmes . . ."; *Histoire de Anne
de Boullant; Wriothesley's Chronicle of the Tudors*, etc.

Lord Rochford had already been caught in the toils which had been woven for Anne's destruction. He was an able and energetic man, strongly attached to his sister ; and it was foreseen that in so dreadful an emergency he would, if left at large, do everything in his power to save her. So he was arrested towards noon at Westminster, and taken to the Tower.[1] Anne's friends were closely watched, but it was not thought necessary to interfere with the liberty of Lord Wiltshire. He was a mean egotist and coward, and from motives of prudence had always disapproved of his daughter's bold and violent courses. There was, therefore, no reason to fear that he would try to defend her.

*Anne in
the Tower.*
At the Tower Anne was received by Sir William Kingston, the constable, of whom Chapuis had reported that he was wholly devoted to Catherine and Mary. To his keeping she was handed over by the commissioners. Up to this moment she seems to have maintained an appearance of firmness ; but when the gates had shut behind the departing councillors, when she found herself surrounded by the gloomy walls of the Tower, in the custody of the constable, her courage gave way. She realised the full horror of her situation, and as Kingston beckoned to her to proceed, fearful visions of loathsome prison cells rose before her mind. She tremblingly asked Kingston whether

[1] E. Chapuis to Charles V., May 2, 1536, *loc. cit.*: " Le frere de la dicte concubyne nomme Rocheffort a este aussy mis en la dicte tour mais plus de six heures apres les aultres et trois ou quatre heures avant sa dicte seur . . . " ; *Wriothesley's Chronicle ;* and Cromwell to Gardiner and Wallop, May 14, 1536, British Museum, Add. MSS. 25,144, fol. 160.

he was leading her to a dungeon. He reassured her, saying that she was to go to the lodging she had occupied before her coronation. This somewhat relieved her distress. "It is too good for me," she exclaimed. But, the tension of the last hour having been too much for her shattered nerves, she fell on her knees and burst into hysterical fits of laughter and weeping. When she calmed down she was taken to her apartment, where four gentlewomen under the superintendence of Lady Kingston had been deputed to wait on her. Suspecting what had happened to her brother, she made a few anxious inquiries about him, and Kingston, who seems to have felt some pity for her, merely answered that he had left Lord Rochford that morning at Whitehall. She asked that the eucharist might be exposed in a closet near her room, that she might pray for mercy ; and then she began to assert her innocence of the crimes with which she was charged. But these were matters to which Kingston would not listen, and he went away, leaving her to the care of her female gaolers.[1]

The news of Anne's arrest and imprisonment ran like wildfire through the city. It was known that she was accused of having committed adultery with Noreys, or with Noreys and Smeton, and that Lord Rochford and others were somehow involved in the case, but as yet nothing was heard of the charge of incest. Rochford was said to have been arrested for having connived at his sister's evil deeds.[2]

[1] Kingston to Cromwell, May 3, 1536, *loc. cit.*
[2] Roland Buckley to Sir Richard Buckley, May 2, 1536, R.O., Henry VIII., 28th, Bundle II. : "Sir ye shall untherstande

CHAP. XVII.

Public feeling.

The fate which had overtaken Anne excited little sympathy. Even among the Protestants, who formed at this time in England but a small class, there were some who disliked her. The great majority of the people, detesting the changes of recent years, accused her and her family of having plunged England into danger, strife, and misery in order to satisfy their own ambition and greed. The difficulties abroad and the consequent slackness of trade, the severity of the new laws and the rigour with which they were enforced, were held to be due altogether to Anne's ascendancy; and it was expected that with her downfall there would be a total change of policy, which would place England once more in a secure and prosperous condition.

Cranmer.

But there was a man whom the tidings filled with dismay. For some months Cranmer had been ill at ease. The ultra reformers, Anne's friends, had not been favoured since her influence had begun to decay; and the archbishop, who relied chiefly on them, had found himself under a cloud.[1] In the country he

that the queene is in the towere, the ierles of Wyltshyre her father my lorde Rocheforde her brother, maister norres on of the king previe chamber, on maister Markes on of the kings preyve chamber, wyth divers others soundry ladys. The causse of there committing there is of certen hie treson comytyde conscernyng there prynce, that is to saye that maister norres shuld have a doe wyth the queyne and Marke and the other acsesari to the sayme . . . "; and E. Chapuis to Charles V., May 2, 1536, *loc. cit.*: "Le bruyt est que cest pour adultere auquel elle a longuement continue avec ung joueur despinette de sa chambre lequel a este dois ce matin mis en ladicte tour, et maistre Norris le plus prive et familier sommeiller de corps de ce Roy pour non avoir revele les affaires . . ."

[1] Cranmer to Cromwell, April 22, 1536, R.O., Cranmer Letters, No. 45.

received a letter from Cromwell, informing him of the
arrest of Anne and of the reasons for it, and ordering
him to proceed to Lambeth, there to await the king's
pleasure, but not to present himself at court. He
obeyed with a heavy heart, for such an order from
the secretary boded no good, and Cranmer was not
the man to face danger calmly. Next morning, at
Lambeth, he indited a letter to the king, beseeching
him not to visit the faults which might be found in
the queen on the Church she had helped to build up.

The archbishop had just finished writing when he
received a message to appear before the council at
Westminster. Such a message at such a time seemed
even more ominous than Cromwell's letter, but it was
peremptory, and had to be obeyed. Cranmer took his
barge, crossed the river, and went to the star chamber,
where he found the Lord Chancellor Audley, the Earls
of Oxford and Sussex, and Lord Sandys. By the
terms of the commission of the 24th of April they
formed a quorum ; and it is probable that they subjected Cranmer to an examination. But he seems to
have been either unable or unwilling to furnish fresh
evidence against Anne. The commissioners acquainted
him with the proof which they had, or pretended to
have, of her guilt ; and the primate, cowed by the
manner in which he was treated, declared himself
satisfied with it. He returned to Lambeth, and there
added a postscript to his letter, saying he was exceedingly sorry such things could be proved against
the queen.[1]

[1] Cranmer to Henry VIII., May 3, 1536, British Museum,
Cotton MSS., Otho C. x. fol. 225, printed by Burnet, etc.

After this, of course, Cranmer made no attempt to help his former patron. Nor do we hear that her friends at court dared in any way to interfere. The only person who tried to be of service to her was a poor lawyer of Gray's Inn, one Roland Buckley, the brother of a friend of Noreys, Sir Richard Buckley, knight chamberlain of North Wales. As soon as Roland heard of the arrest of Anne and Noreys, he

wrote to Sir Richard, who was in favour with the king, beseeching him to come to court and to intercede on their behalf.[1] The letter was entrusted to one of Sir Richard's servants, who rode in haste towards Wales. But in Shropshire the messenger was stopped and examined, and the letter was taken from him. It was sent to the Bishop of Lichfield, the President of Wales, while Griffith—that was the messenger's name—was retained in gaol at Shrewsbury. The bishop forwarded the letter to Cromwell, and inquired what was to be done, so that Sir Richard never knew of his brother's message until it was too late.[2]

While Anne's friends were prevented from acting in her favour, her enemies laboured to complete her

[1] Roland Buckley to Sir R. Buckley, May 2, 1536, *loc. cit.*: "The are lyke to suffyre, all there morre is the pitte, yff it plesyde good otherwyse I praye you macke you redy in all the haste that can be and come downe to youre prynce for you your seffte may do morre than xx men in your absence, therefore mayke haste for ye may be ther or onny a worde be of theyr deth, when it is onnes knowe that the shall dede all wilbe to latte therefore mayke haste . . ."

[2] Council of Wales to Cromwell, May 7, 1536, R.O., *Cromwell Correspondence*, xxv. No. 2.

ruin. They searched eagerly for evidence against CHAP. XVII. her, and examined every one who seemed likely to know anything to her disadvantage. Sir William Fitzwilliam and Sir William Paulet, aided by Sir Edward Baynton, seem to have distinguished them- selves in this way at Greenwich, where Anne's personal servants had remained.[1] Cromwell went frequently to the Tower, and appears to have prin- cipally conducted such little examination of the prisoners as took place.[2]

Anne herself was not examined any further. At *Arrest of* first orders had been issued that, except in the *Weston.* presence of Lady Kingston, she was to hold no com- munication with the four women deputed to serve her ; but it was soon decided that this would neither be practicable nor expedient. So her attendants were allowed to talk with her, on condition that every- thing of any importance which she might say to them should be reported to the constable. In a state of hysterical excitement Anne was unable to weigh her words and to control her tongue. On the morning after her arrest she spoke of Noreys, and told Mrs. Cosyns, one of her attendants, of the conversation she had had with him. She then talked of Weston, whose indiscretion she seemed greatly to fear. The whole conversation was immediately reported to Kingston, who in his turn sent an account of it to

[1] Sir E. Baynton to Sir W. Fitzwilliam, British Museum, Cotton MSS., Otho C. x. 209*b* ; *Wriothesley's Chronicle*, i. p. 37, etc.

[2] Sir W. Kingston to Cromwell, British Museum, Cotton MSS., Otho C. x. fols. 222 and 224*b*.

Cromwell.[1]   The consequence was that Sir Francis
Weston went to swell the number of the prisoners at
the Tower.[2]

*Arrest of
Bryerton.
May 4,
1536.*
About the same time, on the afternoon of Thursday,
the 4th of May, William Bryerton, one of the gentlemen of the king's chamber, was also arrested.[3]   Like
Weston, Bryerton had grown up at court, where,
before receiving the office he held at the time of his
arrest, he had been a page and a groom of the privy
chamber.   He was of a good family; and his uncle,
Sir William Bryerton, or Brereton, one of Henry's
ablest captains, had done excellent service in Ireland.
As young Bryerton had married a lady of small
fortune—the widow of Sir John Savage—his position
was not equal to that of Weston; but he was able to
make a very good figure at court, and, like other gay
courtiers, he was much in the society of Anne and
her friends.   The immediate occasion of his arrest
does not appear; it may have been some further
indiscretion on the part of Anne, or some statement
wrung from her former servants or others about court.

*Wyatt
and Page.
May 5,
1536.*
On the following day the list of prisoners was
completed by the arrest of Thomas Wyatt, Anne's
cousin, and Sir Richard Page.[4]   Wyatt, it will be

[1] Kingston to Cromwell, May 3, 1536, Cotton MSS., Otho C.
x. fol. 225.

[2] Cromwell to Gardiner and Wallop, May 14, 1536, *loc. cit.*;
and *Histoire de Anne de Boullant.*

[3] *Ibid.*; and Constantyne to Cromwell, *Archæologia*, xxiii.
pp. 63-65.   As to the dates of the arrests, see Appendix, Note F.

[4] Histoire de Anne de Boullant:

> " Maistre Waston et Barton le suivirent,
> Pages et Oviet ce mesme chemin feirent,"

remembered, had been suspected—if not more—of
being Anne's lover before she yielded to the king.
Sir Richard Page, a gentleman of the privy chamber,
had been, like the other prisoners, on very friendly
terms with Anne, to whom he had rendered sundry
little services, which she had requited with gifts and
otherwise.[1] Besides the persons who were actually
sent to prison, a good many others were bound under
heavy fines to present themselves before Cromwell or
before the royal council. They were thus kept in
suspense and fear, and could not exert themselves
in favour of the accused.

It now remained to prepare the indictments against *The*
such of the prisoners as were to be brought to trial. *prisoners*
Besides Anne, five of them were singled out. Mark *who were*
Smeton, who had already confessed that he had com- *to be tried.*
mitted adultery with the queen, was one of them.
It was necessary to bring him publicly to trial, for
his confession was the only direct evidence against
Anne which Cromwell was able to produce. By
promises of pardon he might be induced both to
plead guilty and to tell more than he had yet
told, but condemned he must be. The other four
were Lord Rochford, Noreys, Weston, and Bryerton.
Cromwell fully understood that it would be most
dangerous to allow these men to escape. Had it been
Henry's intention, after the death of Anne, to effect
a reconciliation with Rome, the three last named
might have been allowed to escape ; but if he wished

misprinted by Crapelet; and E. Chapuis to N. de Granvelle,
May 18, 1530, Vienna Archives, P.C. 230, i. fol. 90.
[1] List of Anne's debts, R.O., Henry VIII., Box I.

to keep a middle course it was his interest to eliminate
from the party of the reformation as many as possible
of those who might drive it to extremes, and thereby
force the government to lean to the other side. Besides,
Rochford and Noreys, if released, would certainly try
to avenge their own wrongs and the fate of Anne ;
and they would probably be aided by Weston and
Bryerton. It was deemed advisable, therefore, that
they should all die.

*Wyatt
and Page
escape.*
As to Wyatt, he does not seem to have been on very
intimate terms with Anne for some years. He was
arrested rather that he might give evidence than that
he might be brought to trial ; and a few days after his
imprisonment Cromwell wrote to his father, Sir Henry
Wyatt, that the young man would be spared.[1] It was
decided, too, that Sir Richard Page, who was connected with the Fitzwilliams and the Russells, should
be allowed to escape.

*The bills
of indict-
ment.*

*May 10,
1536.
May 11,
1536.*
The examination of the prisoners producing no
further evidence, the bills of indictment were drawn
up. The original documents are still preserved.
There are two findings of the grand juries of Middlesex
and Kent ; and when read together they tell a very
strange tale. Anne was accused of having repeatedly
committed adultery with Henry Noreys, William
Bryerton, Sir Francis Weston, and Smeton, and of
having been repeatedly guilty of incest with her
brother Lord Rochford. She was also accused of
having conspired with these five men to bring about
the death of the king, and of having said that she did

[1] Sir Henry Wyatt to Cromwell, May 11, 1536, R.O.,
Henry VIII., 28th, Bundle II.

not love him, and that after his death she would marry
one of her lovers. It was set forth, moreover, that
Anne and her confederates had by their misdeeds
brought Henry into contempt and had slandered his
issue, and that the sorrow caused by their treasonable
behaviour had so injured his health as to put his life
in danger.[1]

If we consider this long and heavy charge, its
improbability at once becomes apparent. It is unnecessary to dwell on the extreme corruption and
coarseness which it presupposes in Anne and her
lovers; for of the corruption and coarseness of Henry's
court we have ample proof. But even if it be admitted
that Anne was one of the most depraved women of an
extremely base court, it is most unlikely that she
behaved in the manner described in the two indictments. According to her accusers, she never acted on
impulse, but invariably made cool arrangements with
her lovers as to the place and time when and where
she was to meet them, although, according to the very
detailed accounts presented in the indictments, she
ought to have thought herself unobserved and in no
danger of surprise. She is charged, not with giving
way to temptation gradually, but with plunging at
once into a vicious life; and it is assumed that she was
guilty of adultery within a month after the birth of

*Improba-
bility of
the
charges
against
Anne.*

[1] Indictment found at Westminster, May 10, 1536, R.O.
Baga de Segretis, Pouch VIII. Membrane 7, and Pouch IX.
Membrane 18; and Indictment found at Deptford, May 11,
1536, R.O. Baga de Segretis, Pouch VIII. Membrane 11, and
Pouch IX. Membrane 21, most incorrectly abstracted in the
Appendix to the Third Report of the Deputy Keeper of Public
Records.

Elizabeth, and of incest a month before she was delivered of her stillborn babe. There was no evidence whatever to support such accusations as these.

The second part of the indictment, that which relates to conspiring the king's death, is open to even greater doubt than the first. Towards the end of 1535, and in January, 1536, Anne would have been inconceivably foolish had she wished Henry to die. In November Catherine was still in good health, and if Henry had suddenly died there would have been an immediate rising in favour of her and of her daughter. Anne would not have been able to offer even a semblance of resistance, Cromwell himself would have turned against her, Kingston would have shut the gates of the Tower in her face, and the gaolers at Kimbolton and Hatfield would have been the first to try to obtain forgiveness by raising the banner of Catherine and Mary.

At first sight it may seem that Anne was in less danger after Catherine's death. But Anne's enemies were exasperated by that event, and they drew together even more closely than they had done at any previous period. Besides, Anne had at that time the very best reasons for not risking anything. She was with child, and she knew that if she bore the king a son she would be safe. The pretended conspiracy to murder the king, and the alleged promise to marry one of her lovers, seem to have been nothing more than an amplification of Anne's conversation with Noreys at the end of April—the conversation of which she spoke the day after her committal to the Tower. Such amplifications were too common in the time of the Tudors.

But while I am strongly of opinion that the indictments were drawn up at random, and that there was no trustworthy evidence to sustain the specific charges, I am by no means convinced that Anne did not commit offences quite as grave as most of those of which she was accused. She may have been guilty of crimes which it did not suit the convenience of the government to divulge. At the subsequent trial some hints to this effect were thrown out, and although proof was not adduced they were likely enough to have been true.[1]

CHAP. XVII.

Crimes of which she was not directly accused.

[1] E. Chapuis to Charles V., May 19, 1536, Vienna Archives, P.C. 230, i. fol. 82.

CHAPTER XVIII.

ANNE'S LAST DAYS.

Henry shocks his courtiers.

May 2, 1536.

AFTER leaving Greenwich on May Day, Henry went to York place, his new palace at Westminster. Here he spent the night, and here on the following day Lord Rochford was arrested. It was at York place, too, that Henry had the touching scene with the Duke of Richmond described in a former chapter.

The tears shed by the king over the danger which the Duke of Richmond had escaped did not flow long. They seem to have been the only tears the whole affair drew from his eyes, for on the following day he was in excellent spirits. Although accustomed to dissemble, he could not hide his joy that means had been found to rid him of Anne and to enable him to take a new wife. As he had allowed his exultation to appear at the death of Catherine, so he showed his delight at the coming fate of Anne. Never had the court been so gay as now, when the titular queen and some of the foremost courtiers lay in the Tower awaiting sentence of death. Feasts and banquets followed one another, and the inhabitants of the river-banks were often roused from their sleep by the music which

enlivened Henry as he went home in his barge from
some prolonged festivity.[1]

Notwithstanding the coarseness of the age, notwithstanding the indifference of most people of the time to bloodshed, notwithstanding the hatred with which the Boleyns were regarded, Henry's raptures provoked general disgust. Even his courtiers disapproved of his behaviour, and although they vied with each other in providing amusement for him they spoke contemptuously of his merriment. Among others, the Bishop of Carlisle gave a supper to Henry and to some of the ladies at court. Here the king showed exuberant mirth. He spoke with the bishop of the arrest of Anne, and said he had long foreseen that such would be her end. He had even written a tragedy on the subject; and drawing a book out of his doublet he showed it to the bishop. The latter went next day to see Chapuis and told him of Henry's conduct, using expressions, it seems, not very flattering to the king.[2]

---

[1] E. Chapuis to Charles V., May 19, 1536, *loc. cit.*: "Et desia sonne tres mal aux oreilles du peuple que le dict Roy ayant receu telle ignominie sest monstre beaulcop plus joyeulx depuis la prinse de la dicte putain quil ne feist oncques et est presque continuellement alle banquetter deca et dela avec les dames et quelque fois il est demoure jusques apres mynuit et sen retournant par la riviere la pluspart du temps il estoit accompagne de diverses sortes dinstrument et de lautre part les chantres de sa chambre que faysoient leur debvoir que sentoit fort a linterpretation de plusieurs la joyssance destre quicte de maigre vieille et meschante bague avec expoir de reschargement quest chose fort peculieyre et agreable audict Roy."

[2] *Ibid.*: "Il souppa naguaires avec plusieurs dames en la maison de levesque de Carlion, yl monstra une joye desespere

CHAP. XVIII.   But Henry not only pretended that he had foreseen
all that was happening ; it is evident that he took an
active part in shaping the course of future events.
He was regularly informed of every step taken against
Anne and her associates, and he interfered a good deal
with the proceedings.[1]   Although, as on most other
occasions, it was chiefly about matters of detail he was
asked to decide, his wishes probably influenced the form
in which the indictments were drawn up.

The grand juries. May 9, 1536.   The indictments were to be laid before the two grand
juries of Middlesex and Kent, where the crimes were
said to have been committed.   On the 9th of May
precepts to this effect were addressed to the sheriffs,
Humphrey Monmouth and John Cotes for Middlesex,
and Sir Edward Wotton for Kent.[2]   They immediately
returned a list of jurors, of whom those for Middlesex
were to attend at Westminster, and those for Kent at
Deptford.[3]   That these juries were packed there is no

comme me vint dire le lendemain icelluy evesque et me rapporta
aussy que entre plusieurs propoz que le dict Roy luy avoit tenu
particulierement il luy dict quil y avoit desia longtemps quil
presagissoit lissue de ces affaires et que sur ce yl avoit cy devant
compose une tragedie quil pourtoit avec luy et ce disant icelluy
Roy tira de son seing ung petit livret escript de sa main, mais le
dict evesque ne lit point dedans.   Peut estre que cestoit certaines
ballades que le dict Roy a compose desquelles la putain et son
frere comme de chose inepte et gouffe se gaudissoient que leur
feut objecte pour grand et grief cryme."

[1] Sir William Paulet to Cromwell, May 11, 1536, R.O.,
Cromwell Correspondence, vol. xxxiv. ; etc.

[2] Precept of the justices, May 9, 1536, R.O. Baga de Segretis,
Pouch VIII. Membranes 8 and 12.

[3] List of grand juries, R.O. Baga de Segretis, Pouch VIII.
Membranes 9 and 13.

reason to believe. It would have been quite super-
fluous to take so much trouble, the proceedings before
the grand jury being in such cases considered a mere
formality. Never had a bill presented by the royal
officials of the Tudors been ignored, and the confidence
of the government was so complete that the principal
commissioners did not even attend at the sitting. Only
some of the judges presided ; and before them, on the
10th at Westminster, and on the 11th at Deptford,   *May* 10,
true bills were found.[1]   1536.
                                                    May 11,
Even before the indictments had been found, the   1536.
day for the trial of the four commoners had been fixed.   *The trial*
They were to be tried on the morning of Friday the   *of the*
                                                  common-
12th, at Westminster Hall.[2] On the 11th Cromwell   *ers.*
went to Hampton Court (to which Henry had retired)   *May* 11,
and settled with the king the details of the coming trial,   1536.
returning to town in the evening. No one but the king
and the secretary had anything to do with the final
arrangements. The Duke of Norfolk even, who remained at court on the 11th, knew nothing of what
was to happen on the following day. Afraid to commit
himself, he asked Sir William Paulet how matters stood,
but found him equally ignorant. The duke declared
he would not act without special orders from the king,
and sent a message to that effect to Cromwell.[3] Shortly
afterwards he received the news that he was expected
to sit the next morning.

---

[1] Indictments, R.O. Baga de Segretis, Pouch VIII. Membranes
7 and 11.

[2] Baga de Segretis, Pouch VIII. Membrane 6.

[3] Sir W. Paulet to Cromwell, May 11, 1536, R.O., *Cromwell
Correspondence,* vol. xxxiv.

On Friday morning, then, the court over which Audley presided opened at Westminster Hall. With the exception of one of the judges, Sir Thomas Englefield, all the commissioners sat, Lord Wiltshire among them.[1] The four prisoners were brought up by Sir William Kingston; and when the indictments had been read, they were asked whether they would plead guilty or not. Smeton, having already confessed the adultery, pleaded guilty as to this part of the charge, throwing himself on the mercy of the king. As to the rest of the charge he declared himself innocent. Noreys, Weston, and Bryerton pleaded not guilty to all the charges. A jury was immediately sworn to try the case. Here, I must say, the list looks rather suspicious.[2] Of the twelve knights who composed the jury most were royal officials. Sir Thomas Wharton was comptroller in the north. Sir Richard Tempest, a near kinsman of Anne's aunt and enemy, Lady Boleyn, was steward of Wakefield and constable of Sandale. Sir William Musgrave was constable of Bewcastle and keeper of the park of Plumpton, and had a yearly pension of £20 out of the revenues of Sorby. Moreover, he had signed a bond for 2,000 marks to Cromwell and others the king's officers, payment of which might be demanded. Sir Thomas Palmer was one of the ushers of receipts of the exchequer. Sir Edward Willoughby was keeper of Hendley park. Sir William Sidney had been keeper of the great scales of London. Sir Walter Hungerford was the

---

[1] Baga de Segretis, Pouch VIII. Membrane 1.

[2] Baga de Segretis. Pouch VIII. Membrane 5.

son-in-law of Lord Hussey, Anne's bitter enemy, and
had just obtained from royal favour a writ of sum-
mons to the House of Lords. Sir Giles Alington was
the son-in-law of Lady More, Sir Thomas More's
widow. As to the four others, Sir William Askew,
Robert Dormer, William Drewry, and John Hampden,
I have found no proof of their holding any office or
pension under the crown; but they had all been
justices of the peace in their counties, some even
sheriffs. They were, therefore, men trusted by the
government.

Before such a jury the accused had but small
chance. Even had the jurors felt no prejudice
against Anne and her friends, they could not have
approached the consideration of the case with perfect
impartiality; for they knew that if they acquitted
the three gentlemen they would draw on themselves
the anger of the king and his ministers, and that
in the event of Henry trying to take vengeance for their
verdict they would not find any allies upon whom
they could rely. Besides, in the time of the Tudors it
was the accused person who had to prove his innocence
rather than the king's officers who had to prove his
guilt; and in this instance the prisoners were more
than usually hampered in their defence. Until the
indictments were read in court, they probably did
not know the specific acts with which they were
charged: and it was impossible for them, without
preparation, to recall what had happened on the
days when their offences were said to have been
committed. Their condemnation was inevitable, and
a verdict of guilty was returned on all counts. Sir

*The com-
moners
con-
demned.*

CHAP. XVIII. Christopher Hales, the attorney-general, asked for judgment against Smeton on his own confession, against the other three on the verdict; and the court condemned them to suffer the usual torture and death as traitors.[1]

It was now the turn of Anne and Rochford. But as it had become too late to call together a sufficient number of peers for the following day, their trial had to be postponed to Monday the 15th.[2]

Anne in the Tower. By this time Anne had somewhat recovered from the shock she had received on the day of her arrest. She was quieter, and we hear less of such hysterical attacks as were reported on the 3rd and 4th of May. It seems that she did not quite realise her position. She fancied that she was liked by the greater part of the English people, and hoped that the bishops preferred by her influence would interfere in her favour.[3] She had not even heard of Cranmer's cowardice. As to the past she appears to have been undisturbed by scruples of conscience. She felt no remorse for the part she had taken against Catherine, Fisher, More, and the other martyrs; and at that time, and among persons of her class, any crimes of a different kind which she may have committed were scarcely considered to be morally wrong. What she remembered was her steady kindness to her friends and adherents; and she expressed a firm

---

[1] R.O. Baga de Segretis, Pouch VIII. Membranes 2 and 3.

[2] R.O. Baga de Segretis, Pouch IX. Membranes 14, 16 and 19.

[3] Sir W. Kingston to Cromwell, British Museum, Cotton MSS., Otho C. x. fol. 228.

hope that if she died she would go straight to CHAP. XVIII. heaven.[1]

It was only after she had been several days in the Tower that she heard that her brother lay a prisoner in a cell not far from her. She had probably expected as much, for when Kingston confirmed the news she showed no extraordinary emotion. At the same time she was told of the arrest of Weston, Bryerton, Wyatt, and Page. She manifested no fear of them, but chatted about them very freely with her gaolers. Of the two prisoners who escaped, Wyatt and Page, she seems to have said nothing that could expose them to danger.[2]

Even in this time of dire distress Anne abated nothing of her overbearing temper. She had complained of the rudeness of the councillors at Greenwich; she now expressed her astonishment that they did not wait on her to hear her further defence. She complained, too, of the ladies whom the king had deputed to wait on her, and did not hide her dislike for them.[3] Chapuis she greatly abused, ascribing chiefly to his influence the action that had been taken against her. Ever since he had been at court (on the 18th of April), she said, the king's manner towards her had altered.[4]

---

[1] Sir W. Kingston to Cromwell, British Museum. Cotton MSS., Otho C. x. fol. 225.   [2] *Ibid.*

[3] Sir W. Kingston to Cromwell, British Museum, Cotton MSS. Otho C. x. fol. 225 and 228.

[4] E. Chapuis to N. de Granvelle, May 18, 1536, Vienna Archives, P.C. 230, i. fol. 90 : "Celle que la eu en charge et garde ne men scelera chose du monde, desja des le commencement elle menvoya advertir de quelques choses et entres autres que

CHAP. XVIII.

*Peers
summoned
for the
trial of
Anne and
Rochford.
May 13,
1536.*

In this way Anne spent her days in the Tower until the moment arrived for her trial. On the 13th of May the Duke of Norfolk, who had been named Lord High Steward of England for the occasion,[1] issued a precept to summon twenty-six peers in or near London to appear on the 15th at the Tower, there to decide as a jury between Anne and Lord Rochford on the one hand and the king on the other.[2] The peers thus summoned were the Duke of Suffolk, the Marquis of Exeter, the Earls of Arundel, Oxford, Northumberland, Westmoreland, Derby, Worcester, Rutland, Sussex, and Huntingdon, and the Lords Audeley, Lawarr, Mountague, Morley, Thomas Dacres of the South, Cobham, Maltravers, Powes, Mounteagle, Clinton, Sandys, Wyndsor, Wentworth, Burgh, and Mordaunt.[3]

That this panel was quite fairly chosen I have no doubt. The whole lay peerage at that time consisted of sixty-two persons. Of these, four were women, and two under age. Four of the peers—the Earl of Kent, and Lords Dudley, Say, and Talboys—never sat, being too poor. The Earl of Cumberland and Lord Dacres

---

ladicte Messaline ne pouvoit considerer ne imaginer que personne du monde leust mis en disgrace de ce Roy que moy, car oncques puis que fus en la court le dict Roy ne la regarda de bon oeyl. Bien men prent quelle nest exchappee car selon quelle estoit humaine et piteuse elle meust voulu faire menger aux chiens."

[1] Commission to the Duke of Norfolk, May 12, 1536, R.O. Baga de Segretis, Pouch IX., Membrane 17.

[2] Precept to Ralph Felmingham, May 13, 1536, R.O. Baga de Segretis, Pouch IX., Membrane 16.

[3] Panel of Peers, R.O. Baga de Segretis, Pouch IX., Membrane 15.

of the North were employed on the marches towards CHAP. XVIII.
Scotland, while Lord Lisle was deputy of Calais. The
Duke of Norfolk acted as high steward. Of the remaining forty-six (excluding Lord Rochford and
Lord Wiltshire) several had at their urgent request
been excused from attending the parliament which was
going to open, while twenty-six had been summoned
and had appeared.

Among those who sat, there were, indeed, many
enemies of Anne : the Duke of Suffolk, who had opposed
her from the beginning, the Marquis of Exeter,
Catherine's and Mary's staunch friend, the Earl of
Northumberland, whose former passion for Anne had
been changed into hatred, the Earl of Derby and the
Lords Mountague and Sandys, who had joined the
conspiracy against her. But, on the other hand, such
bitter enemies of Anne as Lord Dacres of the North,
Lord Hussey, Lord Bray, and Lord Darcy had not
been summoned, as they would certainly have been
if it had been thought necessary to have a packed
jury. Probably the Duke of Norfolk omitted no peer
whom he knew to be in or near London.

It was not thought fit that a woman who, according
to the statutes, was still Queen of England, should
be led as a prisoner through the city to Westminster.
Anne and Rochford were, therefore, to be tried in
the Tower, and the great hall was prepared for the
court. A platform was erected, benches were made
for the peers, a dais on which was a raised chair
was spread for the high steward, and barriers were
placed to keep off the crowd.[1]

[1] Wriothesley's *Chronicle of England*, edited by W. D. Hamilton.

On Monday morning, the 15th of May, Norfolk and the peers took their seats.[1] The Lord Chancellor Audley sat next to the duke, for although, as a commoner, he could not officially interfere, he might privately advise the high steward. Sir John Allen, the Lord Mayor, with a deputation of aldermen, wardens, and members of the principal crafts of London, attended by order of the king. The part of the hall not occupied by the court was crowded with people who wanted to see a queen of England tried for adultery and treason.[2]

As soon as the members of the court had taken their places Anne, attended by Lady Kingston and Lady Boleyn, was brought in by Sir William Kingston and Sir Edmund Walsingham, the Lieutenant of the Tower.[3] A chair had been provided for her, and she sat down to hear the indictments read.[4] When the reading was over, and the usual question had been put to her, she pleaded not guilty. On behalf of the crown Sir Christopher Hales argued in favour of the indictments,[5] and he was assisted by Cromwell, who, having formerly been a lawyer, appeared as counsel for the king. They did not keep strictly to the indictments, but heaped accusation upon accusation. Anne's conversation with Noreys (reported by Kingston) was adduced as evidence that she had agreed to marry Noreys after the king's death. From this it appeared

[1] Record of Session, R.O. Baga de Segretis, Pouch IX., Membranes 1—6.   [2] Wriothesley's *Chronicle.*

[3] Record of Session, *loc. cit.*

[4] Wriothesley's *Chronicle ;* and *Histoire de Anne de Boullant.*

[5] Record of Session, *loc. cit.*

that they desired his death ; and this, again, was held to prove that they had conspired to bring it to pass. Besides arguing in this tortuous fashion, Hales and Cromwell brought forward new charges. They accused Anne of having given certain lockets to Noreys, from which they concluded that she had contrived to have Catherine poisoned, and had conspired to bring Mary to the same end. They furthermore asserted that she and her brother had spoken contemptuously of the king, of his literary productions, and of the way in which he dressed, and that she had shown that she was tired of him.

In the presence of immediate danger Anne regained her composure, and defended herself temperately and ably. She denied absolutely the crimes laid to her charge. That she had given money to Weston she admitted ; but she had done the same to several other young courtiers—in their case, as in his, without any criminal intent. Although she was, of course, unable to produce rebutting evidence, she spoke so well, and so thoroughly upset the whole structure of the prosecution, that before an impartial tribunal she would scarcely have been convicted.[1] But her efforts were of no avail.

[1] E. Chapuis to Charles V., May 19, 1536, *loc. cit.*: "Ce principallement dont elle fust chargee estoit davoir cohabite avec son frere et autres complices, quil y avoit promesse entre elle et noris de se espouser aprez le trespas de ce Roy, que denotoit quilz luy desiroient la mort et quelle avoit receu et donne certaines medailles audit Noris que se pouvoynt ainsi interpreter quelle avoyt faict empoysonner la feue Royne et maschine de faire le mesme a la princesse. Lesquelles choses elle nya tottalement et a chacune donna assez coulorie responce, bien confessa elle quelle

CHAP. XVIII. The question which presented itself to the minds of the lords was, not whether she was guilty of the charges contained in the indictments, but whether she was to die or not. This question they answered in the affirmative. After the pleadings they retired, and soon came back with a verdict of guilty.

The Duke of Norfolk thereupon gave sentence that Anne, Queen of England, was to be burnt or beheaded at the king's pleasure. She heard the sentence without shrinking, and having obtained leave to say a few words she declared that she did not fear to die. The thing which grieved her most, she asserted, was that the gentlemen included in the indictments, who were absolutely innocent, should suffer on her account, and all she asked was to be allowed a short time to prepare for death.[1]

avoit donne de largent a Waiston comme aussy elle avoit faict a plusieurs autres jeunes gentilzhommes. Il luy fust aussy objecte et au frere aussy quilz sestoient mouque du Roy et de ses habillemens et quelle en plusieurs facons demonstroit ne aymer le dict Roy ains estre ennuye de lui . . . . . . peut etre que cestoit certaines ballades que le dit Roy a compose desquelles la putain et son frere comme de chose inepte et gouffe se gaudis- soient que leur feut objecte pour grand et grief cryme."

[1] E. Chapuis to Charles V., May 19, 1536, loc. cit.: "La concubyne fust condempnee premierement et avoit ouye sa sentence que fust destre bruslee ou davoir transchee la teste au chois du Roy. Elle tint bonne mine disant quelle se tenoit toute saluee de la mort et que le plus que luy deplesoyt estoit que les susmencionnez questoient innocents et loyaulx au Roy deussent morir pour elle et ne supplia autre chose synon luy donner ung peu despace pour disposer sa conscience;" and Histoire de Anne de Boullant:

" Aprez quilz lont coupable publiee
Et que luy ont peine de mort livree

Kingston and Walsingham then led their prisoner
back to her apartment, and her place at the bar was
taken by her brother. Before his trial began,
however, the Earl of Northumberland was obliged,
by illness, to leave the Tower. He was dying of a
nervous disorder, and it may be that although he
had hated Anne of late most cordially, he felt some
compunction for condemning her to death. The
court went on with its work without him.

Rochford was accused of having on one occasion
remained a long time in Anne's room ; and against
charges of this kind, which were neither authenticated
nor proof of guilt, he defended himself energetically.
To the charge that he had used expressions showing
that he doubted whether Elizabeth was Henry's child,
he made no reply. Rash, overbearing, and mocking
as he and Anne were, he may have uttered some

> Le president millort duc de Norfort
> Pour endurer de lespee leffort
> Ou bien du feu selon le bon vouloir
> Du Roy, na faict semblant de se douloir
>
> .   .   .   .
>
> Car jay tousiours au Roy este fidelle
>
> .   .   .   .
>
> Et pour ce veulx que ce dernier parler
> Ne soit que pour mon honneur consoler
> Et de mon frere et de ceulx que jugez
> Avez a mort, et dhonneur estrangez
> Tant que vouldrois que les peusse deffendre
> Et delivrer pour coupable me rendre
> De mille morts, et puis quil plaist au Roy
> Je recepvray la mort en ceste foy. . . ."

The French poet is mistaken when he says that Anne was
condemned after Rochford. This certainly was not the case.

CHAP. XVIII. such jest ; and he was now to pay for it with his life.[1] In the course of his trial it was asserted that Anne had told Lady Rochford that Henry was no longer able to beget children. This statement, which Cromwell did not wish to be made public, was written on a piece of paper, and handed to the accused, who was forbidden to read it aloud. But Rochford, having become fully aware that there was no hope of pardon, disregarded the prohibition, and loudly proclaimed the contents of the sheet.[2]

After the matter had been argued at great length, Rochford defending himself cleverly and stoutly, the peers were once more called upon to pronounce their verdict, and in answer to Norfolk they found the accused guilty on all counts. Judgment was given,[3] and then Lord Rochford was allowed to speak a few words. He said in general terms that he was

[1] E. Chapuis to Charles V., May 19, 1536, *loc. cit.* : " Le frere fust charge davoir cohabite avec elle par presomption quil sestoit une foys treuve longtemps avec elle et de certaines autres petites folies. Et au tout il respondit si bien que plusieurs des assistens voulurent gaiger dix pour ung quil seroit absoublz . . . . . . il luy fust aussy objecte quil avoit deu semer quelque parolles par lesquelles il mectoit en doubte si la fille de sa sueur estoit fille du Roy a quoy il ne respondit riens."

[2] *Ibid.* : " Je ne veulx omectre quentre autres choses luy fust objecte pour crime que sa sueur la putain avoit dit a sa femme que le Roy nestoit habile en cas de soy copuler avec femme et quil navoit ne vertu ne puissance et ce ne luy voulut lon dire devant le monde mais luy fust monstre par escript avec protestacion quil ne le recita. Mais tout incontinent il declaira laffaire au grand despit de Crumuel et aucuns autres quilz ne vouldroient cet endroit engendrer suspicion que pourroit prejudiquer a la lignee que le dict Roy pretend avoir."

[3] R.O. Baga de Segretis. Pouch IX., Membrane 1—6.

worthy to die, but he craved from the king's mercy CHAP. XVIII. that his debts might be paid out of his fortune, which was by the judgment forfeited to the crown. After this he was taken back to his cell, and the court rose.[1]

The condemnation of Anne had been generally *Change of* expected, but it had been believed that her brother *popular feeling.* would be acquitted. At the trial he defended himself so vigorously and so eloquently, that among the common people who were present wagers were laid at ten to one that he would get off.[2] The fact was that during the last few days there had been a strong revulsion of popular feeling. At first the downfall of the chiefs of the Boleyn faction had been hailed with joy by all whom their pride and insolence

[1] R. O. Baga de Segretis, Pouch IX., Membrane 1—6 : "Le frere apres sa condampnacion dit que puis quil falloit quil morut il ne vouloit plus soubstenir son innocence ains confessay quil avoit bien desservy la mort, seullement supplioit au dict Roy vouloir permectre que de ses biens feussent payez ses debtes quil nomma;" and *Histoire de Anne de Boullant :*

> "Il ne sesmeut ne les juges il blasme
> Mais seulement les prie de tant faire
> Envers le Roy quil veuille satisfaire
> A ses amis qui luy avoient preste
> De leur argent a sa necessite
>
> .   .   .
>
> Et cependant en Dieu deliberoit
> Que de bon cueur ceste mort souffriroit."

[2] *Ibid.* ; and Constantine to Cromwell, *loc. cit.* : "There was said that much money would have been laid that day and that [at ?] greate odds that the Lord Rochford should have been quit. . . ." "I heard say he had escapyd had it not byn for a letter." Was this an allusion to the paper shown to Rochford at the trial? I am inclined to think it was.

had galled, by every one who expected some share in
the plunder that was likely to be divided after such
a catastrophe, and by those who hoped that there
would now be a complete political and religious reaction. It had been assumed that there was some
real foundation for the charges brought against the
prisoners ; beyond a very limited circle no one knew
the exact nature of the crimes of which they were
accused, or the kind of evidence that was to be
adduced in proof.

The trial of the commoners at Westminster disclosed the true state of affairs. For the first time
the English people heard of the charge of incest,
which, even in so corrupt a society as that of Henry's
court, was considered almost incredible. The public,
too, were gravely informed that Henry had taken
the infidelity of the queen so much to heart, had felt
such overwhelming sorrow, that his health had been
injured.[1] This they were told at the very time when
they heard the sounds of rejoicing coming from the
royal barge, when Henry was known to be in unusually
high spirits. Moreover, the king's dallying with Jane
Seymour, which now began to be talked about, raised
a suspicion that Anne was to die in order to make
way for an equally depraved rival. When all these
considerations were added to that feeling of good
nature which impels Englishmen to spare a van-
quished foe and to favour the weaker party, the
unpopularity of Anne soon decreased. Many of
those who had been most furious against her became

---

[1] Indictments found at Westminster and at Deptford, *loc. cit.*

anxious that no harm should be done either to her or to Rochford.[1]

But there was no hope for any of the prisoners. An attempt was made to save Sir Francis Weston, whose family was powerful and rich, and had generally sided against the Boleyns. The French ambassadors are said to have interfered in his favour, but their request—if made—was not granted.[2] On the day after the trial of Anne and Rochford, the five men condemned to suffer death were told to prepare for execution on the following morning.[3] This they did as well as they could. They confessed, made out lists of their debts, and wrote farewell letters to their families, whom, it appears, they were not permitted to see. One of these farewell letters, that of Sir

Execution of the male prisoners.

May 16, 1536.

[1] E. Chapuis to Charles V., May 19, 1536, *loc. cit.*: "Combien que tout le monde dyci soit bien joyeulx de lexecution de la dicte putain touteffois yl y a peu de gens qui ne murmurent et treuvent bien estrange la forme qua este tenue a la procedure et condemnacion delle et des autres et se parle diversement dudict Roy et ne sera pas pour appaiser le monde quand lon sappercevera de ce quest passe et se passe entre luy et maistresse Jehanne Semel;" E. Chapuis to N. de Granvelle, May 18, 1536, *loc. cit.*: "Vous ne veites oncque prince ne autre homme que manifesta plus ses cornes ne que les pourta plus alegrement. Je Vous laisse penser la cause;" and Constantine to Cromwell, *loc. cit.*: "Dean: . . I never heard of the queens that they should be thus handled, George: In good faith neither I; neither yet I never suspected, but I promise you there was much muttering of Queen Anne's death. Dean: There was indeed."

[2] E. Chapuis to Charles V., May 19, 1536, *loc. cit.*: Quelque instance quaye faicte levesque de Tarbes ambassadeur ordinaire de France et le Seigneur de Tinteville lequel arryva yci avant hier pour en saulver ung nomme vaston;" and *Histoire de Anne de Boullant.*

[3] Sir W. Kingston to Cromwell, May 16, 1536, British Museum, Harleian MSS. vol. 283, fol. 134; and Singer's *Cavendish*, p. 459.

CHAP. XVIII. Francis Weston, has been preserved at the Record
Office. It is written at the end of the list of his
debts, amounting in all to about nine hundred pounds.
"Father and mother and wife," it runs, "I shall
humbly desire you for the salvation of my soul to
discharge me of this bill, and for to forgive me of all
my offences that I have done to you, and in especial
my wife, which I desire for the love of God to forgive
me and to pray for me, for I believe prayer will do
me good. God's blessing have my children and mine.
By me a great offender to God."[1]

By royal order the scaffold was prepared, not at
Tyburn, but on Tower Hill; and instead of being
hanged, disembowelled, and quartered, the prisoners
were simply to be beheaded.[2] They were allowed to

[1] Record Office, Henry VIII., Anno 1536-37, Bundle I.

[2] Dr. Lingard and Mr. Froude say that Smeton was hanged,
and the former asserts that " the Portuguese writer is certainly
in error when he supposes Smeaton to have been beheaded."
I think "the Portuguese writer" is right. First of all, there
were no gallows on Tower Hill, and the erection of gallows for
the occasion would have caused no little trouble and expense.
Secondly, the account of " the Portuguese writer" is confirmed by Chapuis in letters to Charles V., May 17 and 19,
1536, *loc. cit* : "Sire ce jourdhui a este tranchee devant la
tour la teste au seigneur de Rochefort et aux quatre autres
susnommes;" by the French account, Paris, Bibl. Nat.
MSS. Dupuis, vol. 373, fol. 111 : "Apres le dict Rocheford
furent decappittez quatre gentilzhommes nommez Messieurs
Westen, Norris premier gentilhomme de la chambre du Roy,
Brecter et Marc;" by the *Histoire de Anne de Boullant:*

> "Sinon que Marc . . .
> . . . . Ainsi finablement
> Apres les quatre et suivant leur chemin,
> Receut le coup de sa piteuse fin;"

and by Hall, Grafton, Holinshed, Wriothesley, and the chronicler
of the Gray Friars.

address the people, who had come in great numbers chap. xviii.
to witness their execution. Except in the case of May 17,
Lord Rochford, of whose words conflicting ver- 1536.
sions remain, their speeches have not been
preserved.[1] So much, however, seems certain, that
the prisoners did not assert their innocence, but that
on the other hand not one of them confessed that he
had been guilty of those offences for which he had
been condemned.[2] The former fact has been held to

[1] The account of Lord Rochford's speech given by Wriothesley
in his *Chronicle of England* (edited by Mr. Hamilton for the
Camden Society) agrees best with : "Ce que dict Millor de
Rochefort. . ." Paris, Bibl. Nat. MSS. Dupuis, vol. 373, fol. 111,
and with the account sent by Chapuis: "Execution criminelle
faicte en angleterre le xvieme (*sic*) de May 1536," Vienna Archives,
P.C. 230, iii. fol. 31.

[2] French account, Paris, Bibl. Nat. MSS. Dupuis, vol. 373, fol.
111 : "Qui ne dirent pas grant chose synon que lon priast Dieu
pour eulx et quilz prenoient la mort en gre ;" *Histoire de Anne
de Boullant :*

> " Les quatre qui restent encores apres
>   Ne dirent riens comme si par expres
>   A Rochefort eussent donne creance
>   De parler seul selon leur conscience
>   Sinon que Marc qui tousiours persistoit
>   En son propoz et au peuple attestoit
>   Que telle mort recevoit justement
>   Pour ses meffaictz . . . . . ;"

and Constantine to Cromwell, *loc. cit.* Constantine says that he
was present at the execution and "heard them and wrote every
worde they spake." According to Constantine, Noreys was silent ;
Bryerton said : "I have deserved to die if it were a thousand
deaths ; but the cause whereof I die judge ye not. If ye judge,
judge the best " ; Mark Smeton : "Masters, I pray you all pray
for me for I have deserved the death ;" and Weston : "I had
thought to live in abomination yet this twenty or thirty years

CHAP XVIII. prove that they virtually admitted their guilt; but this is not a legitimate inference. On such occasions condemned persons were permitted to speak only if they promised not to say anything against the king or in opposition to the sentence they had received; and up to the last moment the government had very effectual means of enforcing the covenant. For it might interrupt the execution, and order an offender to be hanged, drawn, and quartered; or his family might be made to smart for the violation of his pledge. Hence scarcely any of Henry's victims dared to maintain their innocence. When Lady Salisbury did so in 1541 she was considered by the government to have been guilty of an extraordinary piece of impertinence; and her family might have fared ill had any of them remained in the king's power.

So Lord Rochford, Weston, Noreys, Bryerton, and Smeton were executed on Wednesday, the 17th of May. Their bodies were exposed to no further ignominy, but thrown into simple shells and buried in the Tower.

Elizabeth is to be declared illegitimate. Meanwhile, attempts had been made to secure the aid of Anne for the accomplishment of a scheme in which the king was profoundly interested. Having no legitimate heir male, and being in doubt whether Jane Seymour would ever contrive to bear him a son, Henry had begun to think of his bastard son, Henry Fitzroy, Duke of Richmond. It occurred to him that if he had no legitimate male offspring it might be possible to obtain the sanction of Parliament for the

and then to have made amends; I thought little I would have come to this."

recognition of the duke as heir to the crown. But as CHAP. XVIII. yet little, Elizabeth stood in the way ; she had been solemnly proclaimed heir presumptive, and her title could not be easily disregarded. It was desirable, therefore, that Anne's daughter should be declared illegitimate.

This object might have been attained if Henry had been willing to adduce proof that Elizabeth was not his child. The words attributed to Rochford, whether really spoken or not, and the general rumour that Elizabeth was the daughter of Noreys, would have been held sufficient evidence by a subservient primate and a willing parliament. But Henry would not hear of this ; he insisted that Elizabeth should be recognised as his daughter, yet be proclaimed a bastard. This *The* was, of course, impossible, unless it were decreed *divorce* that his marriage with Anne Boleyn had been invalid *of Anne.* from the beginning. In support of such a decree Henry might have used the argument which in the opinion of nearly every foreigner and of most Englishmen was the best, namely, that he was legally and validly married to Catherine when he took Anne for his wife. But had this reason been advanced, he would have acknowledged that he had been guilty of adultery or bigamy, and that he had been in the wrong, and had shown bad faith throughout the whole of the proceedings connected with the divorce case. Moreover, by a divorce from Anne based on this ground Mary would have been declared legitimate.

This argument being considered inadmissible, the statements of the Countess of Northumberland with regard to a previous marriage, or a binding pre-contract,

on the part of Anne, were remembered, and Cromwell
was directed to follow up the matter.   On Saturday
the 13th of May, the day after the condemnation of
the commoners, Sir Raynold Carnaby, a friend of
Northumberland, was sent to him to obtain if possible
a retractation of what he had formerly said, and an
admission that there had been a pre-contract between
him and Anne.   But the earl either had spoken the
truth and honestly adhered to it, or he was aware
that he would put himself in serious danger by
making such a confession as was desired.   If a pre-
contract existed, his denial of it before the king's
marriage with Anne might well have been construed
as an act of treason.   So he stoutly upheld his former deposition before Warham, Lee, and the council,
that there was no pre-contract between him and
the queen.[1]

There remained but one other conceivable reason
for a divorce—a forbidden degree of affinity.   Now
Mary Boleyn, Anne's sister, had been Henry's mistress;
and as illegitimate relations, according to the canon
law, formed as strong an obstacle as legitimate
relations, there was a forbidden degree.   Scandalous
as the proceeding might be, the marriage was to be
annulled on this ground.

The person who was required by the new rules
to pronounce sentence was Anne's friend, Thomas
Cranmer.   However loth he might be to take an
active part against his former patron, however annoyed at having to declare invalid that which he had

[1] Earl of   Northumberland to Cromwell, May 13, 1536,
Burnet, *Collectanea*, Part III. Book III. No. 49.

solemnly declared to be valid, he had no choice. He
knew that the king might undo him at any moment;
he had been sufficiently frightened by Cromwell's
peremptory messages ; he was ready for anything that
might be asked of him. On the morning of the day
following the trial of Anne he went to the Tower, and
was admitted to her presence. What he told her and
what she said to him is not known ; but when he
left her, she was convinced that she would be pardoned
and allowed to leave the country. She told the ladies
who were guarding her, that she would be sent to
Antwerp.[1] It is, therefore, probable that the primate
gave her hopes that her life might be spared if she
would consent to a divorce.

On the 17th, at nine o'clock in the morning, the
primate opened his court at Lambeth. The Lord
Chancellor, the Duke of Suffolk, the Earls of Oxford
and of Sussex, Sir Thomas Cromwell, and others of
the king's council were present. Doctor Richard
Sampson appeared for the king, Doctors Nicholas
Wotton and John Barbour for Anne. Whether the
two latter had really received any powers from her
does not appear. They may have been named by
Henry in accordance with the precedent set in 1527
on the occasion of the collusive suit against Catherine ;
but, on the other hand, it is not improbable that one
of Cranmer's objects in going to see Anne at the
Tower was to induce her to appoint Wotton and
Barbour as her proctors.

In any case the two men who appeared for Anne
did nothing to defend her cause. Had they had

[1] Sir W. Kingston to Cromwell, May 16, 1536, *loc. cit.*

CHAP. XVIII. the interest of their client at heart, they might have
raised such difficulties that, if Henry had obstinately
insisted on securing a divorce, he would have been
compelled to come to terms with Anne in order to
obtain her consent, and thus her life might have
been spared. But Wotton and Barbour were royal
officials, anxious to please the king; so Cranmer was
allowed to give sentence. He solemnly declared the
marriage between Henry and Anne to have been
null and invalid from the beginning.[1]

*Anne
prepares
for death.*

May 18,
1536.

Anne might now be allowed to die. Her hopes of
life had not lasted long, for Kingston had soon
undeceived her. After the sitting at Lambeth her
execution was fixed for the morning of the 18th, and
she was told of it. She slept little that night; her
almoner was in attendance, and from two o'clock
onwards she remained in prayer with him. In the
morning she sent for Kingston, and asked him to be
present when she was to receive the sacrament and to
assert her innocence of the crimes laid to her charge.[2]
Shortly afterwards the communion was celebrated,
and both before and after receiving the host she
declared on the salvation of her soul that she had
never been unfaithful to the king.[3] After this she
patiently waited; but as time passed on she became

---

[1] Wilkins' *Concilia,* vol. iii. fol. 804. See Appendix, Note G.

[2] Sir W. Kingston to Cromwell, May 18, 1536, British Museum,
Cotton MSS. Otho C. x. fol. 227.

[3] E. Chapuis to Charles V., May 19, 1536, *loc. cit.* : "La
dame que la eu en garde ma envoye dire en grand secret que la
dicte concubyne avant et apres la reception du sainct sacrement
luy affirma sur la dampnation de son ame quelle ne sestoit
meffaicte de son corps envers ce Roy."

restless, and asked her attendants when she was to die. They answered that she would not be executed before noon.[1] In reality, the execution was not to take place until the following day.

The explanation of this change of plan is not perfectly clear. It seems that Anne, faithful to her French education, considered it more honourable to die by the stroke of a sword than to have her head hacked off with an axe. The hangman of Calais, the only subject of Henry who knew how to behead with a sword, had, therefore, been sent for ;[2] and he may not have arrived at the expected time. It is more probable, however, that the delay was due to a different cause.

The government now regretted that so many people had been allowed to hear the incredible accusations against Anne and her brother, and their able and eloquent defence. Many strangers had been present at the trials ; and it was feared that after their return to their homes they would give a very unfavourable account of the king's proceedings. On Thursday morning, therefore, Cromwell wrote to Kingston that all foreigners were to be expelled from the Tower. In reporting that this

[1] Sir W. Kingston to Cromwell, May 18, 1536, *loc. cit.*

[2] Chronicle of Calais, p. 47 ; and account of Mr. Gostwyk, R.O. Henry VIII. 28th, Box II : "To Sir William Kingston for a composition for such Iuells and apparail as the late queene had in the tower—100*l.* To the same Sir William Kingston for money delyvered unto her to gyve in almes before her deathe— 20*l.* To the executioner of Calays for his rewarde and apparail, C. crownes—23*l.* 6*s.* 8*d.* To the said Sir William Kingston for the said late queenes diett at her being in the tower— 25*l.* 4*s.* 6*d.*"

CHAP. XVIII. order had been obeyed, Kingston expressed the opinion that if the exact time was not made public there would probably be few spectators;[1] and it is not unlikely that the government decided to postpone the execution in the hope that this suggestion would prove to be right.

The day before the execution of Anne. When Anne's attendants told her that she would not die before noon, she sent for Kingston and complained to him of the delay.[2] She had hoped, she said, to be past her pain. The constable tried to console her; it was no pain, he said, it was so quickly done. Anne spoke of the executioner's skill and of the smallness of her neck; and then, the long waiting having unstrung her nerves, she had another attack of hysterical laughter, by which the constable was sorely puzzled. "I have seen many men and also women executed," he wrote, "and that they have been in great sorrow; and to my knowledge this lady has much joy and pleasure in death."[3] The rest of the day Anne spent partly in praying, partly in chatting with her attendants on her past life and on her future fame. Those ingenious persons, she

---

[1] Sir W. Kingston to Cromwell, May 18, 1536, *loc. cit.*

[2] E. Chapuis to Charles V., May 19, 1536, *loc. cit.* : "Elle se confessa hier et comuniqua pensant destre execute et ne monstra oncques personne meilleure vollonte daller a la mort quelle et en sollicitoit ceulx quen debvoient avoir charge; et estant venu commandement de differer lexecution jusque a aujourdhuy elle sen monstra fort dolante priant le cappitaine de la tour que pour lhonneur le dieu il feit supplier au Roy que puis quelle se trouvoit en bon estat et disposee a recepvoir la mort que lon la voulsist depescher incontinant."

[3] Sir W. Kingston to Cromwell, May 18, 1536, *loc. cit.*

said, who had forged so infamous a name for the late
queen would have no trouble in finding one for her.
They would call her Queen Lackhead. And therewith
came another burst of hysterical laughter.[1] There was
but one thing which preyed on her mind, her behaviour
to the Princess Mary. She repeatedly spoke of it,
saying that she had been brought to this end by
divine judgment for being the cause of Mary's ill-
treatment and for having tried to bring about her
death.[2] Of the common story that Anne, kneeling,
asked Lady Kingston to beg Mary to pardon her,
I have found no trace; and it may be dismissed as
an embellishment of later writers.

In this way the time went on. During the night
Anne seems to have taken scarcely any rest, her *May* 19,
nerves being too excited for sleep. She continued 1536.
to talk to her ladies, and conversed and prayed with
her almoner. As the morning of Friday, the 19th of
May, approached, Kingston informed her that she
would shortly be executed, and he handed her a

[1] E. Chapuis to N. de Granvelle, June 6, 1536, Vienna
Archives, P.C. 229½ iii. fol. 12 : " La dame Anne la nuyt avant
quelle fut decapitee commenca a jazer le plus playsement du
monde et entre aultres choses elle dit ces glorieuses et ingenieuses
personnes que forgearent ung nom inaudit a la bonne Royne ne
seront cy empeschez luy en trouver ung car il la pourroient
appeller la Royne Anne sans teste et disant telz propoz se mit a
rire si tres fort que oncques ne fust vu telle chose, bien sachant
touteffoys quelle mourroit lendemain sans nul remede."
[2] *Ibid.* : " Elle dit le jour devant quelle fust executez et depuys
quant lon la voulust mener a lexecution quelle ne pensoit estre
la conduytte par le jugement divin sinon pour avoir estee cause
du male traytement de la princesse et avoir conspire a sa
mort . . . ."

CHAP. XVIII. purse with twenty pounds which she was to dis-
tribute, according to custom, as alms before her death.
A little before nine he returned, and announced that
the moment had come.[1]

Anne is
executed.
During the night a platform had been erected in
the courtyard of the Tower. It rose but a few feet
above the ground, for it had been deemed inexpedient
to raise a high scaffold which might be seen from
afar.[2] In the courtyard the Lord Chancellor, the
Dukes of Suffolk and of Richmond, Sir Thomas
Cromwell, and others of the council were assembled
to witness Anne's death. The Lord Mayor, with some
aldermen and representatives of the crafts of the city,
attended by order ; and as their coming had attracted
attention, they had been followed by a considerable
number of people. But strict watch had been kept
at the gates, and although Englishmen had been
freely admitted, all foreigners had been excluded.[3]

Anne now appeared, led by Kingston and followed
by the four ladies. She wore a dressing-gown of
grey damask, which she had chosen because it was
low round the neck and would not interfere with the

---

[1] E. Chapuis to Charles V., May 19, 1536, *loc. cit.* : " Lexecution
et decollation de la concubyne qua este faicte maintenant a neuf
heures du matin dedans la tour."

[2] French account of Anne's death, Paris, Bibl. Nat. MSS.
Dupuis, vol. 373, fol 112 : "Leschaffault qui nestoit pas plus
hault que de quatre ou cinq marches."

[3] Wriothesley's *Chronicle ;* and E. Chapuis to Charles V., May
19, 1536, *loc. cit.* : " Ou se sont trouvez presents le chancellier et
maistre Cremuel et plusieurs autres du conseil du Roy, et autre
assez grand nombre de subjectz mays lon ny a voulu souffrir
estraingiers . . . ."

executioner's work.[1] For the same reason she had CHAP. XVIII.
tied up her hair in a net, over which she wore the
customary head-dress. In this guise she was handed
over by Kingston to the sheriffs, who led her up to
the platform.

Permission was granted to her to address the
crowd, and she did so in few words and very simply.
She had not come to preach, she said, but to die.
She asked those who were present to pray for the
king, who was a right gentle prince and had treated
her as well as possible. She said that she accused
nobody on account of her death, for she had been
sentenced according to the law of the country. So
she was ready to die, and asked the forgiveness of all
whom she might have wronged.[2] Having said these
words, she herself took off her head-dress, which she
handed to one of the ladies. Then she once more
asked the bystanders to pray to God for her.[3]

---

[1] French account of Anne's death, *loc. cit.*: " Accoustree dune
robbe de nuyt de damas gris fourre pour faire plus beau col."

[2] *Ibid.*: " Lors elle commenca a dire que elle ne estoit pas venue
la pour prescher ains estoit la venue pour mourir, Disant a messieurs les assistans quilz priassent bien dieu pour le Roy, car il
estoit tout bon et quil lavoit tant bien traictee quil nestoit
possible de mieulx et quelle ne accusoit personne de sa mort juges
ne aultres gens quelz quelz fussent, car cestoit la loy du pays qui
la condempnoit, parquoy elle prenoit bien la mort en gre demandant pardon a tout le monde." This account agrees very well
with the versions preserved by Wriothesley and Constantine.
The version of the *Histoire de Anne de Boullant* is a paraphrase
of that just quoted, differing only in a few details. The letter
of the " Portuguese writer " is a mere translation of this account.

[3] *Ibid.*: " Lors elle print elle mesme son accoustrement de
teste et le bailla a une damoyselle et ne luy demoura que une

During the whole time that she had been on the scaffold, she had been nervously looking round[1] towards the place where the executioner stood leaning on his heavy sword. Now she knelt down, and one of her attendants bound a handkerchief round her eyes. After this the ladies also knelt down, silently praying, while she repeated the words: "Oh God, have pity on my soul." The executioner stepped quickly forward and took his aim; the heavy two handled blade flew hissing through the air, and Anne's head rolled in the dust.

Head and trunk were taken up by the ladies, wrapped in a sheet, laid in a plain coffin, and carried to the Tower chapel.[2] Here they were buried with little ceremony. No inscription, except a few letters, was put upon Anne's grave, and the exact spot was soon forgotten. It was discovered only a few years ago.

Such was the end of a strange and eventful career. For a moment it seemed as if Anne would

---

coeffe quelle avoit mise pour tenir ses cheveulx . . . . disant aux assistants quilz priassent dieu pour elle."

[1] French account of Anne's death, *loc. cit.* : " Regardant tousiours derriere elle . . . ."

[2] *Ibid.* : " Et sagenoilla et lune de ses damoselles luy bandist les yeulx; sans se faire tenir aucunement elle attendit la le coup avant quon eust dit une pastenostre, disant tousjours Mon Dieu ayez pitie de mon ame. Lesdictes quatre damoyselles estant tousjours sur leschaffault agenoilles. Et a ceste heure la pouvre dame fut expedyee lune des susdictes damoyselles print la teste et les aultres le corps et midrent tout dedant ung linceul et apres dedans une biere qui estoit toute apprestee et la feirent apporter dedans une eglise qui est devant ladicte tour ou lon dit quelle et les dessusdictz ont este enterrez. Requiescat in pace."

leave no trace in history; but the schism of which she had been the first cause, and to which in one form or another the ruling powers were already deeply committed, could not be undone. Her influence survived, too, in the little girl at Hunsdon, who grew up to be very like her, although Elizabeth never showed a spark of tenderness for the memory of her mother and would have been ashamed to own that she resembled her. From Anne the English people received one of the greatest of their rulers, and for this gift they may well forgive such misdeeds as were not atoned for by long and cruel anxiety and a terrible death. Anne was not good ; she was incredibly vain, ambitious, unscrupulous, coarse, fierce, and relentless. But much of this was due to the degrading influences by which she was surrounded in youth and after her return to England from France. Her virtues, such as they were, were her own. So we may pass no harsher judgment on her than was passed by Cromwell when, speaking confidentially to Chapuis of the woman whose destruction he had wrought, he could not refrain from extolling her courage and intelligence.[1] Among her good qualities he might also have included her warm and constant attachment to her friends.

---

[1] E. Chapuis to Charles V., June 6, 1536, Vienna Archives, P.C. 230, i. fol. 92 : " Et sur ce me louha grandement le sens expert et cueur de la dicte concubyne et de son frere."

CHAPTER XIX.

CONCLUSION.

Silence of the government. FOR more than a week after Anne's arrest, the English government remained silent as to the causes which had led to it and to the imprisonment of so many other persons of note. This reticence gave rise to such very extraordinary rumours both at home and abroad,[1] that Cromwell at last thought it wiser to inform the English agents at foreign courts how the matter was to be spoken of. On the 14th of May *Official account of Anne's arrest.* he wrote to Gardiner and Wallop. " The queen's abomination," he said, " both in inconvenient living and other offences towards the king's highness was so rank and common that her ladies of her privy chamber and her chamberers could not contain it within their breasts, but, detesting the same, had so often consultations and conferences of it, that at last it came so plainly to the ears of some of his grace's council that

---

[1] Charles V. to E. Chapuis, May 15, 1536, Vienna Archives, P.C. 233, iii. fol. 26 : " Le Viconte Hanart a escript au Sgr de Granvelle du ix. de ce mois que au mesme instant il avoit entendu de bon lieu que la concubyne du Roy dangleterre avoit este surprise couchee avec lorganiste dudict Roy."

with their duty to his majesty they could not conceal it from him, but with great fear, as the case enforced, declared what they heard unto his highness. Whereupon in most secret sort certain persons of the privy chamber and others of her side were examined, in which examination the matter appeared so evident, that besides that crime with the accidents, there broke out a certain conspiracy of the king's death, which extended so far that all we, that had the examination of it, quaked at the danger his grace was in, and on our knees gave Him laud and praise that he had preserved him so long from it and now manifested the most wretched and detested determination of the same. Then were certain men committed to the Tower for this cause : that is Marke and Norres, and her brother ; then was she apprehended and conveyed to the same place ; after her was sent thither, for the crimes specified, Sir Francis Weston and William Brereton. And Norres, Weston, Brereton and Mark be already condemned to death upon arraignment in Westminster Hall on Friday last. She and her brother shall be arraigned to-morrow and will undoubtedly go the same way. I write no particularities, the things be so abominable, and therefore I doubt not but this shall be sufficient instruction to declare the truth if you have occasion so to do." [1]

Similar accounts were published in England, but the people declined to believe the official version, and continued secretly to blame the government for the way in which the trials had been conducted. After a time their interest in Anne's fate died out,

Anne's reputation.

[1] Cromwell to Gardiner and Wallop, May 14, 1536, *loc. cit.*

CHAP. XIX. but a few of her adherents always held her memory
dear, and we find among the records of the following
years a note or two of proceedings against persons who
maintained that Henry had put her to death unjustly.[1]
In France poems were written in her honour,[2] and in
Germany the Protestants expressed strong disapproval
of the king's act.[3] About 1544, Jean de Luxembourg,
Abbot of Ivry, wrote an *Oraison de Madame Marie de
Cleves*, in which it is said that Henry was suspected
of having already ill-treated, that is to say murdered,
three wives.[4]   And Constantine, in his memorial,

---

[1] Depositions against John Hill and William Saunders before
the justices of Oxfordshire, June 26, 1536, R.O. Henry VIII.,
28th Bundle ii.   John Hill was accused of having said that the
king had caused Norris, Weston and the others "to be put to
death only of pleasure . ." and "how that the king for a frawde
and a gille cawsed Mr. Norrys, Mr. Weston and the other queen
to be putt to death, bycause he was made sure unto the queenes
grace that nowe is half a yere before."   William Saunders spoke
in a similar manner.

[2] *Epigrammata*, Lib. iii. p. 162, published by Etienne Dolet,
Lyons, anno 1538 : "Regine Utopiae, falso adulterii crimine
damnatae, et capite mulctatae Epithaphium.

> " Quid ? quod tyrannus crimine falso damnatam
> Me jussit occidi, minus me jam laudas ?
> Necnon velut turpe maledicta suffundis ?
> Nulla nota turpis sum, ob acceptum vulnus.
> Nimirum honesta turpido est sine culpa
> Mori, et innocentem cedere aliquando fatis."

I have been unable to find the book itself, so I quote from
Crapelet.

[3] Melanchthon to Camerarius, June 9, 1536, *Corp. Ref.* vol. iii.
No. 1437 : "Posterior Regina magis accusata quam convicta
adulterii ultimo supplicio affecta est."

[4] This book is very rare, and I have never been able to see

reports a saying of the councillors of the Duchess of CHAP. XIX. Milan to the effect that " her great aunte was poisoned, that the second was innocently put to death, and the third lost for lack of keeping in her childbed." [1] By and by, however, those who had known Anne passed away, the real person was forgotten, and fantastic portraits of her were drawn both by admirers and by enemies. And so her history was distorted by party spirit until it became a mere myth.

The fortnight before Anne's execution Henry had spent in the most pleasant manner. After a short stay at York Place he went to Hampton Court, and Jane Seymour was sent to a house of Sir Nicholas Carew, about seven miles from London. [2] Here the king frequently visited her, but he soon found that the distance was too great. On the 14th of May she removed to a house on the Thames, only a mile from the court ; and in this residence she was served with quasi-regal pomp, having numerous servants and living in splendid style. [3] On the 15th she received a message from the king that at three in the afternoon she would hear of Anne's condemnation ; and shortly after dinner,

Henry and Jane Seymour.

May 14, 1536.

May 15, 1536.

---

the original. But there is in the Grenville library an Italian translation from which I quote : " Un re il quale era sospettato dhavere di gia mal trattate tre donne."

[1] Constantine's Memorial, *loc. cit.*

[2] E. Chapuis to Charles V., May 19, 1536, *loc. cit.* : " Et pour couvrir laffection quil a a la dicte Semel il la faict tenir a sept mille dyci en la maison du grand escuyer."

[3] *Ibid.* : " Ce Roy . . . lequel le jour avant la condempnacion dicelle putain envoya querre par le grand escuyer et plusieurs aultres maistresse Semel et la feist venir a ung mille de son logis la ou elle est servye tres splendidement de cuysiniers et certains officiers dudict Roy et tres richement accoustree."

CHAP. XIX. Sir Francis Bryan, Anne's cousin, arrived with the
May 19,   welcome intelligence.[1] When, on the Friday following,
1536.   the death of Anne was announced to Henry, he
           immediately took his barge and went to spend the
           day with Jane Seymour at the place where she lived.[2]
May 20,   Next morning, at six o'clock, she secretly joined him
1536.   at Hampton Court, and there, in the presence of a
           few courtiers, they were married.[3] A few days later
           the marriage was acknowledged, and Jane appeared
           as queen.

Paul III.   The hopes entertained by the conservative and papal
tries to   party after the arrest of Anne were doomed to
win back   disappointment. The first news of her imprisonment
the allegi-
ance of   reached Rome by way of Flanders,[4] about the middle
Henry.   of May. Paul III. at once sent for Gregorio da
May 21,
1536.   Casale, and told him what had happened, saying that

---

[1] E. Chapuis to Charles V., May 19, 1536, *loc. cit.* : " Et ma
dict une syenne parente que disna avec elle le jour de la dicte
condempnacion que des le matin icelluy Roy avoit envoye dire
a la dicte Semel que a troys heures apres mydy il luy envoyeroit
nouvelles de la condampnacion de la dicte putain, ce quil feist par
maistre Briant quil envoya en toute diligence."

[2] E. Chapuis to N. de Granvelle, May 20, 1536, Vienna
Archives, P.C. 230, ii. fol. 22 : " Sil este vray ce que ma este
dit, assavoir quicelluy Roy tout incontinent quil heust hier les
nouvelles de la decapitation de la putain il monta en barque et
alla trouver la dicte maistresse Semel quil a faict loger a ung
mille de luy en une maison sur la riviere."

[3] *Ibid.* : "Jay este adverty de plusieurs et divers bons lieux
comme ce matin aux six heures mestresse Semel est venu par la
riviere secretement au logis de ce Roy et a neufz heures a este
faict la promesse et desponsation et entend le dict Roy que le
tout doit estre tenu secret jusques aux festes de penthecoste. . . ."

[4] N. Raince to Cardinal du Bellay, May 23, 1536, Paris, Bibl.
Nat. MSS. Français, vol. 19,577.

God had enlightened the conscience of Henry. The
pope showed himself most anxious for a reconciliation,
and eagerly pointed out to Casale that by forming an
alliance with the Holy See, Henry would gain so much
authority that he might lay down the law both to
Charles V. and to Francis. He, the pope, had always
been at heart Henry's friend, and whatever he had
done against him he had been forced to do. The
slightest advance Henry might make would be gladly
responded to.[1]

Casale asked the pope whether he might write all
this to the King of England; but Paul III. replied that if
after the insults and injuries he had received he took
the first step in the matter, people would cry shame
on him. Casale was to keep everything that had
been said strictly secret; he was only to assure his
employers of the pope's goodwill, and to urge them
not to miss so fortunate an opportunity of making
peace with the papacy. If Paul III. saw any favourable sign, he would send Messer Latino Juvenale,
Casale's uncle, or some other agent, to England, who
would go nominally for the purpose of transacting
some private business of his own.

Notwithstanding the pope's request that the con-   *May* 27,
versation should be kept secret, Casale gave Henry a   1536.

---

[1] G. da Casale to Henry VIII., May 27, 1536, British Museum,
Cotton MSS. Vitellius, B. xiv. fol. 198 : "Primum igitur se omni-
potentem deum bonorum omnium largitorem deinde M^tem Vram
obsecrare, ut animum inducat sese ita comparare, ut tanta gloria
adeunda occasionem non praetermittat. Quod si V. Regia M^tas
huic Romana Ecclesia conjuncta fuerit, ipsam sine dubio tantum
habiturum auctoritatis, ut caesari simulque Gallorum Regi jubere
possit et utrunque cogere ad pacem. . . ."

full account of it ; and he expressed a hope that the intended mission of Latino Juvenale would not be prevented, as it could do no harm and might do good.[1] Casale seems to have encouraged the friendly disposition of the pope ; for little more than a week after the date of his letter an agent was despatched to England.

The person chosen for this errand was Marco Antonio Campeggio. He received his instructions from his brother, Cardinal Campeggio, who had acted as papal legate in the time of Wolsey. He was to ask that the cardinal should be reinstated in the revenues of his former see of Salisbury ; but this was to be only the ostensible occasion of his visit. If a favourable chance offered itself, he was to urge on the royal ministers that for the honour of God and the quiet of the realm the king ought to seek for a reconciliation with the Holy See, which would deal with him graciously.[2] Henry was to be advised to give proof of a friendly temper by repressing the

---

[1] G. da Casale to Henry VIII., May 27, 1536, British Museum, Cotton MSS. Vitellius, B. xiv. fol. 198 ; and G. da Casale to Cromwell, May 27, 1536, *State Papers*, vol. vii. p. 656.

[2] Cardinal Campeggio to Marco Antonio Campeggio, June 6, 1536, British Museum, Cotton MSS. Vitellius, B. xiv. fol. 205 : " Anchorache la reintegration delle cose mie habi da esser il principal pretesto dell andata vra in anglia pur non restareti se con qualchedun de questi grandi pigliasti confidentia con bon proposito ricordar che a laude de dio quete di quel regno . . . . sarebbe bene che soa m.ᵗᵃ pensasse e facesse ogni opera per reintegrarsi con la sede appostolica quel mi rendo certo che sempre se li renderia benigna, et che per poter conseguir questo il ver principio seria che reprimessi li predicatori di nove heresie. . . . "

preaching of new heresies, and to obtain peace of chap. xix. conscience by begging for absolution for his offences, as his predecessors had often done, earning thereby praise and glory.[1] Those whom Marco Antonio would find favourable were the Dukes of Norfolk and Suffolk, the Bishops of Durham and Winchester, and Campeggio's agent.[2]

As these instructions are now in the British Museum among the Cotton Manuscripts, they must have been formerly at the State-paper Office; and from this I conclude that Marco Antonio really came to England and negotiated with the English ministers. This opinion is confirmed by the fact that at the Record Office there is a letter from Cardinal Campeggio to the Duke of Suffolk, accrediting Marco Antonio.[3]

The pope not only tried direct offers, he had recourse to indirect means. He spoke with Denonville and with Nicolas Raince, strongly advocating the marriage of Henry and the Princess Madeleine of France. Raince wrote to Cardinal du Bellay that the pope had referred to this proposal again and again, and that his holiness could think of no more

---

[1] Cardinal Campeggio to Marco Antonio Campeggio, June 6 1536, British Museum, Cotton MSS. Vitellius, B. xiv. fol. 205: "Anchor vi forzareti far . . . . la conscientia soa procurasse ottener le debite absolutione . . . . . antecessori soi con molta laude et memoria . . . . procurorno. . . ."

[2] *Ibid.*: "Li particulari amici e fautori me . . . . confidentia sono li Ill^{mi} duca di Norfolch, di Sopholch . . . . . . Dunelmen, Wintonien ne voglio scordarmi il nro R^{do} M . . . . . . homo della virtu e bonta che sapete il qual e mio procuratore. . . ."

[3] Cardinal Campeggio to the Duke of Suffolk, June 5, 1536, *State Papers*, vol. vii. p. 657.

effectual way of obtaining a hold over the King of
England.[1]

But on the day after the departure of Marco
Antonio Campeggio, Denonville received letters from
England in which it was said that Henry again
intended to marry one of his own subjects. Nicolas
Raince mentioned this to the pope, who was greatly
disappointed. Paul III. continued, however, to
believe that the French match might be brought
about.[2] A few days later he spoke of a marriage
between the dauphin and the Princess Mary ; and
Denonville and Raince wrote about it to the French
court.[3]

---

[1] N. Raince to Cardinal du Bellay, May 23, 1536, *loc. cit.* :
" De belle prime face Sa S^te levant les mains au ciel me dict quon
ne pourroit mieulx faire que de trouver moyen de faire le mariage
de madame fille aisnee du Roy et du Roy dangleterre comme il
mavoit autrefois dict et mesmement quand je luy dis la premiere
nouvelle de la mort de la Royne Catherine. . . . . Croyez Mgr.
que Nostre dict St. pere a une singuliere devotion au sainct [faict ?]
. . . . et men a parle depuis chacune fois que jay este a luy et
encor aujourdhui et si en parla samedy quand Mgr. lambassadeur
y fust."

[2] N. Raince to Cardinal du Bellay, June 8, 1536, Paris, Bibl.
Nat. MSS. Français, vol. 19,577 : " Je fis lecture a Nostre dict
S. P. de Vre. chiffre a Mondict Sr. de Mascon tant dangleterre
que dailleurs. Sa S^te ne print pas bien cette nouvelle volonte de
mariage en plus basse condition et en eust deplaisir pour ce quil
vouldroit quon parvint a lautre party quil desire comme Vous
entendez bien."

[3] N. Raince to Cardinal du Bellay, July 27, 1536, Paris, Bibl.
Nat. MSS. Français, vol. 19,577 : " Il [the pope] desire fort
dentendre ce que lon repondra a ce que Mgr. lambassadeur et
moy escripvimes par le depesche du 20eme Juin touchant le
mariage de la princesse Marie pour Mgr. le daulphin et ne passe
pas ce propos sans que S. S^te parle de Vous."

It was only in July, presumably after he had heard from Marco Antonio, that the pope understood that Henry was not inclined to give up the spiritual supremacy he had arrogated to himself, and that he did not propose either to ask for absolution or to submit in any way to Rome. Paul III. then spoke angrily of Henry and even more angrily of Cromwell, and abandoned all hope of regaining the allegiance of England by peaceful means.[1]

Henry, Francis I. and Charles V.

Francis I. also heard with annoyance of Henry's marriage with Jane, for—apart from his apparent desire to have the King of England for his son-in-law—he probably foresaw that Henry would soon be perfectly reconciled with the emperor, and that he himself would thereby lose a valuable ally and client. This anticipation was realised. After some time Charles was on very good terms with Henry, although he never gave up his defence of the memory of his aunt. For many years he and Queen Mary of Hungary irritated Henry by addressing him as "well-beloved uncle," and it was with great difficulty that Chapuis at last persuaded them to give up the use of the obnoxious name.

Mary.

Mary gained little by the death of Anne. Contrary to the general expectation, Henry refused to admit her legitimacy or to restore her to her former rank. The Duke of Richmond soon died, but as long as he lived Henry appears to have wished to

[1] N. Raince to Cardinal du Bellay, July 27, 1536, Paris, Bibl. Nat. MSS. Français, vol. 19,577 : " Mgr. Nᵣₑ dict S. P. me parla du Roy dangleterre ainsi comme jescript au Roy en bien grosse colere et se attache continuellement contre Cramouel."

CHAP. XIX. make him his successor, and Mary could escape the danger of imprisonment and death only by laying aside her pretensions to be the Princess of England. During the whole of Henry's reign she continued to play with the idea of flight and of rebellion, but even when the means were at her disposal she shrank from carrying out her purpose.[1]

To Henry's courtiers the death of Rochford and his friends brought a golden harvest. Rochford and Noreys, being royal favourites, had enjoyed numerous pensions and a good many lucrative sinecures. As soon, therefore, as it was known that they had been arrested, an active correspondence took place regarding the sharing of the spoil.

To Gardiner and Wallop Cromwell wrote : " Your lordship shall get in CC £ of the III. that were out among these men . . . the 3rd C is bestowed of the vicar of hell." At the end of the letter he added : " And you master Wallop shall not at this time be forgotten, but the certainty of that ye shall have I cannot tell." [2] Gardiner was by no means satisfied with this arrangement. In 1529, Wolsey had been forced to grant to Rochford and Noreys pensions for life of £200 and £100, out of the revenues of Winchester. These pensions Gardiner had been obliged to pay, but now that the pensioners were to die the bishop thought that all the payments should cease. He protested in vain, however ; he was even sharply reprimanded for complaining, and

[1] E. Chapuis and D. de Mendoça to Charles V., August 31, 1538, Vienna Archives, P.C. 231, ii. fol. 54 ; etc.

[2] Cromwell to Gardiner and Wallop, May 14, 1536, *loc. cit.*

the vicar of hell, as Sir Francis Bryan was called, CHAP. XIX. got his pension. What was the share of Sir John Wallop, I have not been able to make out.

The Duke of Richmond was not quick enough. He wrote on the 8th to the Bishop of Lincoln to secure the office of Steward of Banbury held by Noreys.[1] But, three days before, the bishop had already offered it, with the stewardship of the university of Cambridge, to Cromwell.[2] Robert Barnes applied for the mastership of Bedlam, worth, as he said, but forty pounds.[3] The other offices of the five men executed on the 17th of May were distributed in a similar manner.

In the summer of 1536, seeing that the change of queens had made no great change in politics, the conspirators rose against the king. But they had waited too long. The emperor gave them no help, for he was fully occupied in Provence, and at that very time he was treating with Henry about an alliance against France. Besides, many of the great lords had become reconciled to the new order of things, which, after all, they found rather profitable. Most of them had received considerable grants out of the lands of the dissolved abbeys; and they hoped that their chances of sharing in the spoil were not even yet exhausted. Moreover, the insurgents were embarrassed by the indecision and stupidity of

The pilgrimage of grace. October, 1536.

[1] The Duke of Richmond to the Bishop of Lincoln, May 8, 1536, R.O. 28th Henry VIII., Bundle ii.

[2] The Bishop of Lincoln to Cromwell, May 5, 1536, R.O. 28th Henry VIII., Bundle ii.

[3] Robert Barnes to Cromwell, R.O. *Cromwell Correspondence,* vol. iii. fol. 77.

CHAP. XIX. Mary. She had scruples about encouraging open
rebellion against her father ; and the majority of her
personal friends, knowing her mind, held back from
the insurrection. The pilgrimage of grace, therefore,
was suppressed with comparative ease, and Lord
Darcy, Lord Hussey, and many other adherents of
Mary were brought to the block.

Chapuis. Chapuis remained for several years as ambassador
at the English court, on excellent terms with Henry
March, and with his principal advisers. In the beginning
1539. of 1539, the relations between Charles and Henry
having become less friendly, he was recalled,[1] and the
Dean of Cambray took his place.[2] When the coldness
passed away, and the emperor desired once more to
August, be on good terms with Henry, Chapuis returned to
1540. England ;[3] and he remained there until the king
crossed to Calais to take the command of his army
before Boulogne. Chapuis was present at the siege,
December, and after the campaign he went back with Francis
1544. van der Dilft, who had been chosen to succeed him as
ambassador.[4] Having spent more than four months
in schooling van der Dilft for his new post, he had a
May 4, farewell audience of the king, on the 4th of May,
1545. 1545 ; and Henry did not conceal his regret, for he
had come to like the man by whom he had been so

[1] Mary of Hungary to E. Chapuis, March 10, 1539, Vienna
Archives, P.C. 231, iv. fol. 6.

[2] The Dean of Cambray to Mary of Hungary, March 19, 1539,
Vienna Archives, P.C. 231, iv. fol. 8.

[3] E. Chapuis to N. de Granvelle, September 3, 1540, Vienna
Archives, P.C. 232, ii. fol. 1.

[4] E. Chapuis and F. van der Dilft to Charles V., January 2,
1545, Vienna Archives, P.C. 236, i. fol. 7.

ably and so stoutly resisted.[1] At this time Chapuis was ill and crippled by gout; but he was still vigorous enough to be employed in treating with the English commissioners in the Low Countries. The last mention of him I have found is in 1546; the date of his death I do not know.

All of Henry's German favourites, Juergen Wullenwever, Dr. Adam von Pack, and Marcus and Gerhard Meyer came to a violent end. Having been kept for many months a close prisoner, first at Rotenburg and afterwards at Steinbrueck, Wullenwever was brought to Wolfenbuettel, where, on the 24th of September, 1537, he was sentenced to death and immediately executed. Doctor Pack left Hamburg in March, 1536, to return to England; but while passing through the Low Countries he was detained and thrown into prison. At first Cromwell protested so strongly against his arrest that Chapuis wrote to Flanders; and on the 16th of April he wished to explain why the doctor had been seized. But having by this time heard of the proposals of Charles V., Cromwell did not want to quarrel about minor points; so he interrupted the ambassador with the remark that these were small matters of no importance. The authorities of the Low Countries, finding that Pack was to be left to his fate, tried to extort information from him by putting him to the rack, and soon afterwards he died in prison.

Marcus Meyer held out at Warberg for some time after Henry abandoned him; but in May he was

Henry's German favourites.

September 24, 1537.

March, 1536.

May, 1536.

---

[1] E. Chapuis to Charles V., May 9, 1545, Vienna Archives, P.C. 236, ii. fol. 26.

CHAP. XIX. obliged to surrender.   In direct violation of the terms
on which he capitulated, he was tried by a tribunal
of his worst enemies, condemned, and executed.   A
few weeks later his brother Gerhard shared his fate.

And now I close these pages.   My object has
been to show that very little is known of the events
of those times, and that the history of Henry's first
divorce and of the rise and fall of Anne Boleyn has
still to be written.   If I have contributed to dispel
a few errors, or have in any way helped towards the
desired end, I shall be satisfied.   The task I set
myself will have been fulfilled.

APPENDIX.

APPENDIX.

NOTE A.

THE BIRTH AND EARLY LIFE OF ANNE BOLEYN.

It has been generally held that Anne Boleyn was born in 1507, the authority for this date being a passage and a marginal note in Camden's *History of Elizabeth*. Dr. Lingard, Mr. Froude, and Dr. Brewer accept the statement of Camden as good evidence; but in this opinion I am unable to agree with them. Camden wrote more than fifty years after Anne's death, and in many instances his account of her early life can be proved to be quite incorrect. In this case also he is, I think, mistaken. Happily some evidence has been preserved as to Anne's age. At Basel there is a picture of her, painted by Holbein, which bears the inscription: HR. 1530—*ætatis* 27. It bears also the words (added later): Anna Regina. From this portrait, the authenticity of which is above suspicion, it would appear that in 1530 Anne Boleyn was in her twenty-seventh year, which would place her birth in 1503 or 1504. She may have been rather older, for women so vain as Anne generally give themselves out for somewhat younger than they are.

Most historians have been of opinion that Anne Boleyn was sent to France with Mary Tudor when Mary went to marry King Louis XII. Mr. Brewer strongly opposes

this view.   In the first volume of his *Calendar* he says:
"I take this opportunity of correcting a common error.
It was not Anne, but Mary Boleyn, her elder sister, who
attended the princess into France. . . ."; [1] and in the third
volume he says: "My own opinion is, that she went into
France with her father, Sir Thomas, when the latter was
sent ambassador to that kingdom in 1519, and that she
remained there until 1522.   Those who adopt the popular
statement will have to account for the improbability that
a child not more than seven years of age should have been
sent in the train of Queen Mary in preference to her elder
sister—that she should have been called Miss Boleyn when,
not only in the document referred to, but in others, younger
sisters are distinguished by their Christian names. . . . ." [2]
In the preface to the fourth volume he returns to the subject, and expresses his opinion as confidently as in the
passages just quoted.[3]

But the charge which Mr. Brewer brings against his
opponents, that they have followed, "with little examination,
and some additions," the account which Cavendish gives in
his *Life of Wolsey*, is not justified.[4]   Cavendish's book does
not contain, as Mr. Brewer pretends, "the earliest notices we
have of her career." [5]   Long before Cavendish wrote his *Life
of Wolsey*, notices about Anne's life had appeared in France,
and a long account in verse of her rise and fall had been
published.   A Spanish manuscript chronicle, written before
the year 1552 by some officer in the service of Henry VIII.
or Edward VI.,[6] contains a great many curious passages about
her, and there are references to her in many letters and other
papers of the same period.   English historians have made

---

[1] J. S. Brewer, *Letters and Papers*, vol. i. p. lxv., foot-note.

[2] *Letters and Papers*, vol. iii. p. ccccxxx.

[3] *Letters and Papers*, vol. iv. p. ccccxxxiii. and p. ccccxxxiv.

[4] *Letters and Papers*, vol. iii. p. ccccxxx.

[5] *Ibid.*

[6] *Cronica del Rey Enrico Otavo de Ingalaterra*, edited by the Marquis de
Molins.   Madrid, 1874.

little use of these sources, but abroad some of them have
been known and referred to by a good many writers.

From the account of Anne Boleyn in verse I have already
quoted [1] a passage which distinctly says that she accompanied
Mary Tudor when the latter was married to Louis XII. Of
this account there are two manuscript copies, both apparently
of the first half of the sixteenth century, preserved in the
French Bibliotheque Nationale.[2] In each of them it is stated
that the account was composed on the 2nd of June, 1536—
that is to say, a fortnight after Anne's death. The printed
version published at Lyons in 1545, though differing slightly
from both manuscripts, contains the same statement as to the
date of the composition of the poem.[3]

Charles de Bourgueville, who lived in the beginning and
in the middle of the sixteenth century, wrote a book called
Les Recherches et Antiquites de la Province de Neustrie, which is
a kind of diary mixed with antiquarian, historical, and political
discussions. In this book, among the events of the year 1533,
the writer notes the marriage of the King of England with
"a young lady called Anne Boullenc, who was brought up in
France." "She came there," he adds, "when King Louis XII.
married Queen Mary, sister of the King of England." [4]

So we have two independent witnesses to a fact which
at the time when they wrote must have been known to a
great many persons. Between 1520 and 1550 there must
have been in France many hundreds of men and women
who had known Anne Boleyn while she was at the court of
Francis, and the date when she came over could not have
been so soon forgotten.

[1] Vol. i. p. 41, foot-note.

[2] *Histoire de la Royne Anne de Boullant.* Paris, Bibl. Nat. MSS. Français,
vol. 1742 and vol. 2370, fol. 1.

[3] *Epistre contenant le proces criminel*, etc., par Carles aulmosnier de Mr. le
Daulphin.

[4] *Les Recherches et Antiquites de la Province de Neustrie* par Charles de
Bourgueville. Caen, 1583, p. 123 : "Une demoiselle nommee Anne Boullenc
laquelle avoit ete nourrie en France et y estoit venue lorsque le Roy Louis
douzieme epousa la Royne Marie soeur du Roy d'Angleterre."

In the *Cronica del Rey Enrico Otavo de Ingalaterra* it is said that Anne was most courteous towards Francis I., "because this Anne Boleyn was brought up in France at the court of the king."[1] This could not have been said had she gone to the French court when she was past fifteen, and remained there less than three years.

After the death of Anne a courtier told Chapuis (so Chapuis reports) that Henry had refused the hand of the daughter of Francis I. because she was too young, and because in the said concubine he had had too much experience of what the corruption of France was.[2] If Anne had lived less than three years in France it would have been absurd to speak of her as a sample of French morals.

That Anne remained a Frenchwoman in many of her habits and modes of thought is indicated by little idioms and expressions which she is reported to have used. For instance, she said of Sir William Fitzwilliam that during her examination at Greenwich he was in the forest of Windsor. This phrase puzzled Sir William Kingston, and even Dr. Lingard could not explain it. It is simply an adaptation of a Parisian idiom : " être dans la forêt de Fontainebleau," for being absent in mind.

After what I have said the reader will probably agree with me in thinking that if all this evidence had been known to Mr. Brewer he would have admitted that it was Anne who went to France in 1514. Had he done so, he would have found it difficult to maintain that Anne Boleyn was the younger and Mary Boleyn the elder sister. For, on his own showing, the younger sister remained at home and would not have been called Miss Boleyn.

---

[1] *Cronica del Rey Enrico Otavo*, p. 41 : " Y la Reina Annale hizo muy gran acatamiento porque esta Anna Boloña habido sido criada in Francia in la corte del Rey. . ."

[2] E. Chapuis to N. de Granvelle, June 6, 1538, Vienna Archives, P.C. 229½, iii. fol. 12: " Quil avoit trop experimente en la dicte concubine que cestoit de la pourriture de France." Both Mr. Froude and my copyist read "nourriture," but the stronger expression seems to me to be the true reading.

It is true that Mr. Brewer adduces what he considers good direct evidence for the opinion that Mary was the elder sister. "Any doubt on that head," Mr. Brewer says, "is entirely dispelled by the petition presented to Lord Burghley, in 1597, by Mary's grandson, the second Lord Hunsdon, claiming the Earldom of Ormond in virtue of Mary's right as the elder daughter. It is inconceivable that Lord Hunsdon could have been mistaken in so familiar a fact; still less that he should have ventured to prefer a petition to the queen, in which her mother was described as the younger sister, if she had in truth been the elder."[1]

I do not know whether Mr. Brewer had ever read the letter of Lord Hunsdon to which he refers. It certainly cannot have been present to his mind when he wrote this passage. The letter is not, as Mr. Brewer says, a petition; it is a letter asking for the advice and the favour of the Lord Treasurer, as Lord Hunsdon intends to prefer a petition to the queen. That he ever presented such a petition to Elizabeth there is no evidence to show.

In the letter to Lord Burghley, Lord Hunsdon says :—"My late Lord father, as resolved by the opinion of Heralds and Lawyers, ever assured me that a right and title was to descend on me to the Earledom of Ormond . . . . the brief of whose title was, I well remember, in that Sir Thomas Bullen was created Viscount Rochford and Earle of Ormond to him and his heirs general . . . . the Earledom of Ormond, he surviving his other children before that time attainted, he in right left to his eldest daughter Mary, who had issue, Henry, and Henry myself." Subsequently Lord Hunsdon says that Mary Boleyn was "the eldest daughter and sole heir" of Sir Thomas Bullen, whose manors, lands, and tenements descended to her.[2]

From the fact that Mary Boleyn inherited her father's

[1] *Letters and Papers*, vol. iv. p. ccxxvi.
[2] Lord Hunsdon to Lord Burghley, October 6, 1597, R.O. Elizabeth, Domestic Series, vol. 264, fol. 283.

estates Lord Hunsdon seems to have inferred that she was the eldest daughter; but she was her father's "sole heir," not as his eldest daughter, but as his only surviving descendant; Elizabeth being at that time considered a bastard, and legally non-existent. The argument based on Lord Hunsdon's letter, therefore, falls to the ground; and the fact that he was not recognised as Viscount Rochford and Earl of Ormond, but that his son, after the death of Elizabeth, was created Viscount Rochford, goes some way to prove that Anne was older than Mary.

There is nothing to break the force of Mr. Brewer's argument that it must have been the elder sister who was spoken of as Miss Boleyn, and who was sent to France with Mary Tudor. And as it was Anne who went with Mary Tudor, and who was called Miss Boleyn, she must have been the elder sister.

As to Anne's life in France, Sanders says that she was brought up at first near Briere,[1] and T. Brodeau, in his life of Charles Dumoulin, improving on this statement, asserts that she was brought up in Brie by a relative of Dumoulin.[2] But "near Briere" certainly does not mean "in Brie," but near the little town of Briare, which Englishmen at that time generally spelled Briere. Both the Duke of Norfolk and Peter Vannes spell it so.[3]

It is probable, however, that Anne was brought up neither "near Briere" nor "in Brie." Claude of France, the wife of Francis I., was a very good woman who took pleasure in superintending the education of young girls. She is said to have had large numbers of them at court, as many as three hundred at a time, who were taught by the best masters. "When Mary returned to this country," says the writer of the history in verse, "she [Anne] was retained by Claude, the

---

[1] N. Sanders, *de Origine Schismati*, 1588, p. 16.

[2] J. Brodeau, *Vie de Maistre Charles du Moulin*, p. 7.

[3] Norfolk to Henry VIII. and Peter Vannes to Cromwell, June 23, 1533, *Letters and Papers*, vol. vi. p. 307, 308.

new queen, at whose court she became so graceful that you would never have taken her for an Englishwoman, but for a Frenchwoman born." [1] There can be little doubt, therefore, that Anne spent most of the time she was in France at the court of Queen Claude.

That she returned to England in 1522, about the new year, is proved by the papers cited by Mr. Brewer. These papers also settle the date of the negotiations for her marriage with one of her Irish cousins. Mr. Brewer at first thought that the negotiations referred to Mary Boleyn, but this error he corrected. He continued, however, to be mistaken about the person whom Anne was to marry. The husband proposed for her was not, as Mr. Brewer thought, Sir Piers Butler,[2] but the son of Sir Piers, Sir James.

In speaking of her life between 1522 and 1526, Mr. Froude quotes a letter addressed to a Mr. Melton and speaking of a Mistress Anne, as if there could be no doubt that it referred to Anne Boleyn.[3] A French writer, M. Albert du Boys, translating the letter, fancied that he might safely add to "Anne" the little word "Boleyn." And so he did.[4] But there is not the slightest reason to think that the letter to Mr. Melton belongs to a time when the writer could possibly have alluded to Anne Boleyn as "Mistress Anne." The writer says : "I must

---

[1] *Histoire de la Royne Anne de Boullant, loc. cit.* :—

> " Apres que Marie fust revenue
> En ce pays, elle fust retenue
> Par Claude, qui Royne apres succeda
> Ou tellement ses graces amenda
> Que ne leussiez oncques jugee angloyse
> En ses facons, mais naifve francoyse ; "

and *Cronica del Rey Enrico Otavo de Ingalaterra.*

[2] *Letters and Papers*, vol. iv. p. ccxxxviii.

[3] J. A. Froude, *History of England*, vol. i. p. 184 :—

Mr. Melton.— " This shall be to advertise you that Mistress Anne is changed from that she was at when we three were last together. . ."

[4] Albert du Boys, *Catherine d'Aragon*, p. 146 : "Cette lettre est pour Vous avertir du grand changement qui sest opere dans Anne de Boleyn depuis trois ans que nous l'avons veue, pendant que nous etions ensemble."

go to my master, wheresoever he be, for the Lord Privy Seal desireth much to speak with me, whom if I should speak with in my master's absence, it would cause me to lose my head." Who was this Lord Privy Seal, whom to speak with might have cost the writer his head? It is most improbable that the reference was either to Thomas Rowthall or to his successor Cuthbert Tunstall, for the one was commonly called my Lord of Durham, and the other my Lord of London, the episcopal dignity being considered the higher of the two. I cannot remember any letter in which either of these two bishops is spoken of as "the Lord Privy Seal." The letter, therefore, appears to have been written after Tunstall had relinquished his office to Lord Wiltshire, who was sometimes called Lord Privy Seal. But it was only in 1530 that Anne Boleyn's father obtained the office, and as at that time she was called Lady Anne, the allusion in the letter must be to another of the numerous ladies called Anne, and not to her.

Cavendish's account of the flirtation between Anne Boleyn and Sir Henry Percy is rejected by Mr. Brewer, because in his opinion it cannot have taken place after Sir Henry was betrothed to Lady Mary Talbot.[1] I cannot understand the argument, for Cavendish distinctly tells us that it did take place after the betrothal, and that Sir Henry asked Cardinal Wolsey to have the betrothal annulled. There is nothing impossible or very improbable in this account, and, as Cavendish was certainly with Wolsey at the time, I see no reason to disbelieve his statement. It is confirmed by the fact that Chapuis and other contemporary writers repeatedly assert or imply that Anne was on very intimate terms with young Percy about the beginning of 1527 or about the end of 1526.[2]

---

[1] *Letters and Papers*, vol. iv. p. ccxliii. foot-note.

[2] E. Chapuis to Charles V., May 2, 1536, *loc. cit* : " Yl y avoit des temoigs tous conformes testiffians mariage avoir este passe neufz ans faict et charnellement consume entre elle et le conte nortanberlan."

NOTE B.

WAS MARY BOLEYN HENRY'S MISTRESS?

THE question whether Mary Boleyn was the mistress of
Henry VIII. is now generally answered in the affirmative.
Notwithstanding all the evidence which has come to light,
however, Mr. Froude still maintains the opposite view. He
says:—"The argument from the Pope's silence, and from the
absence of all mention of the Mary Boleyn connection in
every authoritative document where it would most have been
expected, has always appeared to me so weighty as to over-
balance floating scandal, rhetorical invective, and conclusions
drawn by inference from ambiguous legal documents. The
story may have been true, and if it was true it was peculiarly
disgraceful, but it is not proved. In my own opinion the
balance of probability is the other way, but those who believe
it will find their case strengthened by the deliberate words
of the Imperial ambassador." [1]

As Mr. Froude thus states the case for Henry and Mary
Boleyn, I will now state the case against them; after which
the reader may form his own opinion on the subject. I
agree with Mr. Froude that if the story was true "it was
peculiarly disgraceful;" but it is fair to add that as morals
at the English court were at that time extremely low,
Henry's conduct ought not to be judged by a very elevated
standard.

[1] *History of England*, vol. ii. App. p. 655.

Mary Boleyn was married in February, 1521 (not, as Mr.
Brewer says, in 1520), to Mr. William Carey (not, as Mr.
Froude says, to Sir Henry Carey).   Mr. Froude asserts that
" the liaison, if real, must have taken place previous to 1521.
In the January of that year Mary Boleyn married Sir Henry
Carey, and no one pretends that it occurred after she became
Carey's wife.   Nothing was known about it at the time, nor
was it ever heard of till many years after, during the agita-
tion of the first divorce." [1]

This is not the fact.   It has been " pretended " that Mary
Boleyn was Henry's mistress after she became Carey's wife.
There is still at the Record Office a paper containing the
confession of a monk of Syon, in which the following
passage occurs: " Moreover, Mr. Skydmore did show me
young master Care, saying that he was our sovereign lord
the king's son, by our sovereign lady the queen's sister,
whom the queen's grace might not suffer to be in the
court." [2]

Not only, then, was it said that Anne's sister was Henry's
mistress after her marriage, but it was stated that Henry
Carey was the king's son.   I hasten to say that I know
of no other evidence in support of the latter assertion.

In 1527, Henry VIII., wishing to divorce Catherine and to
marry Anne Boleyn, applied for a dispensation to marry any
woman, even if she stood in the first degree of affinity to
him, *ex quocunque licito seu illicito coitu conjuncta*, provided
she were not the widow of his late brother.   Why should
this extraordinary and superfluous clause have been inserted,
if Mary Boleyn had not been the king's mistress?   Mr.
Froude, indeed, contends that the clause proves nothing
against his hero.   " The dispensations," he suggests, " granted
to Emmanuel of Portugal, who married two sisters and afterwards his niece, may have nearly resembled this.   Legal
documents of the kind were made as broad as possible to

[1] *History of England*, vol. ii. App. p. 653.
[2] R. O. 26th, Henry VIII. Box Q, No. 127.

cover all questions which might afterwards be raised."[1]
Had Mr. Froude taken the trouble to make inquiry as to the
dispensations he speaks of, he would have found that they
contain no such clause. I have examined many briefs and
bulls of dispensation, and I have discovered no clause of the
kind in any of them.

Dr. Ortiz, the Spanish theologian sent to Rome to defend
Catherine's interest, was informed by the courtiers of Clement,
that Dr. Knight, who had been deputed to ask for the dispensation, had made no secret of the reasons for which it was
wanted. "It is certain truth," Dr. Ortiz wrote to the
empress, "that some time ago he [Henry] sent to ask his
holiness for a dispensation to marry her, notwithstanding the
affinity between them on account of his having committed
adultery with her sister."[2]

In 1529 Charles V. had already heard of the matter. On
the 5th of January, 1530, he gave audience to Dr. Richard
Sampson, one of the English ambassadors who had been
sent to convince the emperor of the necessity of the divorce.
Charles declared that Henry's conscientious scruples did not
seem to be justified, especially "if it were true, as his said
Majesty had heard (although he himself would not positively
affirm it), that the said king had kept company with the
sister of her whom he now, it was stated, wanted to marry."
To the other observations of the emperor, Sampson replied ;
to this he made no answer.[3] Was not that a tacit admission
of the truth of what the emperor had heard ?

In 1532, Eustache Chapuis speaks of the former adultery
of Henry with Mary Boleyn as a well-known fact of which
there can be no doubt. "Even if," he writes, "he could
separate from the queen, he could not have her [Anne], for

---

[1] *History of England*, vol. ii. App. p. 653.

[2] Dr. Ortiz to the empress, February 7, 1533, British Museum, Add. MSS.
28,585, fol. 217.

[3] Account of the conversation of the emperor with Dr. Sampson, sent to
E. Chapuis, January 5, 1530, Vienna Archives, P.C. 226, ii. fol. i.

he has had to do with her sister." [1]   In the following year several persons were arrested in England because they had blamed the king for marrying the sister of his former mistress.

Before Henry's marriage with Anne, Sir George Throgmorton spoke to him of a rumour that he, Henry, had had improper relations both with her mother and with her sister. The king replied, "Never with the mother;" and Cromwell, who was present, added, "Nor with the sister either." [2]   All this was set forth by Sir George Throgmorton in a letter addressed to Henry himself, after the death of Anne Boleyn. "The sting of the imputation," as Mr. Brewer justly remarks, "consists not in the character of the writer, but in the tacit admission made by the king."

In 1533, Parliament passed an Act promulgating a table of degrees of consanguinity and affinity, within which marriage was forbidden; and it is remarkable that while this table covered the case of Henry and Catherine, it was so framed as to permit marriage with a sister of a discarded mistress. Up to this time the canon law had been in force; and, in that law, so far as forbidden degrees were concerned, no difference was made between legitimate and illegitimate intercourse. As soon as the marriage between Henry and Anne was to be null and void, the provisions of the canon law began again to command respect; and in 1536 Parliament passed a new Act ordering every man who had married the sister of a former mistress to separate from her, and forbidding such marriages in the future.

Before this Act was passed, Chapuis had again stated as an indubitable fact that Mary Boleyn had been the mistress of Henry, and he had added that it was on this ground that Cranmer had pronounced a divorce between Henry and Anne.

Such, in the main, are the arguments for the opinion that

[1] E. Chapuis to Charles V., August 9, 1532, Vienna Archives. P.C. 227, iv. fol. 60.

[2] Brewer, *Letters and Papers*, vol. iv. p. cccxxix. foot-note.

Mary Carey had been the mistress of Henry. The case for the defence, as stated by Mr. Froude in the passage I have quoted, is, that the pope did not take official cognisance of the connection, and that no mention of it is made in any "authoritative document where it would most have been expected."

The answer to the first of these two arguments is very simple. The pope did not take official cognisance of a fact which had never been brought officially before him. For reasons which I have explained in the text, the imperial agents opposed the marriage with Anne, on no other ground than that it was a contempt of court. They asserted that Catherine was Henry's wife; and beyond this they did not need to go. The two sentences of Clement, therefore, simply pronounced the marriage with Catherine to be valid. The bull of Paul III. excommunicated and deprived Henry for a great many acts which were perfectly public and undeniable, such as the casting off of Catherine, the concubinage with Anne, the rebellion against the spiritual authority of the Holy See, and the execution of Cardinal Fisher. It would have been mere folly in the pope to have weakened his case by making any assertion which could have been disputed; for if he had done so, Henry would have complained to all the world that the pope was slandering him. So Paul III. wisely abstained from speaking about Mary Boleyn.

As to the second argument, I know not where Mr. Froude supposes that mention of "the Mary Boleyn connection" ought to be expected. I have shown that it is mentioned in a good many documents which are still preserved. That it is not acknowledged in any document issued with Henry's authority is true, but that proves nothing except that he was, perhaps, just a little ashamed of "peculiarly disgraceful" immorality.

NOTE C.

THE AUTHENTICITY OF THE BRIEF OF DISPENSATION.

THE brief dated the 26th of December, 1503, by which
Julius II. granted a dispensation to Henry and Catherine
to contract marriage, although the former marriage of
Catherine with Prince Arthur had been consummated, has
been frequently spoken of as a forgery. Its authenticity
was denied by Henry VIII. and his ministers; and this view,
which was adopted by Bishop Burnet, has been supported by
Mr. Froude. As the genuineness of the brief has been
considered probable by Dr. Lingard, Dr. Brewer, and
Mr. Pocock, it might have been unnecessary to argue the
question afresh, had not the opinion of Bishop Burnet and
Mr. Froude been defended in the *Quarterly Review*
(January, 1877) in an article attributed to a writer who
enjoys a deservedly high reputation for fairness, ability, and
learning.

"The brief was unheard of," says the Reviewer, "until the
need for it became apparent."[1] This, however, is not proved.
In documents belonging to the years 1504 and 1505 there
are several allusions to a brief which seems to have been
this very parchment. From a letter written on the 17th of
March 1505 by the Bishop of Worcester to Henry VII.[2] we

---

[1] *Quarterly Review*, No. 285, January, 1877, p. 38.
[2] Gairdner, *Letters and Papers Illustrative of the Reigns of Richard III. and Henry VIII.*, vol. i. p. 243.

know that a duplicate of the dispensation was sent in the autumn of 1504 to Queen Isabella of Spain, and this duplicate is nowhere said to have been an exact copy of the intended bull. It is highly probable, therefore, that it was the brief dated the 26th of December, 1503.

"It was unknown to Charles V.," the Reviewer continues, "when, on the 31st of July, 1527, he suggested that the pope should supply the defects of the bull. It was uncertain whether Clement would consent, when, towards the end of the year, the brief made his consent unnecessary. Its existence was unexplained." Unexplained at the time it was, but this is not of much importance if, as I have suggested, the brief was sent to Queen Isabella in the autumn of 1504.

"It was said to have been obtained," adds the Reviewer, "about the time of the marriage, in 1509; but it was dated 1503." In proof of the former statement the Reviewer cites a few lines from a very rare and curious book, *Philalethæ Hyperborei . . . Parasceve*, ascribed by some to Cochlæus, by others to Ludovicus Vives. But he mistakes, I think, the true bearing of this evidence. Philalethes does not say that Catherine, or the emperor, or their agents, pretended that the brief had been obtained about the time of the marriage, in 1509. Nor does he himself give this date. He merely repeats what is said by Catherine's adversaries. They, he declares, point out that the words *forsan cognita* occur in the bull, but that in the brief which Ferdinand obtained about the time of the marriage *forsan* does not occur. This they make use of, "as an invincible ram," to prove that Catherine's marriage was consummated. In opposition to them, Philalethes adduces a letter written on the 23rd of August, 1503, by Ferdinand to Don Francisco de Rojas, his ambassador at Rome, in which the king states that the marriage was not consummated. On the question of the date of the brief Philalethes offers no opinion; and he does not think it worth while to inform his readers whether Catherine's enemies had any good reason for asserting that the document was issued "circiter tempus nuptiarum."[1] This argument of the Reviewer must also, then, be dismissed as proving nothing at all against the brief.

"It was obtained by Ferdinand, yet Ferdinand did not possess a copy." How is this known ? There is not a tittle of evidence to show that Ferdinand had not, besides the original, even several copies of the brief. "It was sent to England, but it was admitted that it had left England before the marriage for which it was required." I know of no evidence for this assertion, and none is adduced by the writer. The brief seems to have been found among the papers left by Dr. de Puebla to his sons, for one of them, Ruiz de Puebla, declared that he had placed it in the hands of the emperor in the beginning of 1528.[2] How it came to be among the papers of the doctor there is nothing to show, and I have nowhere found anything which may be called an admission that it was in England, or that it left that country, at any specified date.

But even admitting that the writer correctly describes the facts, they would not prove his case. The brief sent to Queen Isabella when on her death-bed may have been despatched to England to facilitate the marriage which Ferdinand desired, and when at a later period the bull of dispensation was brought from Rome by the Bishop of Worcester, the brief, being considered superfluous, may have been kept by de Puebla. This is a perfectly natural account of the circumstances, and offers an easy explanation of the difficulty raised by the writer in the *Quarterly Review*.

"Ferdinand did not want it, for, on his theory, it was quite

---

[1] *Philalethæ Hyperborei . . . Parasceve.* Lueneburg, 1533 : " Primum tanquam invincibilem arietem objiciunt, quod cum in ipso dispensationis diplomate, sive bulla habeantur haec verba forsan cognitam, in Brevi vero quod circiter tempus nuptiarum ut conficeretur ab Ferdinando Rege Catholico procuratum est, dudum ex Hispaniis allato simpliciter sit adscriptum cognitam non addito dubitandi adverbio forsan."

[2] Gayangos, *Calendar*, vol. iv. part i. p. 881 ; and Gairdner, *Letters and Papers of Henry VIII.*, vol. v. p. 171.

unnecessary." The writer must have forgotten that he himself had just cited a letter from Ferdinand of Aragon to Don Francisco de Rojas, his ambassador at Rome, which points to the opposite conclusion. In this letter the Catholic king states, indeed, that such a brief is not rendered necessary by the real state of the case, but he adds that as the English are very suspicious and fond of raising difficulties, the ambassador is to obtain a dispensation; and his directions as to the contents of the proposed dispensation exactly correspond to the form in which the brief is made out.[1]

"If he [Ferdinand] had asked for it the brief would have been addressed to him, and a copy would have been treasured up in Spain." This is not a necessary inference. The bull of dispensation was asked for by Henry VII. and by Ferdinand, and it was addressed to neither of them.[2]

The Reviewer asserts that the brief "was addressed to Henry VII."; but in reality, like the bull, it was addressed to Henry, the son of Henry VII., and to Catherine, the daughter of Ferdinand and Isabella.[3]

"But Henry did not want it; for he was more than content with the original bull, which he never intended to use, and could never wish to amplify." True; but this tells rather against than for the writer's argument, for it explains very well why the brief, if it really was sent to de Puebla, did not remain in England, but was taken back to Spain.

"The brief was discovered among the papers of the Ambassador de Puebla, who had left England before the marriage, and who was now dead. A list of all his papers relating to the marriage is still extant, and the brief is not among them." We have no list of *all* de Puebla's papers

---

[1] G. Bergenroth, *Calendar*, vol. i. p. 309; and *Philalethæ Hyperborei Parasceve*, fol. c. iii.

[2] Julius II. to Henry, son of Henry King of England and Catherine, daughter of Ferdinand and Isabella, December 26, 1503, R. O.

[3] Julius II. to Henry, son of Henry King of England, and to Catherine, daughter of Ferdinand and Isabella, December 26, 1503, Vienna Archives, P.C. 228, iii. fol. i.

relating to the marriage. What is known about the matter is that in the beginning of 1528 Ruiz de Puebla handed over the brief to the emperor, that afterwards, about 1529, he was requested to bring up all papers relating to the marriage, that he then made search for them and found those enumerated in the list which the Reviewer asserts to be complete, that several years later he made another search and found more papers relating to the marriage, and that he declared all this in 1545 before a notary in Spain.[1]

"Two men," the Reviewer continues, "were living who could have given valuable testimony. De Puebla's heir, Fernandez, had possession of his papers." From the deposition of Ruiz de Puebla above referred to, it clearly appears that this was not so. It was the brother of Fernandez who had possession of the papers of Dr. Ruy Gonzalez de Puebla.

"He [Fernandez] was reputed an honest man, and it was desirable to have him examined. It appeared, however, that he had just been sent to one of the few places in Europe which were beyond the reach of Henry and the jurisdiction of Charles—to the dominion of the Earl of Desmond." Gonçalo Fernandez was despatched from Toledo in February, 1529.[2] On the 28th of April following, the Earl of Desmond signed a petition to Charles V. which Fernandez was to take back with him; and towards the end of May the English ambassador at the Spanish Court reported that he had returned to Spain from Ireland.[3] The absence of Fernandez, on which the Reviewer lays so much stress, lasted therefore not more than about three months, and on his return the English ambassadors might have questioned him if they had chosen to do so.

"Accolti," the Reviewer proceeds, "the cardinal who in the

---

[1] Deposition of Ruiz de Puebla, September 14, 1515, Gayangos, *Calendar*, vol. iv. part i. p. 881 ; and Gairdner, *Letters and Papers*, vol. v. p. 171.

[2] Instructions to Gonçalo Fernandez, February, 1529, Gayangos, *Calendar*, vol. iii. part ii. p. 907.

[3] Ghinucci and Lee to Wolsey, May 31, 1529, Brewer, *Letters and Papers*, vol. iv. p. 2485.

name of Julius had drawn up the dispensation a quarter of a century earlier, was now the most zealous opponent of the divorce in the Court of Rome. He could have settled the doubt whether a second dispensation had, in fact, been given. Accolti remained impenetrably silent."

The bull and the brief are countersigned by the papal secretary Sigismundus; and from this it would appear that both were drawn up by him. (The bull is also countersigned by D. de Comitibus, by whom it was written out.) There is no evidence that Accolti, who was not a cardinal when the dispensations were granted, had anything to do with the drawing up of the writings; and the Reviewer's assertion that Accolti " could have settled the doubt whether a second dispensation had, in fact, been given," seems to me to be wholly unwarranted.

As to Accolti being the most zealous opponent of the divorce, so far from this being the case, he was for a time considered decidedly favourable to Henry. Under the name of " the old man " he is frequently mentioned by the English agents at Rome, who took his advice as to the way in which they were to proceed. The English agents and he were constantly haggling about the terms on which he would sell his support, and great promises were made to him. His nephew, Benedict de Accoltis, was nominated by Henry to the See of Coventry and Lichfield with a promise of promotion to the more opulent Bishopric of Ely. Under these circumstances it would have been strange indeed if Cardinal Peter de Accoltis had volunteered any statement which might have damaged the cause of Henry. If he knew anything about the issuing of a brief of dispensation, it was certainly not his interest to make a public statement to that effect.

" Though addressed to Henry VII., the brief was unknown in England." I have already stated that the brief was not addressed to Henry VII., and it is impossible to prove that it was unknown in England. It was of the utmost importance to the king that the brief should be held to be spurious, and had any royal official known of a copy of it in England he would have been careful to keep the secret. An Englishman might have lost his head for asserting that there was proof that such a brief had been made out.

"It formed the strongest security for the honour and the legal position of a Spanish princess: yet it did not exist in the archives of Spain." The Reviewer had, no doubt, read the preface to the first volume of Mr. Bergenroth's *Calendar;* but the contents of it seem to have escaped his memory. In that preface Mr. Bergenroth distinctly states that during the reign of Ferdinand and Isabella there were no archives of Spain. The papers were scattered about in strong boxes in different palaces and convents, and in one instance Mr. Bergenroth shows that they were actually deposited abroad.[1] The institution of the royal archives of Spain dates from 1543, when Charles V. decided that state papers were to be preserved in the castle of Simancas.

The circumstance noted by the Reviewer as an argument against the authenticity of the brief, speaks rather in favour of it. If the brief had been forged, the secret would have been confided to as few persons as possible; for the more accomplices there are in such transactions the greater are the chances of detection. Besides Charles himself, no one ought to have known of it but Gattinara, whose aid would probably have been indispensable, and the actual forger. Why should Ruiz de Puebla have been let into the secret? Why was it not simply pretended that the brief had been found by Gattinara in some of the royal arcas? That this was not done is almost sufficient proof (in the absence of contradictory evidence) that the brief was not a forgery.

"It constituted the most extreme exertion of the pope's prerogative known till then: yet Rome preserved no record of its existence." The statement that the dispensation to marry a late brother's wife was the most extreme exertion of the pope's prerogative known till 1503, is open to question.

[1] G. Bergenroth, *Calendar*, vol. i. pp. iv. and v.

The dispensation given to King Henry IV. of Castille to commit bigamy seems to me to go somewhat further.

"In April, 1529, Charles was in doubt as to the value of the brief. He was willing to submit it to the pope. His mind would not, he said, be at rest until he knew whether it had been found in the Roman registers. His doubts were soon satisfied. The registers were subjected to the scrutiny of Spanish and English agents. They found no trace of the brief." This objection would have had some force, had it not been lately shown that the real date both of the bull and of the brief was later than the professed date. According to a letter of the Bishop of Worcester, the brief was made out in the autumn of 1504, the bull perhaps even later.[1] If the English and Spanish agents looked for the dispensation under the date of December, 1503—as they probably did—it was, of course, impossible that they should find it. The Reviewer's argument would have been of some importance if he could have shown that the bull of dispensation had been properly entered in the registers, but that the brief had not been so entered. This, however, nobody has yet shown.

"Errors were detected in the text. A vital flaw was detected in the date." There are a good many errors in the text, and there is a flaw in the date. But it is a mistake to say that the flaw in the date is a *vital* flaw. An error in the date of a dispensation did not then—and would not now —make the dispensation invalid. If it had done so, a great many people would have had to suffer.

There is no doubt that in the end of the fifteenth century it became the custom of the Roman court, in dating briefs, to regard the year as beginning on the 25th of December. A few years after the issue of the bull and the brief of dispensation, the same Sigismundus who had drawn them up dated a brief directed to the Archbishop of Rouen: "Datum Romæ, apud Sanctum Petrum, sub annulo piscatoris die

---

[1] The Bishop of Worcester to Henry VII., March 17, 1505, Gairdner' *Letters and Papers of Richard III. and Henry VII.*, vol. i. p. 243.

XXVIII[a] decembris M[o] D[o] VIIII[o], pontificatus nostri anno sexto." [1] The brief of Clement VII. announcing his escape from the castle of St. Angelo is dated: " Die ultima decembris MDXXVIII pont. nostri anno quinto." [2] But although at the time of the divorce it was laid down at Rome that the year was to be reckoned in bulls from the 1st of January, and in briefs from the 25th of December, this rule was not strictly adhered to; the greatest diversity continued to exist in the computation. There is, therefore, nothing very extraordinary in the fact that the new papal secretary, having in 1504 to make out a brief which was to go forth as one that had been written in the preceding year, dated it either intentionally or by mistake in an unusual manner. The flaw is certainly not, as the Reviewer says, " a vital flaw."

" Charles never sent it to Rome for judgment." This may be admitted; but the emperor strongly objected to part with the brief, and declared his intention of submitting it himself to the inspection of the pope. He did not go to Rome until the spring of 1536 on his return from Tunis, when the divorce suit had long been decided; but in 1529 he met the pope at Bologna, and there, as I believe, he laid the brief before Clement and his cardinals and auditors. That the brief was never sent to Rome, therefore, proves nothing against its authenticity.

The Reviewer adds: " It was no longer necessary. The brief had served to delay action in the legates' court until the pope was reconciled with Spain." From this it might be concluded that after the pope was reconciled with Spain the brief was no more heard of; but the truth is that its authenticity was assumed in all the discussions which preceded the sentences of July and August, 1533, and of the 23rd of March, 1534. In July, 1533, it was decided by the college of cardinals that Julius II. was entitled to grant such a dispensation as that which is contained in the brief; and i

---

[1] Paris, Bibl. Nat. MSS. Français, vol. 2,960, fol. 4.
[2] Paris, Bibl. Nat. MSS. Français, vol. 3,010, fol. 64.

March, 1534, it was considered that for the sentence in favour of the queen such a dispensation was necessary. Soon after leaving the consistory, Cardinal Campeggio told the Spanish agents that if the queen's case had depended on the proof of her virginity he would have had grave doubts about the justice of it. But he had regarded it as settled that the marriage was forbidden only by the human law, and so he had never doubted of the result. It is scarcely correct, therefore, to say that after the reconciliation of the pope with Spain the brief was no longer necessary.

The brief is in the Vienna Archives among the papers which came from Brussels ; and we may safely say that it would not have been preserved had Charles V. known that it was a forgery. And it is incredible that if it was a forgery he was ignorant of the fact. I may add that I have carefully examined the brief, and that I found in it nothing which seemed to indicate that it had been forged. It has been inspected by several other persons well versed in paleography, and from none of them have I heard any expression of doubt as to its authenticity. Unless, therefore, the Reviewer can bring forward more important evidence, or show that impartial and capable judges who have seen the brief agree with him, the document about which there has been so much discussion must be accepted as genuine. It will give me much pleasure if the arguments I have advanced induce him to reconsider his judgment in the matter.

NOTE D.

THE DATE OF ANNE'S MARRIAGE.

ACCORDING to some historians, Henry and Anne were married on the 14th of November, 1532; according to others, on the 25th of January, 1533. The former date has been adopted by all who have wished to make it appear that there was no stain on the birth of Elizabeth. I do not know of any documentary evidence for it, and so far as I am aware none has ever been brought forward by the numerous panegyrists of Henry.

For the later date there is evidence which to my mind seems perfectly conclusive, unless, indeed—as is possible—Henry and Anne were never formally married at all. Cranmer, writing on the 17th of June to Dr. Hawkyns, his successor at the Imperial Court, says that Anne Boleyn's marriage took place about St. Paul's day last; that is to say, about the 25th of January.[1] It has been objected to this that Cranmer was a most inexact man, and wrote nearly five months after the date he mentions. I fully admit that Cranmer was inexact; but it appears impossible that he should have said the ceremony took place in the end of January if it really took place in the middle of November, especially when it was not the interest of the archbishop or his friends to adopt the later date.

[1] T. Cranmer to Hawkyns, June 17, 1533, Gairdner, *Letters and Papers*, vol. vi. p. 300.

Cranmer's statement is corroborated by several passages in the despatches of Chapuis. On the 15th of April, 1533, Chapuis reports that on the 9th the Duke of Norfolk and other commissioners had waited on Queen Catherine, asking her to relinquish her pretensions, and that, when she had refused, Norfolk had declared it did not matter, for, more than two months before, the king had married Anne Boleyn, though none of them had been called to be present at the ceremony.[1] This agrees very well with the later date. If the true date had been the 14th of November, Norfolk would certainly have said that the king had married Anne Boleyn more than four months before.

Shortly afterwards Chapuis wrote that it was generally said the ceremony had been performed on the day of the Conversion of St. Paul.[2]

The statement of Cranmer is, therefore, fully borne out by the Imperial ambassador, and it cannot be fairly denied that the king and his adherents spoke of the 25th of January as the date of the marriage. As they had no reason whatever to adopt a later date than the true one, but, on the contrary, for the sake of the expected prince, had every reason to adopt the earliest date possible, the official account must be accepted as altogether beyond dispute.

[1] E. Chapuis to Charles V., April 15, 1533, Vienna Archives, P.C. 228, i. fol. 41.
[2] E. Chapuis to Charles V., May 10, 1533, Vienna Archives, P.C. 228 i. fol. 61.

NOTE E.

BISHOP FISHER IN THE SPRING OF 1535.

In November, 1534, Fisher and More were treated with greater rigour than at any previous period of their imprisonment; and shortly before Christmas Cromwell advised the bishop to write to the king. Fisher hesitated, as he said, for fear of offending Henry, but he addressed a letter to Cromwell himself, representing his miserable state, and asking either to be released from prison or at least to be allowed to see a priest during the holy days and to have the use of some books of devotion.[1]

Cromwell's answer to this request I have not found, but towards the new year the severity with which the prisoners had been treated was certainly very much relaxed. We hear from William Roper, Sir Thomas More's son-in-law, that about that time Sir Thomas was visited by Cromwell, who spoke in a friendly manner, and assured him that he would not again be pressed with questions, or asked to make any declaration or to take any oath. The king, Cromwell said, was well disposed towards him, and would show him all possible favour.[2]

A few days later it was reported that Fisher and More had made their submission and were restored to the good graces of the king. Of course this was not true; but we know that

[1] T. Fisher to Cromwell, December 22, 1534, *Archæologia*, vol. xxv. p. 93.

[2] More's works, edition of 1557, p. 1,452 ; and Roper's *Life of Sir Thomas More.*

about the middle of January Sir Thomas More was once more allowed to correspond with his friends.[1]

On the 5th of February Palamede Gontier wrote that on the 1st, at the Court at Westminster, he had given the admiral's letters to the Duke of Norfolk, who had inquired about Chabot's health, "and the same did Messieurs of Suffolk and Fischer."[2]

When I first read this passage of Gontier's letter, I felt nearly sure that it was a mistake; but after some time I became less confident. If the name Fischer does not refer to the bishop, it can only stand for Wiltshire. But, according to the French orthography of the time, Wiltshire was written either Wulchier, Vulchier, or Wuilchier; and if Lelaboureur read and printed "Fischer" for any one of these forms, he was guilty of a very gross mistake indeed. That he committed so grave a blunder is highly improbable, for he was well aware that Anne's father was Earl of "Wilt" and Ormond, and that Fisher was a prisoner in the Tower. Besides, there is ample evidence in this letter that when Lelaboureur met with the name of an unknown person he printed it correctly. He printed Ovaston and Borgonny, which are certainly the forms Gontier was likely to use in spelling the names of Sir William Weston and Lord Abergavenny.

There are but two reasons why it might seem probable that there is a mistake. First, in the very long letter no mention is made of the "Comte de Wulchier." But the reader naturally expects to find some reference to Lord Rochford; and his name does not occur any more than that of his father. The truth is that at that time the Boleyns were out of favour. It is significant that when commissioners were designated to treat of the marriage of little Elizabeth with the Duke of Angoulême neither her grandfather nor her uncle were appointed, and that they are not mentioned

[1] More's works, p. 1,450.
[2] Palamede Gontier to Chabot de Brion, February 5, 1535, Lelaboureur. Memoires de Mr. de Castelnau, vol. i. p. 405.

among the guests at a great supper party which was given a few days later by the French ambassador.

The second circumstance which might suggest a doubt whether "Fischer" means the bishop, is that in another part of the letter Gontier says that on the 2nd of February, while he was in the ballroom, "Messieurs of Nortfolk, Suffolk, Fischer, the Chancellor, Cromwell, and others sat in council." This passage would present no difficulty if "Fischer" was Lord Wiltshire; but it needs explanation if Gontier alluded to the bishop, for it is most unlikely that Fisher was called from the Tower to take part in the proceedings of the royal council. But Gontier was not present at the sitting, and, not seeing Bishop Fisher in the ballroom, he may have concluded that he was in the council-chamber. And there the bishop may really have been, for he was very often before the council both at the Tower and elsewhere. Even this passage, therefore, does not prove that the reference is to Lord Wiltshire.

Nevertheless, it would be hard to accept Gontier's statement as it appears in Lelaboureur's volume, were it not that it is supported by other evidence. At the British Museum a paper is preserved setting forth the sums which Sir Edmund Walsingham, the Lieutenant of the Tower, charged the king for the maintenance of the prisoners. When the charge was only for a part of the time during which the prisoners were confined, or when they themselves had paid a portion of the amount due, a note to that effect was made. In this paper we find the following record:—

The Bishop of Rochester for XIIIIth monthys
after XX<i>s</i>. le weke summa . . . . LVI li.[1]

That is to say, the Lieutenant of the Tower charged for the maintenance of Bishop Fisher during fourteen months of four weeks each, or during a year and twenty-seven days. But Fisher was sent to the Tower on the 16th or 17th of April,

[1] British Museum, Cotton MSS. Titus B.I. fol. 165.

1534, and executed on the 22nd of June, 1535, between
which dates one year and sixty-six or sixty-seven days
intervened—forty days more than Sir Edmund charged for.
There is no note that this is a charge only for a part of the
time, or that the prisoner had paid the six pounds which are
not included in the account; and as it cannot be supposed
that Sir Edmund demanded less than he was entitled to
demand, we are driven to the conclusion that between the
17th of April, 1534, and the 22nd of June, 1535, Bishop
Fisher was forty days absent from the Tower.

Dr. Hall, the author of the *Life of Fisher* published by
Baily, tells a long story how the lords of the council first
sent for the bishop and asked him to swear to the Act of
Supremacy, pretending that Sir Thomas More had done so;
how when Fisher refused they sent him to the garden; how
the Lord Chancellor thereupon assured More's daughter,
Margaret Roper, that the Bishop of Rochester had taken the
oath and was at liberty, and restored to the royal favour;
how Margaret believed him, and reported to her father what
she had heard, and begged him to follow Fisher's example;
and how More declined to take the oath, doubting the truth
of Audley's statement. If any of these incidents really took
place, they must have happened early in 1535.[1]

Hall is by no means a perfectly trustworthy historian, and
his account is certainly not altogether correct. But it is clear
from his book that he had seen a good many documents; so
it is more probable that he inaccurately described what he
had read than that he invented the whole story.

After all, there is nothing very improbable in some parts of
the story of Hall or in the statement of Gontier. In the
beginning of 1535 Henry wished to conciliate his enemies,
and he was well aware that for this reason alone it would be
good policy to show some favour to Fisher and More. Moreover, we learn from Roper that, so far as Sir Thomas More
was concerned, the council "in the beginning were resolved

[1] Baily, *Life of John Fisher*, p. 157–163.

that with an oath not to be acknown whether he had to the supremacy been sworn or what he thought thereof he should be discharged." [1] Now if Bishop Fisher had taken such an oath, and had promised (as he was ready to do) that he would not again declare his opinion about the king's proceedings, it would have been excellent policy to set him free. For most people, seeing him at liberty and silent about the king's new laws, would have concluded that he had yielded, which was just what the government wanted, since the supposed submission of one who was so highly respected might induce the malcontents to give way.

On the whole, therefore, I am inclined to think that shortly after Christmas, 1534, Fisher was released on bail on the above stated conditions; that this was the cause of the rumour that he and More had submitted; and that Gontier really saw the bishop at Westminster. When Anne regained her ascendancy, about the middle of February, 1535, this lenient treatment came to an end. She hated Fisher, and was never in favour of conciliatory measures.

[1] W. Roper, *Life of Sir T. More*, p. 89.

NOTE F.

WITH regard to the real cause of Anne's fall, the correspondence of Chapuis has cleared up all doubt. But there still remains the question, What reasons did the government put forward to justify the arrest of the woman whom they called the queen, and of her friends?

There is an old story that Lady Wingfield, on her death-bed, revealed the crimes of Anne, and that it was upon this information that the government acted. It is not said by whom the deposition of Lady Wingfield was taken, nor how it was transmitted to the king. The story presents a good many difficulties, and it is made all the more improbable by the fact that in contemporary accounts no mention is made of any such deposition.

Chapuis gives no information on the subject, except that he expresses strong disapproval of the manner in which the trial was conducted, and animadverts on the fact that depositions were not produced against the prisoners.[1] The writer of the French life of Anne Boleyn gives a very strange and highly-coloured account. One of the members of the privy council, he says, had to reprove his sister for being too gay. The lady, seeing her fault discovered, tried to palliate her guilt by saying that the queen did much worse, and that Mark Smeton might tell the whole story of

[1] E. Chapuis to Charles V., May 19, 1536, *loc. cit.*

her scandalous life. The privy councillor was much frightened by this speech, for, on the one hand, if he kept the
facts secret he might afterwards be blamed and punished;
on the other hand, if he revealed them, he might be accused
of slandering the king's issue. He took the advice of two
of his friends, most intimate servants of the king; and in
the end all three went to Henry and told him what they
had heard. The king ordered them to be silent, and caused
Anne to be watched and finally arrested.[1]

According to a French manuscript printed by Mr. Pocock,
the gentleman in question was Anthony Brown (wrongly
said to be the king's physician), and his sister had formerly
been a mistress of the king.[2] The writer of this paper certainly had access to some documents or other good sources;
nevertheless I am not satisfied of the truth of the French
accounts. They may be merely a reproduction of one of the
many stories that were current at the time both at home
and abroad.

The author of the Spanish *Cronica del Rey Enrico otavo*
reports the story which seems to have been accepted by the
Spanish merchants who resided in London towards the close
of Henry's reign. He gives a very detailed account of the
proceedings. Smeton, he says, was the last of Anne's lovers,
and an old woman called Marguerita, servant to Anne, acted
as their *confidente*. Having before that time been rather
poor, Mark received considerable gifts from Anne, which he
spent on dress, horses, and other showy objects. He became
very overbearing, and treated the other courtiers with insolence.
Finally he had a violent quarrel with Thomas Percy, who complained of him. Anne, on hearing of this, sent for Percy and
ordered him to make up his quarrel with Mark. Percy was
forced to obey, but, bearing the other a grudge, he went to
Cromwell, told him of what Anne had done for Mark, and
pointed out that the musician could not have by perfectly

---

[1] *Histoire de Anne de Boullant.*

[2] Pocock, *Records of the Reformation*, vol. ii. No. ccclix.

fair means all the money he was in the habit of spending. Cromwell thereupon asked Percy secretly to watch his enemy, which Percy did; and the result was, that, on the 29th of April, early in the morning, he saw Mark coming out of Anne's apartment. This he reported to the secretary; and on May-day, in the morning, Cromwell sent for Mark, and subjected him to torture by causing a knotted cord to be violently tightened round his head. Mark, unable to bear the pain, confessed, and said that Noreys and Bryerton had been his rivals. Cromwell wrote down the confession, and sent it to Henry at Greenwich, who received it in the afternoon, and immediately took his barge and left for Westminster. Noreys and Bryerton were secretly arrested, and Wyatt was also sent to the Tower, but treated with great kindness, Cromwell being his friend. The next day Anne and the duke her brother were arrested; and Anne was examined by Cranmer, the chancellor, Norfolk, and Cromwell. By and by she and her brother were sent to the Tower. Then the old woman Marguerita was arrested and put to the rack, when she incriminated Noreys and Bryerton, but swore that Wyatt was innocent. Rochford, Noreys, Bryerton and Mark were all condemned, and executed together; the old woman was burnt at night within the Tower; and Anne after her conviction was beheaded with a sword by the executioner of Saint Omer.[1]

In many particulars this account is of course false. The writer knows nothing of Weston, he calls Rochford a duke, he makes Cranmer the president of the committee before which Anne appeared, and he falls into other and even greater mistakes. He has heard of Mistress Margaret, but he believes her to be an old woman, and evidently confounds her with the Lady Wingfield of Spelman.

The parts of the story, however, which relate to the insolence of Smeton, to his quarrel with Thomas Percy (there was a Sir Thomas Percy at court, brother of the Earl of Northumberland), and to his arrest and extorted confession,

[1] *Cronica del Rey Henrico otavo*, pp. 68—87.

may well be true. They perfectly agree with the account of Constantine and with the official account of Cromwell.

Mr. Froude, in the Appendix to the second volume of his *History of England*, gives one more version of the proximate cause of Anne's arrest. "Lord Howard," he says, "wrote at the same time to Granvelle saying that he understood the 'concubine' had been surprised in bed with the king's organist." [1] In proof of this statement about Lord Howard, Mr. Froude quotes the following passage : "Le visconte Howard a escript a Sr de Granvelle que au mesme instant il avoit entendu de bon lieu que la concubine dudict Roy avoit este surprise couchée avec l'organiste dudict Roy." [2] Unhappily Mr. Froude does not say who was the writer of this extraordinary passage, to whom it was addressed, and where it may be found. Moreover, absolutely nothing is known of the existence of a "Viscount Howard" in the time Henry VIII. There was a Lord Howard, but as he was also the Duke of Norfolk, he was always called by the latter title.

The official account of the causes of Anne's arrest does not go into details. In the letter written on the 14th of May to Gardiner and Wallop, Cromwell does not name the persons who first denounced Anne. He says her servants could not hide "the queen's abomination" any longer; and this perfectly agrees with the Spanish account. Cromwell further says that her servants and others were most secretly examined. This, again, agrees with the account of the chronicler and of Constantine. The plot to murder Henry is, of course, an embellishment of Cromwell's. On the whole, the statements of Cromwell, Constantine, and the Spanish chronicler support each other so well that the balance of evidence seems to be decidedly in favour of the account I have given in the text.

The order in which the arrests were made is now pretty certain. The first arrested was certainly Mark Smeton.

---

[1] *History of England*, vol. ii. Appendix, p. 636.
[2] *Ibid.* foot note.

This appears from Constantine's account (corroborated by Cromwell's, Chapuis's and Bulkeley's letters) as well as from the *Histoire de Anne de Boullant,* from the French account printed by Mr. Pocock, and from the Spanish chronicle. Noreys was certainly arrested on the evening of May-day; Rochford on the 2nd of May about noon. Anne was called before the council in the morning, and taken to the Tower about two o'clock in the afternoon. Weston and Bryerton were both arrested on Thursday, the 4th of May. In the account of Constantine, printed in the *Archæologia,* Bryerton is said to have been arrested on Thursday *afore* May-day.[1] But from the context it is clear that Bryerton was arrested after the other men were in the Tower, so that *afore* is either a clerical error or a misprint for *after.* Any doubt on this head is dispelled by Cromwell's letter to Gardiner and Wallop. As to Page and Wyatt, they seem to have been arrested about the same time as Bryerton and Weston, or at latest on the day following; for it appears from the letter of Kingston to Cromwell that Anne was told of the arrest of the two former on the same occasion on which she was told of that of Rochford and the two latter gentlemen.[2]

According to the writer of the Spanish chronicle, Wyatt was told on the day before the execution of Rochford—that is, on the day after the conviction of Anne—that he would not be proceeded against. Thereupon, the chronicle proceeds, Wyatt wrote a letter to the king; and in this letter he took credit for having warned Henry not to marry Anne Boleyn, because she was a bad woman. For his boldness he had been banished from court for two years. Now he wished to state that his reason for speaking as he had done was that Anne Boleyn had been his mistress.[3] Whether this be

---

[1] Constantine's account, *Archæologia,* vol. xxiii. pp. 63—65.

[2] Sir W. Kingston to Cromwell, British Museum, Cotton MSS., Otho C. x. fol. 225.

[3] *Cronica del Rey Enrico otavo de Ingalaterra,* pp. 88—91.

true or not, it is difficult to say ; but it is certain that Thomas
Wyatt admitted that he had committed some kind of moral
offence, for reference to it is made in the letters of his father,
Sir Henry Wyatt, to Cromwell and to the king.[1]   The
chronicler correctly states that Wyatt was immediately
restored to royal favour, and that he was shortly afterwards
sent as ambassador to Spain.

[1] Sir Henry Wyatt to Cromwell, May 11, 1536, *loc. cit.* ; and Sir Henry
Wyatt to Henry VIII., no date, R.O. Henry VIII. 28th, Bundle I.

NOTE G.

GROUNDS FOR THE DIVORCE OF ANNE.

DR. LINGARD, in his *History of England*, expressed the opinion that the marriage between Henry and Anne was decreed by Cranmer to have been null and void from the beginning, because of the former relation of the king to Anne's sister Mary Boleyn. For this he was taken to task by an "eminent writer." In the Appendix to the fourth volume of his *History* he replied to his critic; and every impartial reader will, I think, be convinced by his able and temperate answer.[1] Mr. Froude, however, rejects the theory, repeating some of the old arguments of Dr. Lingard's opponent, and adding others which he considers very important.

It may be well, therefore, to re-state briefly the whole case. I have already given my reasons for believing that Mary Boleyn had been the mistress of Henry VIII.; but I fully agree with Mr. Froude that the two questions are to a certain extent independent of one another, and that, even if Mary Boleyn had been Henry's mistress, the divorce may have been granted by Cranmer on different grounds.

The first of Mr. Froude's arguments is that in the statute by which Elizabeth was disinherited there occurs in the preamble the following passage: " . . . certain just true and lawful impediment unknown at the making of the said Acts and since that time confessed by the said Lady Anne before

---

[1] Lingard, *History of England*, vol. iv. Appendix, note K.

the most reverend father in God Thomas, archbishop of Canterbury, Metropolitan and Primate of all England, sitting judicially for the same by the which plainly appeareth . . ."[1] In answer to this it may be said, first of all, that if preambles to Acts of Parliament were to be accepted as trustworthy evidence as to the facts they recite, English history would be a very strange tale—even stranger than it appears in Mr. Froude's pages. Again, the Act sets forth that Anne confessed an impediment before Cranmer "sitting judicially for the same." Now, when Cranmer sat at Lambeth on the 17th May, Anne was represented by Dr. Wotton and Dr. Barbour; and, as Dr. Lingard urged some forty years ago, any confession which she may be said to have made must have been made in her name by her proctors. Mr. Froude evidently feels that there is some force in this argument, for to strengthen his case he says of Anne that: "On Wednesday she was taken to Lambeth, where she made her confession in form, and the Archbishop, sitting judicially, pronounced her marriage with the king to have been null and void."[2] But Mr. Froude adduces no evidence for this remarkable statement. It is most unlikely that if Anne had been taken from the Tower to Lambeth and back, no reference would have been made to the fact by chroniclers and newsletter writers, by Kingston, and by Chapuis. The official record of the court held by Cranmer expressly excludes the possibility of her having appeared before him at that time. All the persons who were present are enumerated, and her name is not in the list. It is stated that she was represented by N. Wotton and J. Barbour, and the words *personaliter comparens*, which are always found in such records when the party chiefly concerned was in court, are wanting. No weight, therefore, can be attached to Mr. Froude's argument, unless he can show that Cranmer held two different courts for the same purpose, that Anne was really taken to Lambeth to appear

---

[1] *Statutes of the Realm*, 28th Henry VIII., chapter vii. paragraph i.

[2] Froude, *History of England*, vol. ii. p. 395.

at one of them, and that her marriage was twice annulled by the archbishop.

In a Chronicle of England under the Tudors, written apparently by some cousin of Thomas Wriothesley, who became Lord Chancellor and Earl of Southampton, occurs the following passage: "And the same day in the afternoon at a solemn court kept at Lambeth by the Lord Archbishop of Canterbury and the doctors of the law, the king was divorced from his wife, Queen Anne, and there at the same court was a privy contract approved that she had made to the Earl of Northumberland afore the king's time, and so she was discharged and was never lawful Queen of England, and there it was approved the same." [1] Mr. Froude accepts this as sound evidence; but he does not say that the only copy of the manuscript of the Chronicle known to exist is certainly later than the year 1592. Though it is pretty certain that the original Chronicle was written by a contemporary, all we have of it is a copy made at a much later date by a scribe who can be proved to have taken considerable liberties with the text. It is, therefore, impossible to decide how much of the manuscript is the work of the author, and how much is due to interpolations and alterations by the copyist.

This fact detracts considerably from the authority of the Chronicle. The phrase about the divorce stands quite apart from the statement that a pre-contract was proved, and the latter explanatory sentence may well have been an interpolation.

But even admitting for argument's sake that the passage was written by the chronicler himself, it cannot be regarded as an important contribution to the discussion of the question. The writer was certainly not a man of high station who had access to the very best information. At the time when his chronicle seems to have been written, his cousin, Thomas Wriothesley, had not risen to eminence, and Sir Thomas

---

[1] C. Wriothesley, *A Chronicle of England*, edited by W. D. Hamilton, for the Camden Society, 1875-77, vol. i. p. 40.

Audeley, who appears to have been his patron, was wise enough not to tell the secrets of the king. The chronicler, therefore, had no special knowledge as to secret events; and even about matters regarding which he might have been expected to have accurate information he falls into some very palpable mistakes. He asserts that Henry and Jane Seymour were secretly married at Chelsea, while all other evidence tends to show that the ceremony was performed at Hampton Court.[1] And in the passage quoted by Mr. Froude there are also some very grave errors as to fact. For the chronicler says that the court was held on the afternoon of the 17th of May, while it appears from the official record that it was held between nine and eleven o'clock in the morning. He says, moreover, that Cranmer sat with the doctors of the law, while Cranmer (according to the same official account) sat alone.[2] A writer who makes two such mistakes is certainly not a very trustworthy authority, and his assertion (if it be his) is not to be taken as of equal weight with that of Chapuis.

It is true that Mr. Froude tries to discredit the account of Chapuis by asserting that he had at first offered two explanations of the divorce.[3] But in the despatches of Chapuis I have not found these two explanations. The ambassador did say in a letter to Granvelle that he had heard from some people that Cranmer had declared Elizabeth to be the daughter of Noreys, and not of the king, while, according to others, Cranmer had decreed that the marriage between Henry and Anne was invalid on account of the king's former cohabitation with Mary Boleyn.[4] I think it is only Mr. Froude who will call this two explanations of the divorce. Chapuis, in June, simply confirmed his first statement as to the grounds of Cranmer's sentence.[5]

[1] Wriothesley's *Chronicle*, p. 43.   [2] Wilkins, *Concilia*, iii. p. 803.

[3] *History of England*, vol. ii. App. p. 651.

[4] E. Chapuis to N. de Granvelle, May 19, 1536, Vienna Archives, P.C. 230, i. fol. 90.

[5] E. Chapuis to N. de Granvelle, July 8, 1536, Vienna Archives, P.C. 230, i. fol. 145.

A further reason for disbelieving the account of the chronicler and the theory of Mr. Froude is that, if the marriage had been pronounced void on account of a pre-contract, this would have had some consequences of which we do not find any trace. First of all, it would have prevented Elizabeth from being declared a bastard, for the good faith of even one of the parents was sufficient to legitimate the issue. As Henry could not well have said that when he married Anne he knew there was a pre-contract with Northumberland, he would necessarily have been held to have acted in good faith. Secondly, the same pre-contract which would have annulled the marriage of Anne and Henry would have annulled that of Lord and Lady Northumberland. We know that the countess wished to be separated from the earl; she would certainly, therefore, have asked for a divorce if it could have been obtained. There is not the slightest evidence that she even thought of making such an application after Anne's death.

If all these arguments be added to those adduced by Dr. Lingard, it cannot be seriously doubted that the cause of nullity which Henry was afraid to avow, was his former connection with Mary Boleyn.

INDEX.

INDEX.

A.

B.

M.

THE END.